BENEATH DARK WATERS

The Legacy of the Empress of Ireland Shipwreck

EVE LAZARUS

ARSENAL PULP PRESS
VANCOUVER

BENEATH DARK WATERS

SECOND PRINTING: 2026

ARSENAL PULP PRESS
Suite 202 – 211 East Georgia St.
Vancouver, BC V6A 1Z6
Canada
arsenalpulp.com

The publisher gratefully acknowledges the support of the Canada Council for the Arts and the British Columbia Arts Council for its publishing program and the Government of Canada and the Government of British Columbia (through the Book Publishing Tax Credit Program) for its publishing activities.

Arsenal Pulp Press acknowledges the xʷməθkʷəy̓əm (Musqueam), Sḵwx̱wú7mesh (Squamish), and səlilwətaɬ (Tsleil-Waututh) Nations, custodians of the traditional, ancestral, and unceded territories where our office is located. We pay respect to their histories, traditions, and continuous living cultures and commit to accountability, respectful relations, and friendship.

Cover and text design by Jazmin Welch in collaboration with Jasmin Linton
Edited by Catharine Chen
Proofread by JC Cham
Indexed by Stephen Ullstrom

Printed and bound in Canada

Library and Archives Canada Cataloguing in Publication:
Title: Beneath dark waters : the legacy of the Empress of Ireland shipwreck / Eve Lazarus.
Names: Lazarus, Eve, author
Description: Includes bibliographical references and index.
Identifiers: Canadiana (print) 20240441249 | Canadiana (ebook) 2024044132X | ISBN 9781551529738 (softcover) | ISBN 9781551529745 (EPUB)
Subjects: LCSH: Empress of Ireland (Steamship) | LCSH: Shipwrecks—Québec (Province)—Saint Lawrence River Estuary.
Classification: LCC G530.E4 L39 2025 | DDC 910.9163/44—dc23

BENEATH DARK WATERS

For Mike, Mark, Megan, Matthew, and Max

And in memory of all the passengers and crew who travelled on the *Empress of Ireland* on May 28, 1914

CONTENTS

Eve Lazarus and Hugh Verrier at the wreck site, August 22, 2019 | Mike Dunn

INTRODUCTION
Rimouski

IT'S THE MORNING OF August 22, 2019, and I'm in a Zodiac bouncing along the waters of the St. Lawrence River. The boat is piloted by François Hazel, a French Canadian marine biologist and diving instructor. The Zodiac can hold six divers and all their gear, but this morning there are only six of us—no gear. Far from being divers, we are curiosity seekers from New York, Vancouver, London, and Montreal, all obsessed with the sinking of the *Empress of Ireland*, which claimed 1,014 lives in 1914. Until a few years ago, I had never heard of the *Empress of Ireland* and its disastrous end. And that's staggering because the loss of passenger life outnumbered that of the *Titanic* and the *Lusitania*.*

I'm sitting next to Hugh Verrier, the New York lawyer who heads up one of the world's largest law firms and who is responsible for our trip out to the wreck and for this book. Hugh is originally from Montreal, and since the 1920s his family has owned a summer property near Rimouski, close to where the *Empress of Ireland* sank. Hugh swims in the St. Lawrence River most summers and has always known about the tragedy, but in recent years he has developed a fascination for the story of survivor Gordon Charles Davidson.

---

* An estimated 836 passenger lives were lost on the *Empress of Ireland*, compared to 832 on the *Titanic* and 788 on the *Lusitania*.

Gordon Davidson was a PhD candidate from Union, Ontario, who lived in Vancouver, British Columbia, when he wasn't studying at UC Berkeley in San Francisco. He had reportedly survived the sinking of the *Empress* by swimming 6.5 kilometres (4 miles) to shore. When Hugh looked into this, experts told him this wasn't possible—not at that time of year and not for that distance. But Hugh wanted to make sure. He wanted to verify the information that had been repeated in newspaper articles and regurgitated in books and even at Davidson's own memorial service almost a century before. Whatever happened, Hugh wanted to set the record straight.

A few years earlier, I had given a talk at a Vancouver lawyer's fiftieth birthday party about the human stories behind several heritage houses. A lawyer from Hugh's firm had attended and told him that I do this kind of genealogical research, tracking down descendants of long-dead people. So, on November 6, 2017, Hugh hired me to research Gordon Davidson. In an email to me, he attached Davidson's 1922 obituary, an article about his miraculous swim to shore, and a photo of him receiving medical treatment at the Château Frontenac following the shipwreck. "I have not found any record of him speaking or writing about swimming to shore," Hugh wrote. "He did not have any children. So, this is not going to be easy to find out about." He wasn't wrong. This has been my biggest challenge to date—an amazing research project and a story about so much more than one swim.

We leave the Rimouski Marina at nine in the morning and stop first at Pointe-au-Père, or Father Point, as it was also known in 1914. It was the station for the St. Lawrence ship pilots, a lighthouse, and the Marconi telegraph station. It takes us another forty-five minutes to reach the site of the wreck, barely glimpsing another vessel as we watch land and the tall white steeple of the Sainte-Luce Catholic Church recede in the distance.

Thunderstorms are predicted for later in the day, and the sky is dark and cloudy, but there is none of the dangerous fog that can swiftly descend on the St. Lawrence River. I feel a little like I'm on a roller coaster; the small waves are choppy, lifting us up and then slapping us back down as we clutch tightly to the rope handholds. We feel the spray of water in our faces, and it's freezing cold, even in late August.

I expect something large to mark the site of the wreck, but there is only a white buoy with a brown handle floating next to a bright-orange ball. It would be impossible to find without the coordinates to look for it. The buoy designates this as a federally protected National Historic Site of Canada as of 1999 and one for expert divers only. Unfortunately, by then, divers had had decades to pillage souvenirs, taking everything from smashed-up suitcases, china, tables, chairs, and light fixtures to human bones. Many of these finds are spread about in various museums across Canada, but even more of them have found their way into private collections all over the world.

Out in the middle of it, the St. Lawrence River seems impossibly wide—it's about 50 kilometres across. From this vantage point, I consider a swim to land. It would be difficult in perfect summer daylight conditions and seemingly impossible in late May in the middle of the night, with freezing water and only a half moon for light.

The sonar equipment on our Zodiac clearly shows the outline of the *Empress* lying in a shallow trench below us. François passes around a laminated photo produced by Parks Canada that shows the ship resting on its starboard side at a 65 degree angle. The longitude and latitude coordinates are here, and the photo shows the bow at the highest point, where a hole was made in 1914 to retrieve mail and silver bars 30 metres down and rudders and propellers at 45 metres.

As well as transporting divers to the wreck site, in 2019 he has the contract with Quebec's Ministry of Culture and Communications to

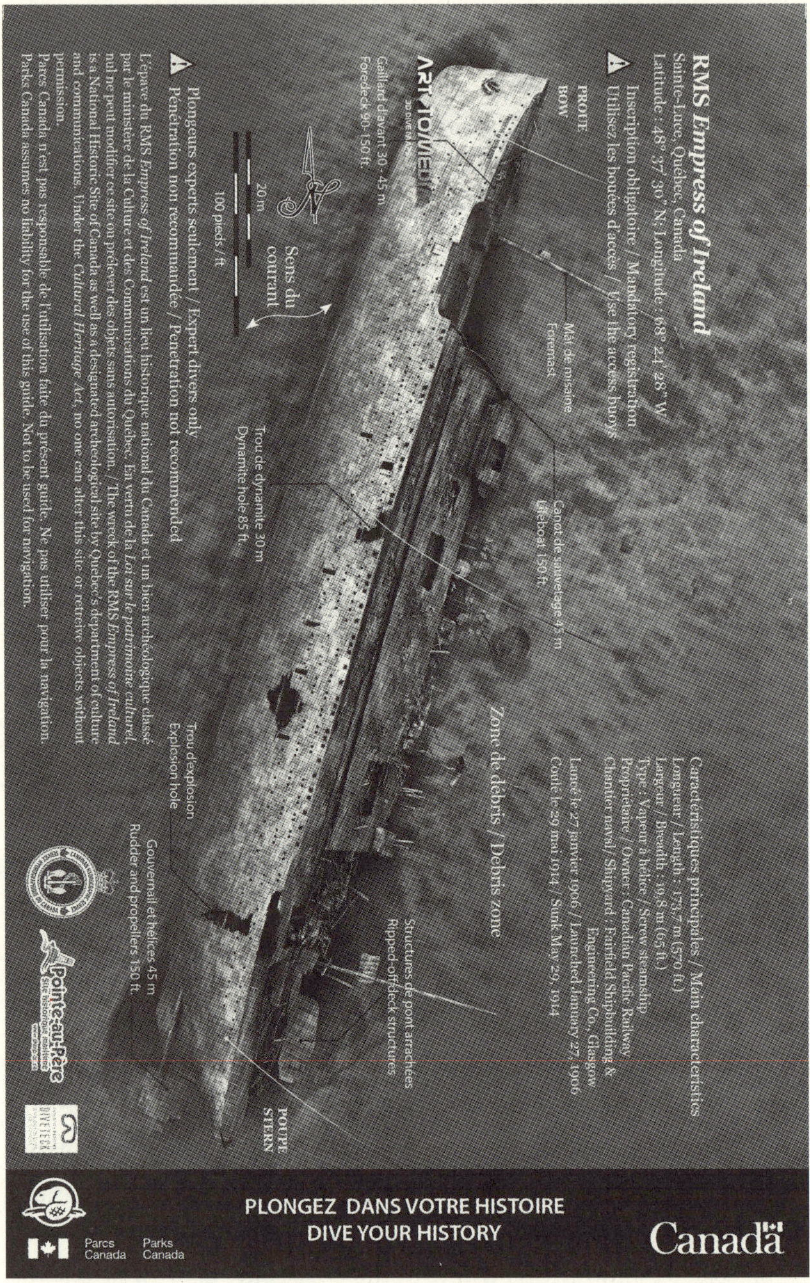

Dive map of the Empress of Ireland *wreck site* | *Parks Canada and Arto Media, developed by Parks Canada in 2014 using archaeological and historical data and information gathered from local divers*

put out the marker and a line down to the wreck every May and bring it up again the following September.

As dive sites go, it's not very deep. Depending on the tides, the wreck is accessible at 30 to 45 metres, but the dive is fraught with danger. The water temperature of the St. Lawrence River is just above freezing, even in summer. The water is murky and turbulent, the currents are challenging, and it's a long way from shore. While it takes only a few minutes to follow the rope down to the wreck, divers have an hour at most to explore the 150-metre-long liner, because they must swim slowly back to the surface, pausing often along the way so as to avoid decompression sickness, more commonly known as "the bends." Divers take in extra nitrogen from the compressed air they breathe, and this nitrogen dissolves into the blood. If they rise too quickly (so that the surrounding water pressure decreases too rapidly), the nitrogen forms gas bubbles in the blood or tissues, causing intense joint pain, ruptured blood vessels in the lungs, heart attacks, strokes, and sometimes even death. François tells us that several divers have died exploring the wreck.

After the *Empress* sank, she remained hidden and forgotten about for the next half century. Then, in 1964, articles were published on the fiftieth anniversary of her sinking, and a group of divers decided to search for her.

We spend half an hour at the wreck site. Every now and then we drift away, and François restarts the motor to take us back to the marker. Even though the water is calm, the unpredictability of the weather and the knowledge that we're floating above hundreds of souls trapped in the wreckage below are unsettling. What was it like for them in the fourteen minutes it took for the ocean liner to sink? I consider the panic of searching for lifebelts in the cabins, of water spilling in, of being thrown into the pitch dark in an unfamiliar setting. And, for those who did make it to the deck, of discovering that, due to the list of the ship, it was only possible to release four of the forty lifeboats.

The *Empress of Ireland* carried more than 117,000 people between Liverpool, England, and Saint John, New Brunswick, and later Halifax or Quebec City, depending on the season, in ninety-six round trips between 1906 and 1914. A million or so Canadians from coast to coast can trace their roots back to an ancestor who came to Canada on this ship. The *Empress of Ireland* and her sister ship, the *Empress of Britain*, were owned by the all-powerful Canadian Pacific Railway (CPR), and in many ways, she was this country's *Mayflower*.

1. Captain Kendall and the London Cellar Murder

CAPTAIN HENRY GEORGE KENDALL stood on the bridge. Resplendent in his suit of blue serge with brass buttons and gold braid, he greeted many of his passengers by name as they came aboard the SS *Montrose* at Antwerp, Belgium.

The Canadian Pacific–owned steamship was a step up from Kendall's last post as captain of the *Monmouth*, but the *Montrose* was still a workhorse, built for the immigrant trade and outfitted to carry eighteen hundred third-class passengers and seventy in second-class. For this trip in July 1910, she would carry just 266 passengers to Quebec City.

At thirty-six, Kendall was a rising star in the Canadian Pacific network. He'd started his career as a fifteen-year-old deckhand on a sailing ship; his status now as captain transcended his working-class background. A non-drinker, Kendall was good looking, charming, and articulate, making him popular with passengers. He was respected by his crew and often made a point of strolling his ship at different times of the day, anticipating any problems and keeping on the lookout for sloppy uniforms or tarnished fittings.

For me, Kendall is one of the most interesting and ultimately flawed characters in the story of the *Empress of Ireland*. This is why I've decided to start the book with him, right at the point when his career is really about to set sail. The fact that this happens on the back

TOP: *Captain Kendall walking along the deck of the* SS Montrose, *circa 1910 | Société d'Histoire du Bas-Canada, Guy D'Astous collection;* RIGHT: *Dr. Hawley Crippen, 1910 | Public domain*

of a particularly gruesome murder, in real time and with the whole world watching, is as compelling as the murder stories in any of my previous books.

Like millions of others around the world, Kendall was well versed in what the newspapers were calling "the London Cellar Murder." The two suspects—Dr. Hawley Harvey Crippen and his young lover, Ethel Le Neve—had fled London and were wanted for questioning. Just that morning, Kendall had read the latest newspaper reports over breakfast and closely examined their photographs while catching up on the police investigation. Scotland Yard believed the couple would attempt to escape England and had staked out ships that were preparing to leave port, asking their captains to keep a lookout for the couple.

American-born Crippen had studied medicine and homeopathy in Michigan and Ohio, specializing in eyes and ears and training in compounding medicines and opiates. He married Charlotte Bell in 1887. Their son, Otto, was born two years later. When, in 1892, Charlotte died in childbirth, Otto was shipped off to live with his grandparents. Crippen, now thirty, moved to New York, where he met Cora Turner, a want-to-be opera singer. They married in a private ceremony in 1894. Between 1896 and 1898, Crippen operated the Toronto office for Dr. Munyon's Patent Medicine, and by 1900, he was working for the company in London, England. Cora's acting and singing had flatlined in the States, and she saw the move as a way to jump-start her career in musical theatre. Once in England, she took the stage name Belle Elmore. She towered over her mild-mannered husband and chose his clothes for him.

Crippen was not an attractive man. He was short—under five foot four—and balding. He had bulging blue eyes and wore large glasses with wire rims and thick lenses. People described him as kind and gentle, but his marriage was tumultuous. Elmore burned through

Crippen's money, and he seemed happy to let her. He bought her expensive clothes and jewellery, converted to Catholicism for her, and managed her career.

And then he fell in love with Ethel Le Neve.

39 HILLDROP CRESCENT

The last time anyone remembered seeing Elmore was at a dinner party given by the Crippens at their rented home on Hilldrop Crescent in Camden on January 31, 1910. Two days later, Elmore unexpectedly resigned by letter from the position of treasurer of the Music Hall Ladies Guild. In the letter, she said that she had to leave for the United States, having just learned of the illness of a close relative. The letter was not in her handwriting and, even more suspicious, the signature on the letter was spelled "Ellmore," not Elmore.

Mrs. Crippen, a.k.a. Cora Turner / Belle Elmore, 1910 | Library of Congress Prints & Photographs Division (Washington, DC) ID ggbain.05164

Meanwhile, Crippen moved Le Neve, his twenty-seven-year-old secretary, into his house and told people she was his housekeeper. The couple were seen around town, with Le Neve dressed in a sealskin coat and broach that looked remarkably like ones worn by Elmore.

When people asked after his wife, Crippen told them that she'd gone to California, became seriously ill, and then died. Two months after Elmore had supposedly left for the States, and around the time Le Neve was telling her stunned family that she had married Crippen at a London registry office, Crippen placed a notice of Elmore's death in the local paper and in a theatrical paper called *The Stage*. When Elmore's friends demanded details, Crippen said she had left for California on the SS *La Touraine*, but there was no record of her on the ship's manifest, and Crippen would not produce a death certificate. On June 30, Elmore's friends paid a visit to Chief Inspector Walter Dew at Scotland Yard.

Crippen explained to the inspector that he had lied because he was too humiliated to tell the truth: Elmore had left him to join her lover in the States, and as far as he knew, she was alive and well. Inspector Dew and his men searched Crippen's house, but the only thing they thought was odd was that Elmore had left most of her clothes and expensive jewellery behind. Crippen told them that she hadn't wanted to take anything that he had bought for her. While Dew thought Crippen's story sounded credible, he was concerned that no one had heard from Elmore.

Had the forty-eight-year-old Crippen stayed put, the police investigation likely would have ended there, but the doctor panicked. He hacked off his young lover's long brown hair, ordered a boy's suit and boots, dressed her up as a sixteen-year-old boy, and fled with her to Europe.

Once he realized they had gone, Dew ordered a more extensive search of the house. This time police found a mutilated human torso buried in quicklime under the bricks of the coal cellar. Skin and internal organs, including liver, stomach, lungs, and heart, were wrapped in a pyjama top. Identification was impossible because the remains were missing head, hands, feet, and bones, but some skin was found bearing a scar similar to one Elmore had on her stomach. There was also a hair curler and bleached hair the same colour as Elmore's found near the remains. Toxicology tests revealed traces of hyoscine hydrobromide, which Crippen used for homeopathic preparations and was lethal in large doses.

Winston Churchill, at the time the home secretary, authorized a 250-pound reward for information leading to the arrest of Crippen and Le Neve.*

SUSPECTS FLEE LONDON

Two hours after leaving Antwerp, Kendall was standing on the bridge and happened to look out onto the boat deck. He was surprised to see a man squeezing the hand of his younger male companion. Rather than assume they were a gay couple, Kendall decided to follow them. He took his cigar out onto the deck and started up a conversation. The older man, speaking with an American accent, told Kendall he was John Philo Robinson, a businessman from Detroit taking his sixteen-year-old son, John Junior, to California. They both wore brown suits, grey hats, and white canvas shoes.

The photo of Crippen that Kendall had seen in the police circular and that was splashed on the front pages of newspapers all around the world showed a man with round glasses and a moustache. Although Robinson didn't wear glasses, the indentation on either side of his nose suggested that he had until recently. Kendall also took note of Robinson's protruding eyes. He didn't have a moustache but had started to grow a beard.

---

* About $43,000 CAD in 2024.

Kendall checked the passenger manifest and saw that father and son had booked a four-berth cabin in Brussels and given their address as the Hotel des Ardennes, which fit with the information given in the newspaper. The Robinsons had not brought any baggage.

Kendall went back to his cabin to take another look at the photos in the English newspaper he'd brought aboard. He covered up Crippen's moustache and glasses with some chalk. Then he cut a hole in a piece of white paper so he could look at Le Neve's face without her hair or hat. He was almost certain that Dr. Crippen and Ethel Le Neve were the Robinsons. But before he wired authorities, he needed to be positive.

Kendall turned out to be quite a detective. Noticing that the Robinsons hadn't booked a table in the dining room, he invited them to join him at the captain's table. When they were seated, Kendall went to Cabin 5, where they were staying. The first thing he noticed was two hats. The larger was stamped with "Jackson, Boulevard du Nord," a shop in Brussels. The smaller hat was packed with newspaper to make it fit a smaller head. Under the couch was a locked black box.

Kendall returned and took his seat at the head of the table. Young Robinson was seated on his right, the older man next to him. Kendall noted that young Robinson was quite "ladylike" in his manner and the way he ate and that his father seemed to pay a lot of attention to him.

Back in his cabin after dinner, Kendall wrote, "Le Neve has the manner and appearance of a very refined, modest girl. She does not speak much, but always with a pleasant smile. She seems thoroughly under his thumb, and he will not leave her for a moment. Her suit is anything but a good fit. Her trousers are very tight about the hips and are split a bit down the back and secured with safety pins."[1]

He continued to watch the odd couple closely.

Once, when he saw them on the deck, Kendall called out to Mr. Robinson. The man didn't answer. When Kendall called out a second time, Robinson apologized for not hearing him, saying that the cold weather made him deaf.

Kendall was sure he could make out the outline of a revolver in Crippen's hip pocket. He went to his cabin, loaded his own revolver, and took to wearing it around the ship. "He meant taking no chances when threatened with arrest," wrote Kendall. "If he turned and fired on me, I would shoot him dead."[2]

THE CAPTAIN'S STORY

Passengers loved to hear Kendall talk about his adventurous background, and he was more than happy to tell them stories of his exploits. He'd grown up in Liverpool, and his father died when he was ten, throwing the family into poverty. When he turned fifteen, he got a job aboard the *City of Berlin*. His whole family came to see him off, and for luck his grandfather gave him a thin gold chain he'd worn during the Crimean War. His mother told him to never drink, get tattooed, or chew tobacco. These were the last words he ever heard from her, and he followed her advice.

After a couple of voyages with the *City of Berlin*, he signed on with the *Iolanthe*, a windjammer bringing steel rails to Australia for a railway being built between Normanton and the Croydon Goldfield. Five months later, the ship reached Queensland. On the long voyage over, Kendall and another sailor witnessed the stabbing of a shipmate. The other sailor was poisoned as a result and died before the ship reached port. Kendall testified against the murderer, but the man got off and threatened revenge. Frightened he'd become a third victim, Kendall deserted ship and headed to the goldfields to try his hand at gold mining. He failed miserably, and now flat broke, he stowed away on a mail ship called the *Yaralla*. When the captain discovered he had a stowaway on board, he dumped Kendall at Thursday Island, a remote pearl fishing town in northern Queensland. Kendall tried harvesting pearls, and when that didn't work, he found a berth aboard a Norwegian sailing ship with a cargo of seabird excrement bound for England.* The journey home took seven months.

By 1901, Kendall, now twenty-seven years old, was married to Jane Wright and was a father. He was second officer on the SS *Lusitania* when it was wrecked in fog off the coast of Newfoundland.† No lives were lost, and now with a newly minted master's certificate, Kendall was appointed second officer on the SS *Lake Champlain*. His favourite story from those days was of taking the ship to British Columbia with a cargo of large animals en route to a zoo. The animals were caged on the shelter deck. One night at 2:00 a.m., a boatswain woke Kendall to tell him a leopard was loose and roaming the ship. By the time Kendall arrived on the scene, the animal had managed to shut itself in one of the bathrooms. Kendall tried a mix of ether and chloroform from the ship's dispensary to knock out the animal. It worked, but the fumes also knocked out six sailors. The leopard stayed unconscious long enough to be dragged back to its cage.[3]

The Beaver Line was purchased by the CPR in 1903, and Kendall was promoted to first officer. Three years later he was named first officer of the *Empress of Ireland*. "During the twelve months that I was serving on the *Empress of Ireland*, we carried many illustrious personages, including Earl Grey, Governor-General of Canada; Viscount Lascelles; Prince Fushimi, the emperor of Japan's cousin; Rudyard Kipling, Marconi; and others," wrote Kendall in his memoir.[4]

Soon afterward, Kendall was given his first command on the SS *Milwaukee* and then on the *Montrose*, one of only sixty ships in the world equipped with wireless telegraph equipment, which enabled messages to be sent from ship to shore.

---

* Seabird excrement, also known as guano, was highly valued as an agricultural fertilizer because of its high content of nitrogen, phosphate, and potassium.

† An earlier ship of the same name as the *Lusitania* that was torpedoed by a German U-boat in 1915.

Built as a cargo liner in 1896, the SS Montrose *was sold to the* CPR *in 1903 and converted into a passenger ship | Société d'Histoire du Bas-Canada (Beloeil,* QC*), Guy D'Astous collection*

THE CHASE

In July 1910, Kendall was steaming toward Canada with a ship full of passengers. The range for sending a message from the *Montrose* was less than 250 kilometres (150 miles). Kendall would soon be out of range, so he had to make a decision. Fast. If he was wrong, it would be career suicide. But he wanted to be the man who caught London's most famous murderer; he wanted the attention this would bring.

"I was 99 percent sure that this was the fugitive whom Scotland Yard wanted for murder," wrote Kendall. "It was both my duty as a decent law abiding individual and shipmaster to let Scotland Yard know about these mystery travellers. On the other hand, I was asking for a full measure of trouble should my opinion turn out to be wrong. I should be accused of forming irresponsible judgments and if the suspected passengers turned out to be above suspicion who could say that some law action for damages might not result?"[5]

Kendall made his decision. He sent a telegram via the ship's wireless operator to the CPR's managing director in Liverpool on July 22.

> Have strong suspicions that Crippen London Cellar murderer and accomplice are amongst saloon passengers. Moustache taken off growing beard. Accomplice dressed as boy. Voice manner and build undoubtedly a girl. Both travelling as Mr. and Master Robinson. Kendall[6]

Kendall decided it best not to arrest the suspects or let on that their real identities had been discovered. He was concerned about the effect this might have on other passengers, the lack of manpower to guard them, and what a desperate Crippen might attempt to do to himself. Kendall went about the ship collecting all the newspapers that mentioned Crippen and the murder and locked them away.

It would be a few days before the ship was in range again to receive or transmit messages. Kendall had no idea that his message had been received, that CPR officials had contacted Scotland Yard, and that Inspector Dew was on board the White Star liner *Laurentic*, in pursuit.

Typically, the *Montrose* took eleven days to reach Quebec City, while the much faster *Laurentic* could do the trip from Liverpool in seven days. Inspector Dew left port three days after the *Montrose*; he planned to be waiting just outside Rimouski, Quebec, to arrest Crippen and Le Neve.

Newspapers in England and North America were running front-page stories about the pursuit. The *Montrose* had the world's attention. As telegrams flew back and forth, the newspapers printed daily updates, and screaming headlines kept the public informed as the drama on the Atlantic played out. Maps and charts showed the distance between the *Laurentic* and the *Montrose* so the public could follow the chase. The case had all the elements of a murder mystery, and readers could follow along in real time. It was also the first time Marconi's invention of the wireless telegraph was used to catch a criminal.

The *Laurentic* had a full load of passengers. Wishing to remain anonymous, Inspector Dew registered under the name Mr. Dewhurst, but he was quickly identified by a reporter for the *London Daily Mail* who was travelling on the same ship.

"There was something intensely thrilling, almost weird, in the thought of these two passengers travelling across the Atlantic in the belief that their identity and whereabouts were unknown while both were being flashed with certainty to all quarters of the civilized world."[7]

As the days continued, Kendall kept watch over the fugitives while the *Montrose* stayed out of communication with the rest of the world. He enjoyed Crippen's company. Both men were well travelled, and Kendall easily got Crippen talking about the places he had lived, including Toronto, Detroit, and San Francisco. Both men loved reading murder mysteries, and Kendall loaned Crippen a regular supply of books. Among these were *The Pickwick Papers* by Charles Dickens, *Nebo the Nailer* by Sabine Baring-Gould, and *The Murder of Delicia* by Marie Corelli—a story about a man who murders his wife. Crippen returned the favour by loaning Kendall *The Four Just Men* by Edgar Wallace. He said it was about a murder set in London with a five-hundred-pound reward.

"There were two Crippens, but until about the fifth day out I was acquainted only with the quiet spoken little man who turned out to be one of the most charming passengers I ever had with me," wrote Kendall. "Well mannered, the very essence of politeness, a great reader, always ready to hear a good story."[8]

On July 28, eight days after leaving Antwerp, the *Montrose* was back in communication with the mainland. The ship's marconi operator was inundated with messages from the world's media, the CPR, and Scotland Yard. Kendall's modest ship was the most famous vessel afloat, and he had an audience of millions around the world waiting for scraps of information. He sent a marconigram to the editor of the *Montreal Star*; his story appeared on the front page the next day.

> Dr. Crippen and Miss Le Neve I am confident are on board
> He is still shaving his moustache growth and he is growing a beard
> Dr. Crippen has no suspicion that his identity is suspected
> The other passengers also are ignorant of his identity
> Miss Le Neve refrains from talking
> The pair have no baggage
> They cannot be parted and are very reticent
> Dr. Crippen has stated that he has travelled much
> He puts in much of the time reading books
> He is very sleepless at nights
> I first suspected the identity of the couple two hours after leaving Antwerp, when I got the first clue
> Dr. Crippen says, with regard to his companion (who is disguised as a boy), that he is taking him to California. The boy, says the doctor, is in bad health
> They spend much time together in their room
> Ordinarily they are bright and cheerful; but at times both show signs of decided worry
> Dr. Crippen is booked as a merchant
> The woman, disguised as a boy, is booked as a student
> This is the first account given to any newspaper
> KENDALL, Commander[9]

When the *Laurentic* overtook the *Montrose*, Inspector Dew telegraphed Kendall to inform the captain that Dew would be awaiting their arrival at Father Point just outside Rimouski. He also wanted Crippen to remain unaware he had been discovered in case he tried to kill himself by jumping overboard or by taking poison.

New-York Tribune.

NEW-YORK, MONDAY, AUGUST 1, 1910.—TWELVE PAGES. ** PRICE ONE CENT

HOSPITAL ELEVATOR FALLS

Thirty Visitors at Bellevue Go to Basement—None Hurt.

LINER IN WITH MENAGERIE

Many Contributions for Hornaday All Way from Tasmania.

AMERICAN DENTIST AND HIS STENOGRAPHER ARRESTED ON STEAMER MONTROSE.

DR. HAWLEY HARVEY CRIPPEN.

MISS ETHEL CLARE LENEVE.

CRIPPEN AND GIRL ARRESTED ON SHIP

American Dentist and Ethel C. Leneve Taken Into Custody on the Montrose.

DEW MAKES IDENTIFICATION

Crippen Expresses Relief That Suspense Is Over—Prisoners Taken from Ship at Quebec Early To-day.

Quebec, Que., Aug. 1.—The Canadian Pacific liner Montrose, with Dr. Hawley Harvey Crippen and Ethel Clare Leneve prisoners aboard, reached Quebec, the end of her journey from Antwerp, shortly after 1 o'clock this morning. Closely guarded, the pair were taken from the vessel at 1:35 a. m.

Soon after the vessel's arrival the prisoners were landed and driven to jail. Miss Leneve seemed half senseless as she emerged from her cabin and had to be supported down the steep gang plank. The police had difficulty in keeping the crowd back.

While they were guarded on the passage between Father Point and Quebec, Dr. Crippen and Miss Leneve were allowed to see each other.

No effort was made by Inspector Dew to secure a confession from Dr. Crippen. The jewels found on the prisoner, it is said, furnish the only incriminating evidence found.

NO BAR TO LEE'S STATUE

President Taft Approves of Its

DRUG VICTIM A SUICIDE

Seemingly Cured, Springs into

AUTO'S GEAR SAVES BABY

Half a Block Under Machine, Swinging by Her Dress.

HAD TO JILT SOME ONE

Brooklyn Girl, in Quandary, Has

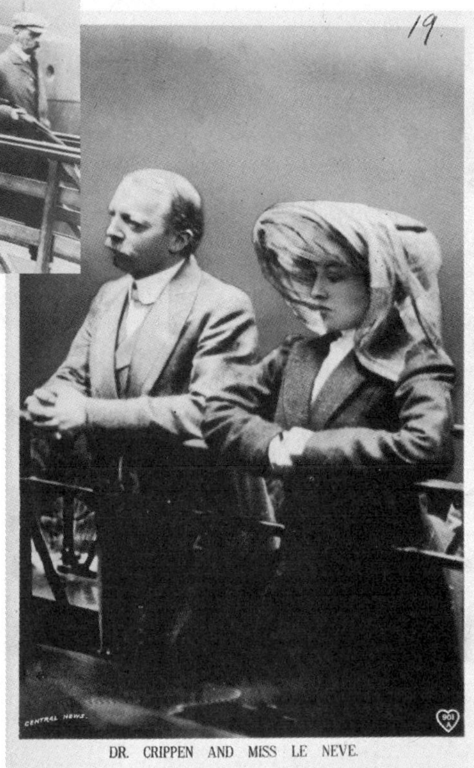

DR. CRIPPEN AND MISS LE NEVE.

CLOCKWISE FROM TOP: New York Tribune, *August 1, 1910; Hawley Harvey Crippen and Ethel Le Neve | Arthur Bennett, 1910, V0026226 Wellcome Library, London; Chief Inspector Walter Dew of Scotland Yard arrests Dr. Crippen on the gangplank of the* SS Montrose | *Public domain*

At 4:30 a.m. on Sunday, July 31, Kendall blew the *Montrose*'s whistle to alert Father Point and Inspector Dew of the ship's imminent arrival.

Once ships reached the St. Lawrence River, they were required to take aboard an experienced pilot who would navigate the treacherous river to Quebec City. The government steamer *Eureka* would bring a pilot out to meet the ship near the Father Point station.

So as not to spook Crippen, Dew and members of the Dominion Police disguised themselves as pilots, dressing in the standard blue suits and white caps. They arrived in a rowboat from the *Eureka* rowed by four sailors. Worried that Crippen might find it suspicious that there were four pilots instead of one, Kendall told him that the ship regularly carried pilots returning to Quebec City.

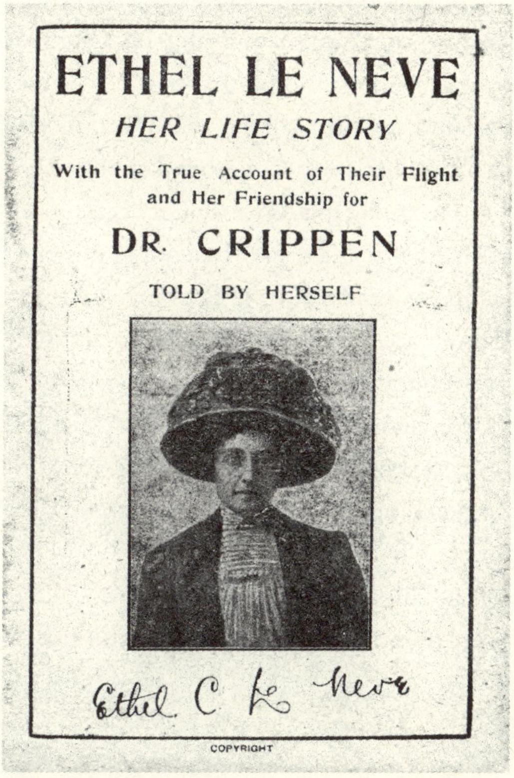

The cover of a sixty-four-page booklet issued in 1910 | Société d'Histoire du Bas-Canada (Beloeil, QC), Guy D'Astous collection

When Dew came on board, Kendall pointed out the man he thought was Crippen. "That is my man; is he yours?"[10] It must have been a stressful moment for Kendall when Dew couldn't immediately identify Crippen and said he would need to see him face to face.

Crippen was quickly and quietly arrested in Kendall's cabin. "Thank God it is all over," he told Kendall. "I couldn't stand it any longer. The suspense has been too great."[11] Crippen was taken to an unoccupied cabin and stripped of his clothes. Dew found a linen belt containing five of the doctor's dead wife's diamond rings, earrings, a stickpin, and a ten-dollar bill. He wasn't carrying a revolver; Kendall thought he must have thrown it overboard so as not to cause them problems entering Canada. A shocked Le Neve was arrested in their cabin, a search of which turned up a diamond broach and sixty dollars.

Once the suspects were confined to separate cabins, the *Montrose*'s whistle signalled the captain of the *Eureka* to bring his cargo of twenty-five reporters, who were waiting to board the *Montrose* and travel to Quebec City. At around nine that night, the *Montrose* was greeted in port by a squad of fifty police and a large crowd of onlookers.

Crippen was arraigned the next day in a Quebec City courtroom and sent back to London to stand trial at the Old Bailey. He was convicted of murder and hanged in November 1910 at Pentonville Prison. Le Neve, who was charged as an accessory to murder, was acquitted.

Kendall received the 250-pound reward. He was also offered a proposal of marriage from a woman in Philadelphia, twenty thousand dollars for a twenty-week theatre engagement, and another five hundred to have his face cast and exhibited at a waxworks museum. He politely declined all three offers.[12]

The great chase made Kendall a celebrity, and he rose quickly within the company. In 1914, he was named captain of the stately *Empress of Ireland*.

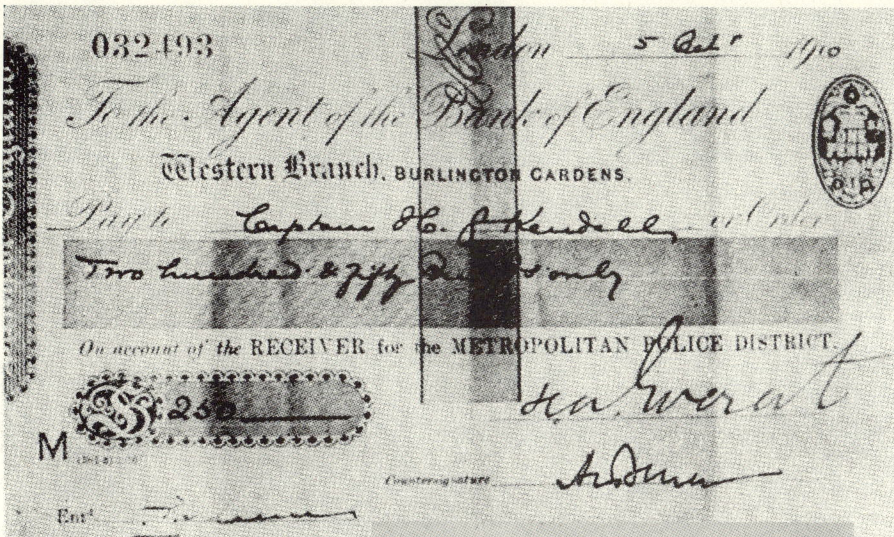

032493

London 5 Oct 1910

To the Agent of the Bank of England

Western Branch, BURLINGTON GARDENS.

Pay to Captain H. G. Kendall or Order

Two hundred & fifty pounds only

On account of the RECEIVER for the METROPOLITAN POLICE DISTRICT.

£250

M

Countersignature

Entd

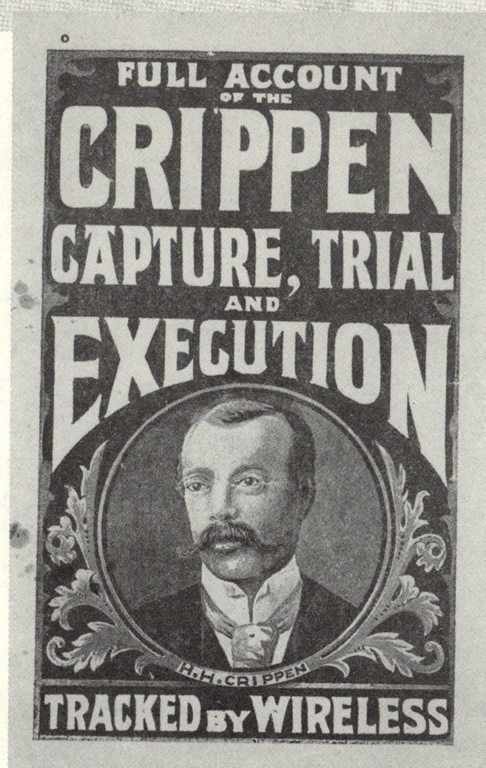

ABOVE: *Captain Kendall's reward* | Adventures on the High Seas *(Hurst & Blackett Limited, 1939)*; RIGHT: *the cover of a thirty-two-page booklet issued in 1910 | Société d'Histoire du Bas-Canada (Beloeil, QC), Guy D'Astous collection*

The Empress of Ireland *in Saint John, circa 1908 | Société d'Histoire du Bas-Canada (Beloeil, QC), Guy D'Astous collection*

2. Travelling to Quebec

ON THE MORNING OF May 28, 1914, the port at Quebec City was buzzing with activity. Nearly three thousand immigrants, tourists, and returning Canadians would disembark from seven different ocean liners that day, and workers were unloading the cargo from two colliers that carried coal from Cape Breton to Montreal. The Dominion Coal Company operated fourteen colliers, including the Norwegian-registered *Storstad*.

The RMS *Empress of Ireland* towered above the wharf. She was 14,191 tons of Edwardian elegance. She had been in Quebec City for five days, and this next sail would be her 192nd trip across the Atlantic. She was under the command of the newly promoted Captain Henry George Kendall, the youngest captain of the large Atlantic liners. The *Empress of Ireland* and the *Empress of Britain* also paid the highest in the fleet; Kendall was taking home 850 pounds a year.* This would be his third crossing as commander of the *Empress*. On May 1, he had taken the ship from Halifax—the Canadian winter terminal—to Liverpool and returned via the Gulf of St. Lawrence and up the now thawed St. Lawrence River to Quebec City. The trip out had been uneventful, and the *Empress* had arrived safely at port with 1,100 passengers aboard.

---

* About $143,000 CAD in 2024.

The *Empress of Britain* and the *Empress of Ireland* were large and fast and offered a safe, comfortable weekly service from Liverpool. They could travel up to 20 knots (37 kilometres per hour) at sea and, during summer, they could make this trip in six days (which included two days on the St. Lawrence River), a selling point for nervous passengers wary of the turbulent waters of the North Atlantic.

Kendall and his officers got little time off while in port, as they had to oversee thousands of details. On this trip, they would be loading 2,400 tons of coal to fuel the trip to Liverpool, as well as over 1,000 tons of cargo and passenger luggage. The *Empress* would be carrying over three hundred bags of mail bound for Europe and 212 bars of silver, which newspapers such as the *New York Times* and the *Ottawa Citizen* valued at a million dollars.

The huge liner required a variety of skill sets to operate; these were spread over three departments and 423 crew members. The deck department was responsible for navigation, the purser's department for passenger service, and the engineering department kept the ship's furnaces stoked and the engines running in temperatures that could reach 50 degrees Celsius. Aside from officers, quartermasters, marconi operators, a surgeon, a barber, a storekeeper, and a master at arms, there were boatswains, a printer, butchers, electricians, barkeepers, assistant pursers, a bugler, and bellboys.

A SAFE SHIP

After the sinking of the *Titanic* had shocked the world just two years earlier, the *Empress* had tightened up her safety protocols and was now considered a very safe ship. She was outfitted with sixteen steel lifeboats and twenty-six wood-and-canvas lifeboats—twenty Engelhardt and six Berthon—more than enough to hold every passenger and member of the crew in the event of an emergency. Even if the unimaginable happened and the *Empress* sank, the passengers and crew took it for granted that they would be rescued.

Safety drills were performed before every crossing, and this one was supervised by Hugh Staunton, CPR superintendent of life-saving appliances and marine superintendent, on May 23, 1914, the day after the *Empress* arrived from Liverpool. Staunton checked that the lifebelts in the cabins were in good condition and watched as crew members lowered three lifeboats. Each lifeboat weighed 2.5 tons, and it took ten crew members between one and three minutes to launch one. The lifeboats were stocked with enough water and rations to last for several days at sea.[13]

Twenty-one-year-old Joseph Singer apprenticed as a tailor and was one of a hundred assistant stewards aboard the *Empress*. His role was to help the servers and cabin stewards while the ship was at sea, and he was also responsible for loading baggage. He was trained to operate a lifeboat and, in the event of an emergency at sea, he was assigned to close one of the twenty-four watertight doors in under four minutes. The horizontal door operated with rack and pinion gears. During the safety drill, Singer went to the upper deck immediately above his assigned door, took out a metal crank key, and inserted it into a square-headed pinion. He turned the key for one minute until the door was closed. In theory, if all the watertight doors were closed in time, the system would keep the ship afloat, even if two of the eleven compartments were flooded.

Michael McAleavey and his cousin Patrick worked in different parts of the ship. Patrick was a scullion with the cleaning crew, and Michael, a trimmer, delivered coal to stokers like William Clark, a forty-something Irishman who had survived the sinking of the *Titanic* two years earlier. As a fireman, Clark worked in the boiler room, doing the hot, dirty work of feeding the ship's furnaces and shovelling coal from the bunkers into the boilers. The stokers shovelled fifteen tons of coal an hour to produce the steam that drove the ship. The engine room was the nerve centre of the ship. Each shift had forty men. Five looked after the engines, while the others tended nine coal-fired cylindrical boilers that supplied steam to the two quadruple-expansion engines.

Stewards went from cabin to cabin, checking that each one was stocked with at least one lifebelt per person. Ever since the sinking of the *Titanic*, the *Empress* ships carried over 2,200 lifebelts, more than enough for a full contingent of passengers and crew.

Particular attention was paid to the first-class amenities. The grand piano in the music room was tuned, oak trim was polished, and teak decks were washed. The glass dome in the main lounge was shined, silverware was set, and the writing room was equipped with fresh notepaper.

The return trip would carry 1,056 passengers, far less than the maximum allowed.

GORDON DAVIDSON

Gordon Charles Davidson was a good-looking, serious young man of twenty-nine. He had dark hair, dark-brown eyes, and an athletic build and stood just shy of six feet. Later he would grow a moustache, but for this trip across the Atlantic, he was clean shaven and wore his hair parted slightly to the left in an attempt to smooth down an unruly cowlick that had dogged him since childhood.

Gordon had spent his childhood on the family farm in Union in the Elgin County of Ontario. After finishing high school, he moved to Vancouver, British Columbia, to study and to live with his brother, James, a science teacher at the Columbian Methodist College in New Westminster, an offshoot of Toronto's Victoria College. In 1906, Gordon became one of two students to receive the first bachelor of arts degrees awarded in British Columbia. When he wasn't studying,

Gordon Davidson, circa 1913 | Courtesy of Margaret Patmore

he was a standout swimmer and a player and coach of the university's soccer team.

The Davidsons lived on West Twelfth Avenue in Fairview Slopes, a largely middle-class area situated below the mansions of Shaughnessy Heights. It was a suburb developed for the rich by the CPR in 1909 and named after company president Thomas Shaughnessy.

Gordon was travelling to England to continue research for his PhD in history at UC Berkeley, thanks to a grant from the Native Sons of California. He was booked in second class with a tourist-class sleeper on the CPR's *Imperial Limited* train, which departed Vancouver for Montreal nightly at 8:00 p.m. The sleeper was similar to that of a first-class sleeping car, but without all the luxury fittings and at half the price.

FRONT-PAGE HEADLINES

When Gordon Davidson read the local papers on the day of his departure, he would have learned that the Jack Kong murder trial, which had dominated the headlines for weeks, had concluded with a surprise verdict of manslaughter. Kong, a sixteen-year-old Chinese houseboy for the Millard family in Vancouver's West End, had killed his mistress, cut up her body, and burned it in the furnace. He was sharing the headlines with a well-known local singer named Madame Este Newton. She was in hospital fighting for her life after her husband, John, shot her and killed himself.

The other front-page headline concerned the arrival of the *Komagata Maru*, a Japanese steamship carrying 376 passengers from the province of Punjab in British India. The passengers were hoping to immigrate to Canada but were refused entry into Vancouver. Another disturbing headline concerned the sinking of the new lightship, *Halifax 10*, off the coast of Nova Scotia. She had been on her way to take up service as a lighthouse near Halifax Harbour. The entire crew of twenty-five was lost.

Despite the recession that had hit Vancouver with such force the previous year, construction around the city continued, though at a much slower pace. As Davidson arrived at the CPR depot at the foot of Granville Street, he would have seen that the new station was almost finished. Even on a late Saturday afternoon, the men were still at work, with the noise of the riveting gun and a chorus of hammers and saws going to work on the new four-storey, steel-frame terminus building. It would be the third station built since intercontinental trains had started arriving in Vancouver in 1887. This meant that the current station's days were numbered; it had lasted just fifteen years, an ornate castle-like building built in the CPR's early chateau style, with two massive turrets and an arched entranceway.

View from the water of the second CPR station at the foot of Granville Street, Vancouver, 1903 | City of Vancouver Archives (BC), AM54-S4-Can P194

PASSENGERS FROM THE WEST

I contacted the CPR's archives to see if they had a train manifest that would tell me the names of the other *Empress* passengers from Western Canada who were on the train with Davidson. Frustratingly, the manifests don't exist; they've been either lost or thrown out decades ago. Adding to the confusion, passengers were listed by the office where they booked, not by where they lived or departed from. Davidson was listed in the newspapers as an American from California, even though he was Canadian and his trip originated in Vancouver.

Eighty people travelling on the *Empress of Ireland* booked out of the Vancouver office, and many would have been on the same train as Davidson. They included people from other BC cities such as Victoria, Nanaimo, and Silverton, as well as Washington state, and nearly thirty were from the Kootenays. While Davidson was on a study trip, others were travelling for business, some were starting a European holiday or on their honeymoon, and still others were immigrants to Canada returning home to visit family and show off their children.

Many of the passengers were part of the Salvation Army, travelling to London to the group's International Congress in England, the first in ten years. Over two thousand Canadian delegates, from Victoria, BC, to St. John's, Newfoundland, were heading there. The Salvationists booked passage aboard several different liners, but the majority were travelling aboard the *Empress of Ireland* and the *Alaunia*, which departed two days later.

The 161 Salvationists, including forty-one musicians and Commissioner David Rees, the top dog in Canada, travelling on the *Empress* made up the bulk of the 255 passengers booked in second class—with the exception of a few travelling in third class.*

Salvationists travelling on the *Empress* from Vancouver included Annie Cook, who was combining the Congress with a trip to visit her sick mother in England; John Fowler and William Wakefield, who were part of the Salvation Army band; and the Delamonts, who booked on the train at Moose Jaw, Saskatchewan. John Delamont and his sons, Leonard and Arthur, as well as Archie Brown and Charles Wilkes, had been chosen to play in the Salvation Army Staff Band at the Congress. John's wife, Seraphine, and his daughter, Lizzie, were also travelling with them.

On the *Imperial Limited*, despite travelling in different classes, passengers met while wandering the aisles, sitting in the smoking room, or enjoying the spectacular views from the special observation lounges at the rear of the train that acted as a living room.†

---

* The first- and second-class cabins on the *Empress of Ireland* were designed to be interchangeable. On this trip Commissioner David Rees and Colonel Sydney Maidment were given first-class cabins but dined with their families and comrades in second class.

† Before the Connaught Tunnel opened in 1916, trains couldn't pull heavy dining cars along the mountain regions between Vancouver and Lake Louise. Instead, the train stopped for meals at CPR hotels in North Bend, Glacier, and Field.

TOP: *the* Imperial Limited *CPR train leaving Glacier, circa 1900–1920 | Wallace B. Chung and Madeline H. Chung Collection, Books and Special Collections, University of British;* BOTTOM: *Dufferin Terrace and the Château Frontenac in Quebec City, 1908 | McCord Stewart Museum (Montreal, QC), MP-1981.94.5.2 and Columbia Library (Vancouver, BC), CC-TX-283-1*

Five days after leaving Vancouver, the train arrived at Windsor Station in downtown Montreal. From there passengers would catch one of the special boat trains to Quebec City. First-class passengers spent the night at the CPR's flagship hotel, the Château Frontenac, its lobby already filled with steamer trunks belonging to those sailing on CPR liners the following day. The company's second- and third-class passengers spent their night in lesser luxury in hotels such as the Neptune, located on Côte de la Montagne close to the harbour.

MORE SALVATIONISTS ARRIVE IN QUEBEC

Twenty-five-year-old Captain John Edward Dodd was on the train from Toronto with Violet, his bride of just ten days. Dodd was a journalist and subeditor of the Salvation Army *War Cry*, played bass in the staff band, and was combining the conference with a honeymoon and his duties as a *War Cry* correspondent. His first report, "Travel Jottings," would outlive them both. The train was running an hour late. "Little groups of Salvationists were to be seen at the entrance to the depot right until the train departed. It was hard to say goodbye. Very hard for some," wrote Dodd. "Who would blame them even if they were envious."[14] The sidewalks were crowded with well-wishers, noted Salvationist Major George Attwell: "In all this wide world, I doubt whether a happier party ever set out on a long journey."[15]

The train stopped briefly at Montreal to pick up more Army members, including Major Nettie Simco of Vancouver, who was in Montreal visiting friends. She told Colonel W.J. Turner that she'd had a vision of sorts in which she saw the bodies of her Army comrades being carried ashore in coffins. The passengers disembarked at the station by the wharf where the *Empress* was docked. Their trunks and valises were carried to the dock in wheelbarrows and then taken up the gangplank. Some trunks were taken to passenger cabins and staterooms, others stored below deck.

"From the train to the *Empress of Ireland* was but a few steps, and the transfer of passengers and baggage was so silent and swift that one would have thought that the party was entirely composed of seasoned globe-trotters instead of people many of whom had never crossed the Atlantic," wrote John Dodd. "We were on our way to the I.C.C. and the next stop is Liverpool."[16]

Salvation Army Captain Hal Beckett worked with immigrants entering Quebec City, and he had brought his wife and eighteen-day-old baby daughter down to the wharf to see their friends off. "It was like gala day at the wharf," wrote Beckett.

> Everyone was in high spirits. I can feel the warmth of the excitement now after all these years. The staff bandsmen were arrayed in new uniforms, with maple leaves on their epaulettes. I served with many of them on Territorial Headquarters, and I felt a pang that I was not to be of the happy party. Pointing to my infant I said: "If it had not been for you my dear, I might have been going too." I asked Commissioner Rees, if on his return, he would dedicate the baby, and, with a smile, he shrugged his shoulders. It was as if he had said: "If I come back."[17]

"I find my heart strangely moved as I write and recall our entry into Quebec, on that memorable Thursday afternoon, and the gay scene as we boarded the *Empress*," wrote George Attwell. "I can vividly picture our first rush to see what our cabins looked like, our first glimpse at the dining room, and the sense of satisfaction at the thought that there seemed to be nothing to mar our comfort."[18]

The Empress of Ireland *in Liverpool, circa 1912* | *Société d'Histoire du Bas-Canada (Beloeil, QC), Guy D'Astous collection*

PREPARING TO SAIL

By 2:00 p.m., preparations were complete, and Captain Kendall was waiting to greet his passengers. Memorizing the names of his first-class passengers was part of the job so that he could greet each one by name. On this trip, his VIPs included British actors Laurence Irving, his wife, Mabel Hackney, and Sir Henry Seton-Karr; John Abercrombie and Charles Lindsay Claude Bowes-Lyon, the eldest son of the Earl of Strathmore; and Wallace Leonard Palmer, the twenty-nine-year-old associate editor and special correspondent for Canada of the *Financial News* in London, who had been in the country for three months with his wife, Ethel. And there was another Ethel, Ethel Sabina Grundy Paton, a wealthy socialite from Sherbrooke, Quebec. Most of the passengers boarded with a small bag to hold their valuables. Many gave friends and relatives a tour of the ship's public areas.

John Langley, a good-looking athletic man, just under six feet with blue eyes and dark-brown hair, cut a dashing figure as he boarded the *Empress* at 2:00 p.m. He made sure that his suitcase and kit bag were safely stowed away in Cabin 555 and then went up to the first-class deck to take a few photos. Twenty-seven-year-old Langley had immigrated to Canada from Ireland just six months earlier. His wife, Bessie, was staying home with two-year-old Patricia and baby Joan at Willow Grange, their 640-acre cattle ranch in Canford, BC. Langley was travelling back to Ireland to take care of some property matters.

He ran into Elizabeth Rhodes Hailey from Vancouver, mother of Alfred Hailey, the captain of the *Empress of India*. They chatted about her son, who, after spending nearly two decades sailing around the world on windjammers and tramps, had worked his way up to commander of passenger liners such as the *Empress of China* and the *Empress of India* on the trans-Pacific route.

At 4:00 p.m. the whistle sounded, warning those not sailing that it was time to leave the ship.

Less than thirty minutes later, Captain Kendall gave the order to cast off all lines. Friends and onlookers gathered on the pier included a contingent from the Salvation Army who had come to say goodbye.

Then it happened. Emmy, the ship's orange cat, had never missed a voyage, as legend had it. She jumped off the ship and ran away. A terrible omen for those who believed in such superstitions.

John Langley at Knockanure Manor, the Langley family home in Tipperary | Langley family collection

3. Departing Quebec City

GORDON DAVIDSON WAS UNAWARE that Emmy the cat had left the ship and was watching him sail away from the roof of the shed at Pier 27. Even if he had known, he wouldn't have thought much of it. There was so much else to take in as the ship prepared to leave.

Members of the Salvation Army Staff Band were dressed in new red tunics and brought along RCMP-style Stetsons chosen to proudly represent and promote Canada in England. They collected their instruments from the piles of luggage and gathered on the promenade deck for an impromptu concert, playing "O Canada" and "Auld Lang Syne" at the dock and launching into "God Be with You Till We Meet Again" as the *Empress* glided out into the river. Many of the passengers pressed against the ship's railings to wave to family and friends who had come to see them off.

VIPS

Tugboats manoeuvred the ship into the St. Lawrence River. It was a clear day, and smoke poured from the liner's two yellow-and-black funnels. Captain Kendall stood on the bridge with his second-in-command, Chief Officer Mansfield Steede, a forty-one-year-old Irishman who had been at sea since he was fourteen. Kendall may have started as a cabin boy on a sailing ship but was enjoying his

TOP: *The* Empress of Ireland, *circa 1906–1914 | Library and Archives Canada (Ottawa,* ON*) / Co-operative Commonwealth Federation and New Democratic Party Fonds;* RIGHT: *Commissioner David Rees and Colonel Sydney Maidment aboard the last voyage of the* Empress, *May 28, 1914. Written on the back of the photo: "Picture snapped by Captain George Goodhew at the dock in Quebec City just before the* Empress *sailed." | Used by permission of the Salvation Army Canada and Bermuda Archives (Toronto,* ON*), photo 53694*

new status as captain of the CPR's flagship liner. He was looking forward to entertaining his first-class passengers with his stories and spending time with renowned British actor and playwright Laurence Irving and his wife, actress Mabel Hackney. Their troupe had just finished a three-month-long Canadian tour performing four plays—*Typhoon*, *The Unwritten Law*, *The Lilly*, and *The Importance of Being Earnest*—and had given their final performance at Walker Theatre in Winnipeg on May 23. They had originally booked passage home on White Star's *Teutonic*, but the Irvings, their maid, Hilda Haggeston, and two other cast members—married actors Elsie and Harold South—had decided to leave three days earlier and rebooked on the *Empress*, the Irvings in first class and the Souths in second.

There were two nineteen-year-olds in first class. Montreal's Grace Kohl was already a seasoned traveller. She had just returned from a trip to England to attend a wedding with her mother and older sister, Kitty. The women had sailed on the *Empress of Ireland* under the command of Captain James Murray. This time she was on her own and planned to stay with an aunt in Surrey, England.

The other nineteen-year-old, Cedric Aubrey Woolls Gallagher, was travelling to England with his mother, Charlotte. Cedric's father, the manager of the Royal Bank in Winnipeg, had stayed behind, and Cedric's six-year-old sister, Evelyn, was with her aunt in Montreal. This was Cedric's first trip overseas. As the ship steamed down the St. Lawrence, Cedric, a tall, thin young man, and Charlotte, his elegant mother, started to explore their impressive surroundings.

The ship had eight decks. The most ornate ones were on the highest levels of the ship and housed the music room, the smoking lounge, the library, and a well-stocked café on the lower promenade deck that supplied drinks and snacks throughout the day. These decks were filled with plush velvet, taffeta, leather furniture, and thick carpets

CLOCKWISE FROM TOP: *decks on the* Empress of Ireland | *Library and Archives Canada (Ottawa,* ON*) / Andrew Audubon Merrilees fonds / e004665745; first-class entrance on the lower promenade deck, with stairs leading up to the music room and down to the dining saloon* | *Bedford Lemere & Co, public domain; the first-class cabin occupied by the Duchess of Connaught in 1911* | *City of Vancouver Archives (*BC*)* AM*54-S4-:*LP*97; first-class dining saloon on the* Empress of Ireland, *1906* | *Bedford Lemere & Co, public domain*

surrounded by sculpted oak, mahogany, and teak woodwork, with a central atrium that rose from the dining room.

Once the ship was at sea, the upper decks of first class were out of bounds for anyone not paying the hefty premium, but there was still much to see, eat, drink, and do for those not as privileged. Passengers in second and third class had music rooms with a piano for whomever felt like playing, and parents of small children took advantage of the sandbox located on the upper deck toward the front of the ship. The upper deck and the shelter deck included cabins for second-class passengers and many of the crew members and the first-class barbershop. The three lowest decks—the Orlop deck, the lower deck, and the main deck—housed most of the third-class passenger cabins and the dining room.

The class structure aboard the Empress followed class lines in the UK and Canada at the time. The wealthy and educated filled first class. The white collar and middle class took up the majority of the cabins in second. Third class, at least on this voyage, was filled with a mixture of women and children, several Salvationists, and farmers and immigrant workers returning home from the States.

SECOND CLASS

John Langley made his way to Cabin 412 on the second-class deck to check on Eleanor Hunt, a family friend from Dublin now living in Vancouver. He found her sharing a cabin with Mary Katherine Hepburn, also of Vancouver, and her two children, three-year-old Barbara and baby Owen. It was the start of a year-long holiday for the Hepburns, who were meeting up with Mary Katherine's mother in England. Her husband, Frank, planned to join his family the following Christmas. Red-headed Barbara was around the same age as Langley's little daughter, Patricia, and he took the girl for a walk around the deck while the women dressed for dinner.

Elsewhere, stewards were busy helping disoriented passengers find the library, dining room, and saloons. They brought blankets and books and took drink and food orders for those sitting on the main decks to take in the scenery.

Just before 6:00 p.m. Gordon Davidson joined the other passengers in the dining room. Second-class passengers ate first, and the Salvationists dined in their dazzling new uniforms.

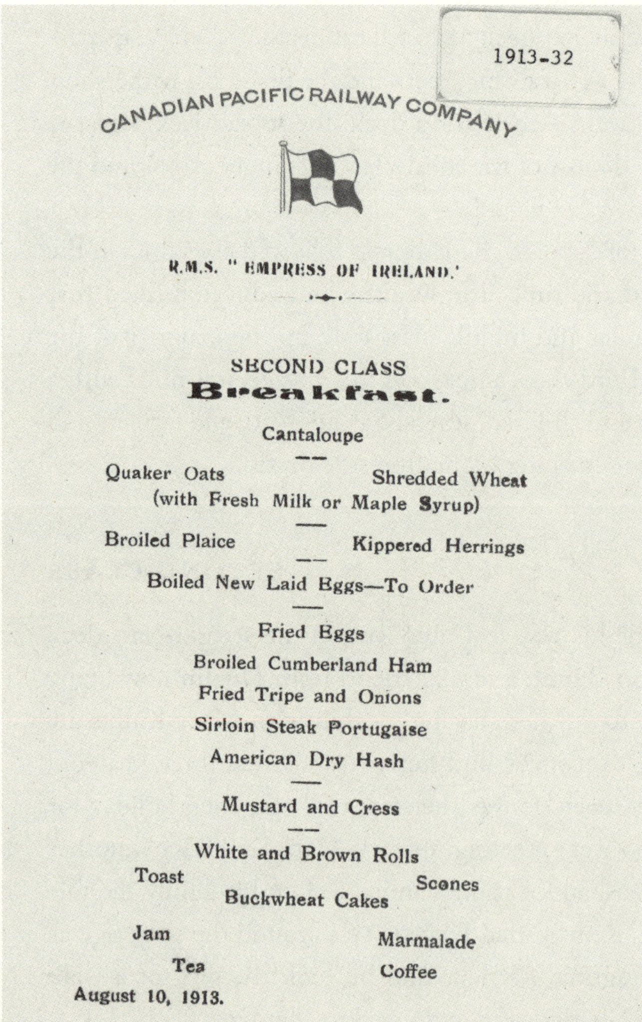

1913-32

CANADIAN PACIFIC RAILWAY COMPANY

R.M.S. "EMPRESS OF IRELAND."

SECOND CLASS

Breakfast.

Cantaloupe

Quaker Oats — Shredded Wheat
(with Fresh Milk or Maple Syrup)

Broiled Plaice — Kippered Herrings

Boiled New Laid Eggs—To Order

Fried Eggs
Broiled Cumberland Ham
Fried Tripe and Onions
Sirloin Steak Portugaise
American Dry Hash

Mustard and Cress

White and Brown Rolls
Toast — Scones
Buckwheat Cakes

Jam — Marmalade
Tea — Coffee

August 10, 1913.

Menu from the Empress of Ireland's *second-class dining room, 1913* | *City of Vancouver Archives* (BC), PAM *1913-32*

Meals for the 715 third-class passengers were split into three seatings. Those at the last seating would have to wait until 9:00 p.m. to eat in a cafeteria-style dining room. Their dinner was less fancy but decent, consisting of bouilli soup, ragout of veal, roast mutton, parsnips and semolina, and pudding for dessert.

TOP TO BOTTOM: *drawing of the first-class music room from a* CPR *brochure, circa 1906; drawing of the first-class café from a* CPR *brochure, circa 1906; drawing of first-class diners in the* Empress *from a* CPR *brochure, circa 1906* | *Société d'Histoire du Bas-Canada (Beloeil,* QC*), Guy D'Astous collection*

IMMIGRANT WORKERS

About three hundred of the third-class passengers were immigrant workers who had recently been laid off from the assembly lines of car factories in Detroit, Michigan, and Windsor, Ontario, and were heading home to Europe. Others had come from countries such as Russia and Germany and were working as labourers in the US. Some immigrants had given up on North America and were returning home for good.

Egildo Braga, twenty-six, was one of the twenty-seven Italians in the *Empress*'s third class who were working in Minnesota mines and returning home to see families or to flee the violent strikes plaguing the mining sector. He had arrived at Ellis Island in December 1908 and married his wife, Carolina, three years later, and now the couple were travelling home to show off their toddler, Rino, to their family in Italy.

Passengers enjoying a game of deck golf on the Empress of Ireland, *circa 1913 | Société d'Histoire du Bas-Canada (Beloeil, QC), Guy D'Astous collection*

Of the twenty-five Norwegians who were travelling in third class from various destinations in Canada and the US, Arthur Evenson, Christian Samuelson, Johannes Gard, and Magnus and Sarah Luren were travelling home to Stavanger to celebrate the hundredth anniversary of Norway's independence from Sweden.

THE SHIP'S SURGEON

At 7:00 p.m., Cedric, Charlotte, and the other first-class passengers were summoned to their dining room by a bugler and then entertained by the ship's five-piece orchestra. There was a separate dining room for the children. As Dr. James Grant, the newly hired ship's surgeon, would later tell his wife, the meals were the best that he'd ever had.

Grant grew up in Cumberland, a small coal mining town in the Comox Valley on Vancouver Island, and had recently finished an internship at Montreal General Hospital after graduating from McGill University. Grant's boss, Dr. William Alexander Molson, had thought that twenty-six-year-old Grant's health could be improved by some sea air and arranged for him to act as ship's surgeon. This was Grant's third crossing on the *Empress* and his second as ship's surgeon. He was missing his wife and little boy on Vancouver Island.

Passengers went out on deck to watch the sun setting behind the mountains. "It was a beautiful sight and one that you wanted to look at for a long time," wrote Bert Greenaway.[19]

Later, a large number of passengers, ship's officers, and crew gathered around a piano in the music room as Ensign Oliver Mardall of Vancouver led about fifteen members of the Salvation Army band in an impromptu concert. Some sang loudly while others joined in with the harmonicas, fiddles, accordions, and other instruments they had brought with them. Mardall led the choruses of "Rocked in the Cradle of the Deep," making everyone dip their knees on the

Passengers gathered on the deck of the Empress of Ireland, *circa 1910 | City of Vancouver Archives (BC), Am54-S4-: Bo P117*

word *deep*. "I never knew Ollie to be so happy as he was then," wrote George Attwell. "We sang a few lively songs at first then a few sentimental ones and ended with hymns. Most of the boys went to bed about 11:30 p.m."[20]

Dr. Grant listened to the band play and then went to the café, where some of the passengers were playing bridge. He ordered a coffee and a sandwich and headed back to his cabin on the upper deck around 12:30 a.m.

SALVATIONISTS

Seven-year-old Grace and her mother, Edith Hanagan, watched Grace's father, Ted Hanagan, conduct the concert. Afterward, the family headed to their cabin. There was a sink, a bed under the porthole, and two berths. With the *Titanic* still fresh in her mind, Grace asked her parents to put her on the top bunk. "I didn't want to sleep on the bed by the porthole because if the boat went down, the water would come in there first," she said.[21]

Teddy Gray was an illustrator for the *Toronto Daily Star* and volunteered with the Salvation Army's *War Cry*. He drew a picture of a Salvationist holding a baby with the words "Who'll be next?" for his old roommate, Hal Beckett, who had been at the wharf in Quebec City to see them off. Then Gray drew himself in the centre of a card, passed it around for his friends to sign, and on the other side wrote, "I thought you would like this. It is plain—but a novelty."[22] This second card was addressed to his fiancée, Sadie Bilham, who Gray planned to marry when he returned to Ontario. He popped the cards into the mail for Rimouski. Gray was nervous about sailing; a few days earlier, he had taken out a $2,000 insurance policy, leaving everything to Sadie.

Hattie Attwell stayed on the deck with her friends and fellow Salvationists after the band finished their last song, "Sweet and Low."

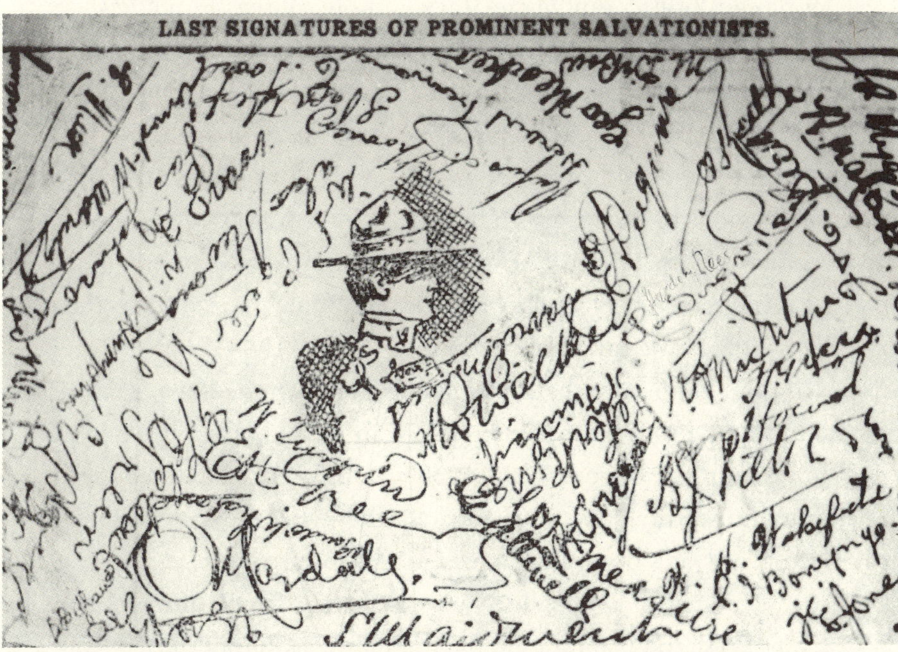

Self-caricature by Teddy Gray, with signatures from many Salvationists aboard the Empress, *May 28, 1914 | Used by permission of the Salvation Army Canada and Bermuda Archives (Toronto, ON), photo 65591*

"The moon was shining down, and everything was peaceful and lovely. The boat was silently gliding through the water," Hattie said. "A beautiful breeze blew gently. We sat for a time, until presently the commissioner came along and said to his wife [Ruth Rees], 'My dear, you must come away, you'll be tired tomorrow.'"[23]

It had been a long day of travel, and one by one, the Salvationists disappeared to write letters or retire to their cabins.

PARTY OF FIVE

Sebena Barbour and her little girls, three-year-old Evelyn and eight-year-old Florrie, Sebena's fiancé, Robert Crellin, and family friend Billy Barry made up a party of five from Silverton, BC. Sebena had married Thomas Barbour in Cumberland, England, and left for Canada shortly after, landing in Three Forks in southeastern BC, where Robert Crellin, Billy Barry, and other Cumbrians were already working in the silver mines.

But I'll let Florrie tell you her story: "I was born in 1906, and they named me Florence Lorraine Barbour. When I was christened, Bob Crellin stood for me as my godfather, and a lady who was a French Canadian and was called Lorraine Sloan was my godmother."

Florrie remembers Crellin and Barry as frequent visitors to their house. Crellin, she says, played the concertina.

In 1913, Thomas Barbour was taking a load of ore down from the mines when a rock slide startled his team of six horses, and he was thrown from the wagon. "Uncle Bob and Billy Barry took us to the hospital to see my dad and I asked Mother what the ice was for on the back of Dad's head, and she said it was to stop the bleeding. Dad just smiled and said we had to be good girls and look after Mother for him."[24] Barbour died nine days later and is buried in the New Denver cemetery. Sebena and her two little daughters moved down to Silverton so that Florrie could start school.

The following year, Sebena decided to take her girls to meet their grandmother. She planned to marry Crellin, Florrie and Evelyn's "Uncle Bob." Barry was engaged to a young lady from his hometown, and he wanted to marry her and bring her back to Silverton. The two men shared a cabin on the *Empress* adjacent to the Barbours. The group had dinner together, but the girls were tired, and Sebena took them back to their cabin. The girls' grandmother had sent two fancy dresses for them to wear in England, but they were too big, so Sebena spent some time making alterations. Crellin and Barry headed for the smoking room.

BELOW DECK

John Fowler, a car inspector with the CPR in Vancouver, was no stranger to Atlantic crossings. On this trip he was travelling to London as the deputy band sergeant from the Salvation Army No. 1 Corps. His wife and three small children had stayed at home. Fowler was one of a handful of Salvationists travelling in third class, and he was sharing Cabin 656 with three others. He'd been feeling off since the start of the trip, and even though he'd retired early to his cabin, he was finding it hard to sleep.

Brothers Chris and Theo Bartschi had arrived in Canada from Switzerland eleven years earlier. They'd barely managed to catch the *Empress* before she left the dock at Quebec City. Once aboard, they'd found their berths in Cabin 731 but were unhappy with their cabin-mates and asked to be moved. The steward found them a new cabin higher up and nearer the centre of the ship. Now the brothers were enjoying the music and joining in the dancing and singing.

At 10:00 p.m. the Bartschis went to the saloon, where they played several games of whist with two English travellers. They retired to their berths at 11:00 p.m. After the long day they'd had, both were soon asleep.

Frank Brooks, a joiner by trade, played the trombone in the Salvation Army band. He was sharing a second-class cabin with fellow band members Ernie Foord and George Felstead. Ernie's wife, Alice, and their young daughter, also named Alice, were sharing a cabin with Frank's wife, Henrietta, and their nine-year-old daughter, Dorothy. The Brooks had immigrated to Toronto in 1905 and were excited to be taking Dolly to England to meet their families for the first time.

George Felstead's wife, Louise, and their two children, fifteen-year-old William and twelve-year-old Gladys, were sailing in third class. The Felsteads had lived in Toronto for eight years, and as well as attending the Congress, they planned to visit family in London. George was a carpenter with the Robert Simpson Company, but his passion was music.* He was considered the best horn player in the Salvation Army's Toronto band.

Kenneth McIntyre from New York was travelling with the Canadian staff band as a baritone horn player and sharing a cabin with fellow Salvationists and band members William Measures, Ernie Aldbridge, and Teddy Gray. It was almost midnight when McIntyre put the letters and postcards he had written to family and friends into the ship's mailbox and headed to his cabin. All three of his cabinmates were asleep but had left the lights on for him. Though he was exhausted after the long day, McIntyre couldn't sleep. "I was extremely tired but somehow was unaccountably led to read all the fine print instructions, framed under glass, on how to put on a life preserver. I had no sense of fear, but I opened the locker-wardrobe door on my side of the stateroom. There on the shelf were two of the old-style life preservers—cork blocks sewn in canvas."[25]

McIntyre decided to learn the layout of the ship and find a route to the upper deck. He closed the locker door, stepped out into

* Later a major department store chain known as Simpson's, and still later, part of the Hudson's Bay Company.

the passage, and followed it until he came to a landing. "A broad stair came up from the deck below. Two narrow stairs led up into the second-class dining room saloon. In rough weather one could grasp both handrails in the climb. Crossing the dining saloon, I went directly to one of the storm-proof doors, slid it open and stepped out onto the After Boat Deck. The night was clear, the air crisp and the *Empress* was plainly up to full speed, taking us, I thought, toward the gulf and the Atlantic and Liverpool."[26]

McIntyre retraced his steps back to his cabin and fell into a deep sleep.

THE CREW

Captain Kendall was in the wheelhouse, directing the ship from the bridge. With him was second officer Roger Williams, three other crew members, and river pilot Adelard Bernier. It was standard practice while travelling up or down the St. Lawrence River for any ship over 30 metres (100 feet) long to have an experienced pilot aboard. Bernier was a veteran of the waterway and well equipped to deal with the river's temperamental weather, shoals, tides, and narrowing shores. He had worked with Canadian Pacific for seven years.

At 9:00 p.m. chief steward Augustus Gaade commenced his nightly walk through the sleeping quarters. The saloon stewards were cleaning up after the first- and second-class sittings and preparing the table settings for the next day's breakfast. Those on the deck had watched the sun set on the port side of the ship. It was a clear night, and they could see the lights on the shore.

Around 10:00 p.m., Gordon Davidson went to Cabin 524. It was an outside room on the starboard side of the main deck, and he was sharing the room with Arthur Stillman, who was visiting his parents in England. Rena Belle, Stillman's wife of two years, had stayed at home in Calgary.

As Davidson entered his room, a cabin steward was leaving, having just closed the porthole. Stillman had the top berth. Their cabinmate James Lennon had moved into another unoccupied cabin.

Davidson, Stillman, Lennon, and Martin Gill had met on the train trip from out west. They made an interesting travel party: Davidson was a thirty-year-old academic; Stillman was a twenty-five-year-old assistant manager with the Great West Permanent Loan Company in Calgary; Lennon was a thirty-one-year-old insurance agent from Winnipeg; and twenty-three-year-old Gill worked at the No. 1 mine in Ainsworth, BC.

Gill now made his way down to third class, where he was sharing a six-berth cabin with five other men. The third-class cabins and public areas were basic but comfortable.

At midnight, the second shift came on, and first officer Edward Jones took over from Williams on the bridge.

Shortly after midnight, the poker players from first class finished their games in the lounge.

At 12:30 a.m. the *Empress* sailed into a fog bank. She slowed her speed and sounded one long blast of her fog signal. She emerged from the fog bank before another blast was needed.

Shuffleboard on the deck, 1914 | Public domain

4. The Storstad

JUST AFTER 9:00 P.M. Captain Thomas Andersen was finishing up on the bridge of the *Storstad*, getting ready to join his wife in their cabin and grab a few hours of sleep. He was a big man in his midthirties with a red face and a large moustache. His uniform was a blue serge suit and a peaked cap. Many of the officers set up homes in Sydney, Nova Scotia, for their families while working on contract for the coal companies. Anna Andersen, a no-nonsense, pleasant woman with chestnut hair and blue eyes, often sailed with her husband.

The *Storstad* was on its way to Montreal, carrying more than ten thousand tons of coal. She had a reinforced hull that could slice through winter ice, and at that moment she was headed to Father Point to collect a pilot who would navigate the ship up the St. Lawrence.

Andersen had gone to sea at fifteen as a deck boy on the SS *Najaden*, working his way up to earn his captain's ticket at nineteen. He had been captain of the *Storstad* for three years now, taking over command a few months after she launched in 1910.

Andersen handed over the ship to his second-in-command, thirty-three-year-old Alfred Toftenes, and told him to wake Andersen either when the collier reached Father Point or in the event of fog.[27] The captain's cabin was directly under the bridge. Alfred Toftenes was chief officer and a highly respected member of the thirty-six-man

The pilot boat Eureka *meets the* RMS Empress of Britain *at Rimouski, 1907* | *McCord Stewart Museum (Montreal, QC), M2003.28.137*

crew. He had sailed with Andersen for three and a half years and had been promoted to second-in-command six weeks earlier.

The *Storstad* was travelling at full speed: 10 knots (18.5 kilometres per hour).

The next few hours were uneventful as the *Storstad* passed the lighthouse at Matane and Pointe Mitis.

RIMOUSKI

At 1:30 a.m. the *Empress* met up with the steamboat *Eureka*, which collected the mail and took pilot Adelard Bernier from the *Empress* to the lighthouse station at Father Point.

The *Empress* was now past the most dangerous part of the St. Lawrence River, and Bernier's job was finished. He shook hands with Captain Kendall. "I don't think you should run into much fog for the rest of the night. Good luck, Commander," he told Kendall.[28]

Kendall ordered full speed ahead. He would wait until they were on open seas before handing command over to chief officer Mansfield Steede, who was now asleep in his cabin.

The *Empress* was in the widest part of the St. Lawrence River—50 kilometres (31 miles) across—and she was going about 17 knots (31 kilometres per hour). John Carroll, the lookout, rang the crow's nest brass bell once to notify the bridge of a vessel on the starboard side.

Kendall took the stairs to the compass platform for a better view. He could see the distant lights of an incoming ship and estimated that it was about 10 kilometres (6.2 miles) away. The crew of the *Empress* were aware that the other ship would have to move closer to shore to pick up its pilot. The weather was clear and fine, and Kendall saw no reason for concern. He adjusted his course to north 73 magnetic, north 76 east, believing he was far enough out in the channel to easily pass the other vessel.[29]

FOG

Over on the *Storstad*, chief officer Toftenes was hugging the coast while assessing the speed of both vessels and ensuring that they were on safe parallel courses.

Moments later a thick bank of fog rolled in from the south shore, slowly creeping across the water in a northwest direction and blanketing the *Empress* and the *Storstad*. Both ships were now hidden from each other.

Two years earlier, the liner's sister ship, the *Empress of Britain*, under Captain James Murray, had collided with the collier SS *Helvetia* in the fog on the St. Lawrence River. Like the *Storstad*, the *Helvetia* was under charter to the Dominion Coal Company.[30] In that instance, the *Helvetia* had sunk. No lives were lost, but the *Empress of Britain* was blamed, owing to her excessive speed prior to the accident. While

Murray hadn't undergone any disciplinary action, Kendall didn't want to make the same mistake.

At this point, the stories of the surviving crew members from the two vessels go in markedly different directions. Both say their engines were stopped and that the other ship was going fast.

At the time of the collision, there were five men on the bridge of the *Storstad*: Toftenes, third officer Jacob Saxe, two sailors, and a fireman. Toftenes said that at the first sign of fog, he slowed his engines, and when he could no longer see the *Empress* through the fog, he ordered the engines to stop.

About five minutes later, Toftenes said, in order to counteract the current that was pulling the *Storstad* to the shore, he gave an order to port the wheel to the right. Because the *Storstad* was stopped in the water, the vessel didn't respond, and Saxe took it upon himself to turn the wheel as far as it would go. The *Storstad* still refused to budge. To gain control of the vessel, said Toftenes, he ordered slow ahead and then he called his captain.

Toftenes told Captain Andersen about the fog, but not that there was another ship in the area. Andersen asked if he could see the Father Point light, and Toftenes answered, "It's just closing off now."[31]

ARE YOU ANXIOUS?

Andersen quickly dressed. "Are you anxious?" Anna asked her husband. "I don't know why but I am," he told her.

On the bridge, Andersen went straight to the ship's compass to check the *Storstad*'s position. Then he looked up and saw the lights of the *Empress* straight ahead. He immediately ordered his ship's engines to full astern (to be thrown in reverse) and sounded three long blasts of the ship's horn to warn the *Empress* of his intentions.

Meanwhile, Anna got up and began to dress. "I was just putting on my fur coat when the collision came. It was not a hard bump, because

I was standing up and the shock did not throw me across the cabin." She joined her husband on the bridge. "I saw the *Empress* lying across our bows. I said to my husband, 'I suppose we're going down?' He said: 'We might be.' He told me to just take things easy and not to cry. I didn't get scared. I felt quite coolheaded."[32]

At the same moment, Kendall was standing on the navigation bridge, staring in horror as the *Storstad*'s bow emerged from the fog and headed straight toward them. The collier rammed the passenger ship dead centre, slicing through the *Empress* and leaving a huge gaping hole.

A depiction of the Storstad *colliding with the* Empress of Ireland, *drawn from telegraphic descriptions and commissioned by the American Press Association, 1914* | *Société d'Histoire du Bas-Canada (Beloeil, QC), Guy D'Astous collection*

5. The Collision

CAPTAIN KENDALL GRABBED HIS megaphone and commanded the crew of the *Storstad* to maintain full speed ahead in order to plug the hole in his ship and slow the flow of water pouring through it. Captain Andersen of the *Storstad* complied, but it was too late. The impact of the collier and the forward motion of the *Empress* caused the *Storstad* to swing out from the liner and slide back into the fog.

Kendall gave the order to stop the engines and close the bulkhead doors of the watertight compartments. He told Jones, his second-in-command, to ready the lifeboats. Then he sounded the siren to abandon ship. The ship was in a state of emergency.*

The *Storstad* was filled with Cape Breton coal en route to Montreal. Her bow was reinforced to push through ice on the St. Lawrence River, and her sharp prow ripped through the *Empress*'s steel plates and cabins, tearing a 32.5 square-metre hole in the ship's starboard side, well below the waterline. The collision was barely felt by the crew of the *Storstad*, but one of her bow anchors had penetrated a midship cabin on the *Empress* and sliced through sleeping human flesh. The

---

* Sound signals are vital communication tools at sea. The crow's nest bell is rung to alert the crew to the presence of sightings in the vicinity of the ship. One ring signals a sighting to starboard, two rings a sighting to port, and three rings a sighting straight ahead. In fog, the steam whistle is sounded every two minutes to alert other vessels of the ship's presence. When the siren is sounded, it means abandon ship and do what you can to save yourself. (Source: exhibit placard, Site Historique Maritime de la Pointe-au-Père.)

door plate from Cabin 328 was later found on the collier's prow near the crumpled stern, showing that the *Storstad*'s bow had penetrated 5.5 metres (18 feet) through the liner's side, almost exactly in the middle measured from stern to stern.[33]

More than 200,000 litres (53,000 gallons) of water a second poured into the *Empress*, causing catastrophic flooding in the engine rooms and lower decks. Charles Spencer, a fifteen-year-old bellboy, ran down to third class to wake up his co-workers so they could get to the bulkheads and close the watertight doors. But when he got there, the water was already more than half a metre (1.6 feet) deep, and he struggled to get through it. Finding it impossible, he took off back up the stairs to the boat deck.

In just thirty seconds, the *Empress* had taken on almost half her own weight in water. After a minute and a half, the boiler rooms were flooded with the equivalent of nine Olympic swimming pools of water. Water poured along the corridors into the third-class cabins.

SOS

Ronald Ferguson, who had worked for Marconi Marine Company since 1910, was, at twenty, the senior marconi operator. He rushed to join Edward Bamford in the marconi wireless room. Ferguson tapped out: "Stand by for distress signal: we have hit something." A minute later, chief officer Mansfield Steede ran into the room and told Ferguson to call SOS. His next message to the station at Father Point was "SOS have struck something, sinking fast: send help."[34]

The telegraph operator at Father Point just had time to relay that the government steamers *Eureka* and *Lady Evelyn* were on their way before all power on the *Empress* was lost.

Chief officer Steede was at his assigned post at lifeboat no. 8 on the port side of the ship, directing crew members to launch the lifeboats. But the increasing list of the deck made this impossible. As he

The Marconi wireless station at Father Point | Library of Congress (Washington, DC), LC-B2-3079-11

directed the passengers, a couple of boats came loose from their davits and skidded across the deck, crushing several passengers to death. Steede was swept away by falling machinery and disappeared into the water. As the *Empress* began to tilt to starboard, water poured through the open portholes.

The furnaces flooded. The power went out.

The ship was thrown into darkness before most of the sleeping passengers could even grasp what was happening. Those who had managed to leave their cabins were left groping around in the pitch dark, trying to find a way out, clawing their way up the tilting stairs. Because they had boarded the ship mere hours earlier, they were unfamiliar with the ship's layout.

Dear Father and Mother;-

I have been wanting to write you for a long time, but have not seemed well enough to do so, and I have been trying to get Tom to write telling you the exact facts about our wonderful rescue but I cannot seem to get him at it.

In the first place, I want to say how disappointed I feel at not getting to see you all, especially Ma, as I have been so building upon it, but it was through no fault of ours and we shall just have to wait. Of course, I do not ever expect to come to see you It must be you all coming to see me next.

Well, words fail to describe the awful experience which we all passed thro. The few of us who are left, I suppose, can tell to a certain extent just the experience those who are gone passed thro, at any rate what they experienced on the decks that awful morning.

I was lying on the lower berth, awake, and thought how smoothly the 'Empress' was moving. (but now I know that it was not moving at all.) Just then I heard three whistles, and it seemed only a second whenbthe awful grinding and tearing took place. My first thought was that the Empress had run upon a rock, and her bottom was being torn off. The impact was so great that it knocked me against the back of the berth. I immediately got out on the side of the berth and called Tom. He would not get down at first and I called him sharply and said "Come quick now Tom, let's go up on deck something awful has happened". Tom got down very slowly and said "Don't be nervous Dear, it is only a little ice-berg and we shall be all right" but I said"no, come on now", and the ship then began to list so much that Tom had to put his hand against the side of the cabin

June 1914 letter from Margaret Greenaway to her in-laws | Courtesy of Denise Reynolds

JOHN FOWLER SAVES FELLOW PASSENGER

Vancouver Salvationist and CPR employee John Fowler was woken by the whistle and looked out of his open porthole to see the *Storstad* bearing down upon them. "She seemed to bore her way through the ribs and plates almost down to our screws. It was not a big impact and there was not very much noise, but the effects of the collision were tremendous. Before I realized what had happened, my cabin began to fill with water."[35]

Fowler woke his two sleeping cabinmates and went out into the corridor. He gave his lifebelt to a woman who was struggling up the stairs with her two small children. Remembering a promise he'd made to his friend George Cook to look out for Cook's wife, Annie, he went by her cabin in second class but found it empty.

Fowler, a small man at just five foot seven, with a slight build, saw passenger Eliza Willmot struggling to get up the stairs, water lapping around her legs. Every time she got up a step, she slipped back down again. Fowler found a rope and threw it to her. He was able to pull her up, and they made their way to the top deck. Those farther back were not so lucky and drowned as water flooded the ship's gangways.

By now the ship was almost on its side. Rather than immediately jump in the water as others were doing, Fowler sat on the rail and tried to gather his strength. He saw the ship's two funnels crash into the water. Then he heard what sounded like an explosion and found himself going down with the ship. As he fought his way to the water's surface, he started to swim toward a lifeboat and was helped aboard.

ANNIE COOK FINDS A LIFEBOAT

Annie Cook, a Salvation Army member from No. 1 Corps in Vancouver and a forty-three-year-old mother of three, was travelling to London for the conference and to visit her sick mother. The crash woke her up. She wasn't concerned at first and said to one of her cabinmates, Salvation Army staff captain Emma Hayes, that it was probably just the pilot boat banging against the ship. But Cook got up anyway and put on her stockings and boots, left the cabin, and saw people rushing toward the stern, water already up to their waists. She yelled at her two other cabinmates, Major Nettie Simco and Ensign Anna Knudson, to hurry, but they didn't seem to understand the urgency of the situation. Cook soon found herself caught up in a determined crush of people who were propelling her forward.

As she struggled up the stairs, a man grabbed her. "Oh, don't pull me back," she said. "I won't pull you down, missus," he replied, and he let her go.[36] Cook finally made it to the upper deck, which was so slippery that she couldn't stand. She clung to the rail on the side of the listing ship, shut her eyes, and prayed to her god to save her. A man put a lifebelt in her hands, but she couldn't figure out how to put it on. She saw two lifeboats out on the river, one with people in it and already half full of water.

The ship's masts were now hanging right out over the water. Cook grabbed a rope and swung herself out over the water, as close to the lifeboats as she could get. All around her, people were swimming and struggling to stay afloat, and she could hear the screams of the dying. She begged the men in the boats to help her and soon felt herself pulled into one of the little boats, away from the hands of a stranger who was hanging on to her, trying to save himself from drowning. But the boat was already overloaded and there were too many to save.

THE DELAMONTS LOSE A SON

Salvation Army bandsman John Delamont had sailed on a number of ocean liners, so when he heard the ship's siren, he knew something serious had just happened. "I jumped out of bed, switched the light on and was dressing hurriedly when I was violently knocked back. I

The Delamont family band in Moose Jaw, circa 1910 (left to right: Walter, Arthur, John, Herb, Leonard, and Frank) | Courtesy of Warfleet Press and the Delamont Library, Metro Guides

thought we had come into contact with an iceberg, I did not imagine that men could have been so careless as to steer their vessels into each other." He woke his sons, Leonard and Arthur, and told them to put on their lifebelts and get up on deck. Then he threw on some clothes and ran to the cabin where his wife, Seraphine, and daughter, Lizzie, were sleeping, but he couldn't open the door. He threw his weight against it, and the door came unstuck. The three made their way up to the deck.

"People were pushing and struggling to get to the top. My daughter caught hold of my coat. As we were climbing the stairway a man pulled a handful of hair out of my daughter's head. Poor girl. My wife turned to her and said, 'Never mind, my girl,'" said Delamont. "It was heart-rending to see the dear little children looking for their mothers and fathers. Their cries and sobs were terrible to hear. It is a scene that I shall never forget; to see these dear little ones falling off the side of the ship into the icy water. It was undoubtedly the most terrifying quarter of an hour of my life." As the ship started to sink, twenty-five-year-old Leonard Delamont crawled along the side of the ship to his parents and sister. "Leonard turned to me and said, 'Do you think she is going under, Dad?" I replied, 'Yes, my boy, she is going to the bottom.' Seeing that his mother wasn't wearing a lifebelt, Leonard unfastened the one that he was wearing and put it around her. He kissed her, said, 'Goodbye Mother' and dived into the river."[37]

After the ship sank, Seraphine surfaced and frantically began searching for her daughter. She saw Lizzie hanging on to an upturned lifeboat and swam to join her. They were adrift for about an hour when they heard John Delamont's voice calling out to a passing lifeboat for help. Delamont had never learned to swim but had found a piece of wreckage to keep him afloat. The people in the lifeboat didn't hear him, but his wife and daughter did, and he joined them in clinging to the upturned lifeboat until they were eventually rescued and taken to the *Lady Evelyn*.

Twenty-two-year-old Arthur Delamont didn't know where the rest of his family was or if they were even still alive. He drifted until he was picked up by a rescue boat and reunited with his friend Archie Brown.

"I couldn't swim, and the only thing which kept me up was my lifebelt," said Brown. "I paddled away until a lifeboat came along. They would not take me in, but they put a piece of wire under my shoulders and tied me to the side, and paddled away until I woke up to find myself in the bunk of some other boat."[38]

ALICE BALES LEARNS TO SWIM

Dressed in his pyjamas and a raincoat, Salvation Army staff captain David McAmmond handed his lifebelt to twenty-one-year-old Alice Bales and watched as she crawled down the side of the ship and jumped into the water. It was the first time Bales had been in water, and she had no idea how to swim. "There was a man swimming beside me with a lifebelt on and I caught hold of his belt. He said: 'Don't take hold of my belt, I'm dying.'" Bales asked him to show her how to swim and started to imitate his strokes. She made her way to a nearby lifeboat using the same strokes as the man with the lifebelt. "A man came up and grabbed hold of my belt and I said: 'Don't hold my belt, I'll go down and die if you do.'" He held on for a minute then his head fell over and he was dead." Bales kept screaming out, "Save me for my mother's sake," and eventually someone in a lifeboat heard her. "They put out a long pole and I caught it, and they pulled me in."[39]

The man whose strokes she had imitated drowned.

David McAmmond swam to an overturned lifeboat, and a stranger helped him get a firm hold. They clung to the lifeboat until they came across one of the crew struggling with another lifeboat that was overturned. The three men were able to get the lifeboat turned right side up and find the oars. They began to pick up several people from the water. When McAmmond was taken aboard the *Lady Evelyn*, he was happy to see George and Hattie Attwell and several other Salvationists. "They were stark naked when they were rescued and the only way to save their lives was to rub them with heavy towels. It seemed dreadful to see the lifeboats coming along with three or four dead people, each lying in the bottom," said McAmmond. "I saw [George] Wilson lying in another boat almost exhausted. He had to be pulled on deck with a rope about his body. Then he was taken to the engine room and there we rubbed him and got him back to a state of living."[40]

NEWLYWEDS SEPARATED

Bert Greenaway, twenty-four, was sharing Cabin 537 with three other members of the Salvation Army band. Earlier in the evening they had all tried on their lifebelts before retiring to their berths for the night. Just before 2:00 a.m. Greenaway and Ernest Green were woken by Jim Jones, who was talking in his sleep. "I woke him and mentioned that he had said very distinctly, 'We are on our last lap.' Three times he said this and each time louder. We all agreed that Jones had said this, but just laughed."

After the collision all four young men left their cabin, forgetting to grab their lifebelts. "Ernest Green opened the door but fell down the sloping corridor. The lights were on, but the water was pouring in the portholes," said Greenaway.[41] When he reached the main deck, he took off his coat and gave it to a man holding a naked baby. Greenaway managed to get into a lifeboat and was taken to the *Storstad.*

Bert Greenaway's older brother, Tom, had married Margaret Dalzell the week before. They were combining the International Congress with their honeymoon. Margaret woke to the sound of three loud whistle blasts. Minutes later, the impact of the collision knocked her against the back of the berth, and she heard "an awful grinding and tearing." Her first thought was that the *Empress* had run into a rock and that the sound she heard was the ship's bottom being torn off. "Come quick now, Tom," she called to her husband. "Let's go up on deck. Something awful has happened." Tom climbed down slowly and told her not to worry; he thought the ship had hit an iceberg and everything would be fine. Then the ship began to list, and Tom had to lean against the side of the cabin to hold himself up.

Margaret ran out of the cabin and straight into Salvation Army captain John Dodd, who was also combining the Congress with his honeymoon. He told her not to worry; it was just a fire. "It's not a fire,

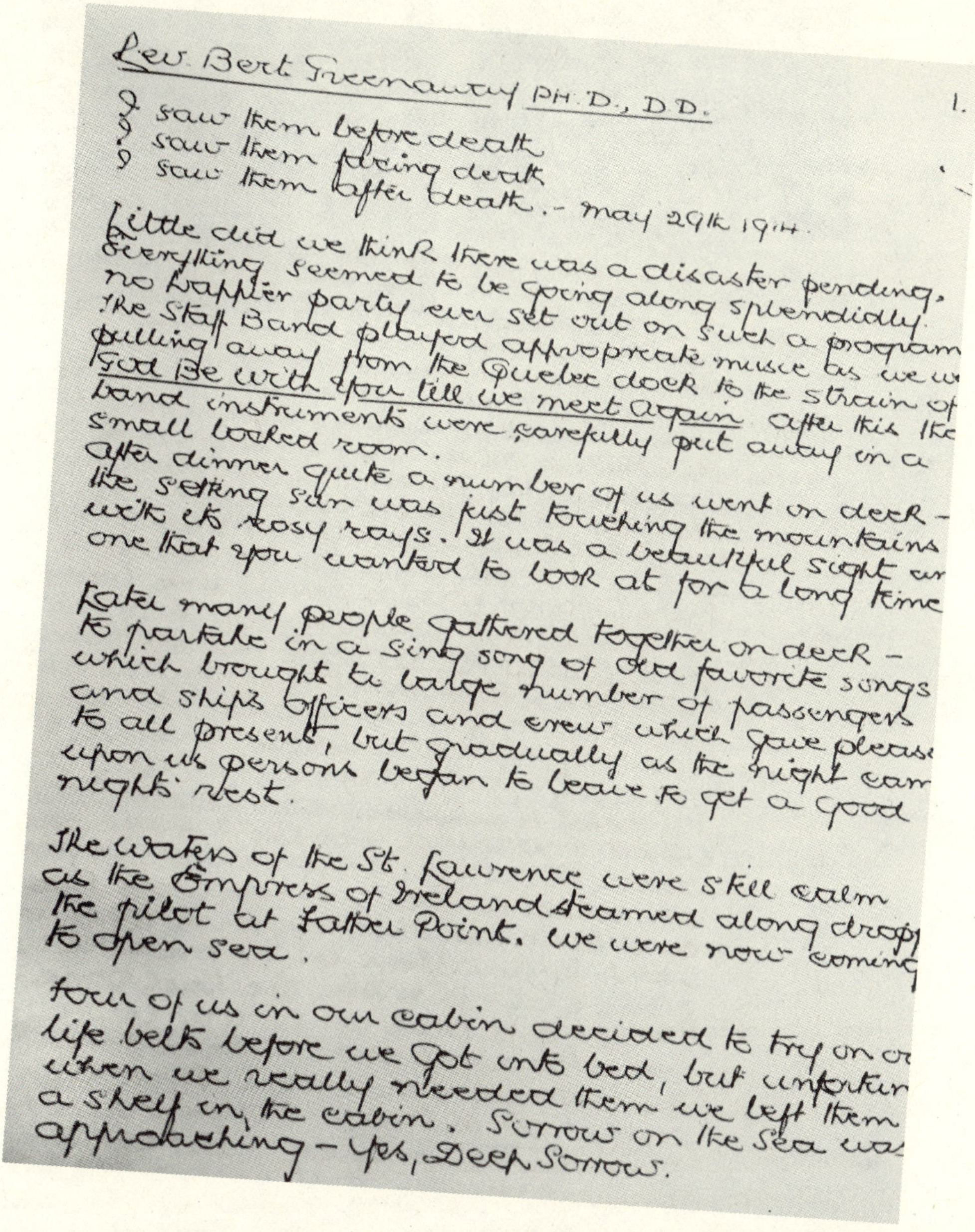

Rev. Bert Greenaway PH.D., D.D. 1.

I saw them before death
I saw them facing death
I saw them after death. – May 29th 1914.

Little did we think there was a disaster pending. Everything seemed to be going along splendidly. No happier party ever set out on such a program The Staff Band played appropriate music as we w pulling away from the Quebec dock to the strain of God Be with you till we meet again. After this the band instruments were carefully put away in a small locked room.

After dinner quite a number of us went on deck – the setting sun was just touching the mountains with its rosy rays. It was a beautiful sight an one that you wanted to look at for a long time

Later many people gathered together on deck – to partake in a sing song of old favorite songs which brought the large number of passengers and ships officers and crew which gave pleas to all present, but gradually as the night cam upon us persons began to leave to get a good nights rest.

The waters of the St. Lawrence were still calm as the Empress of Ireland steamed along dropp the pilot at Father Point. We were now coming to open sea.

Four of us in our cabin decided to try on o life belts before we got into bed, but unfortun when we really needed them we left them a shelf in the cabin. Sorrow on the Sea was approaching – yes, Deep Sorrow.

Letter from Bert Greenaway | Used by permission of the Salvation Army Canada and Bermuda Archives (Toronto, ON)

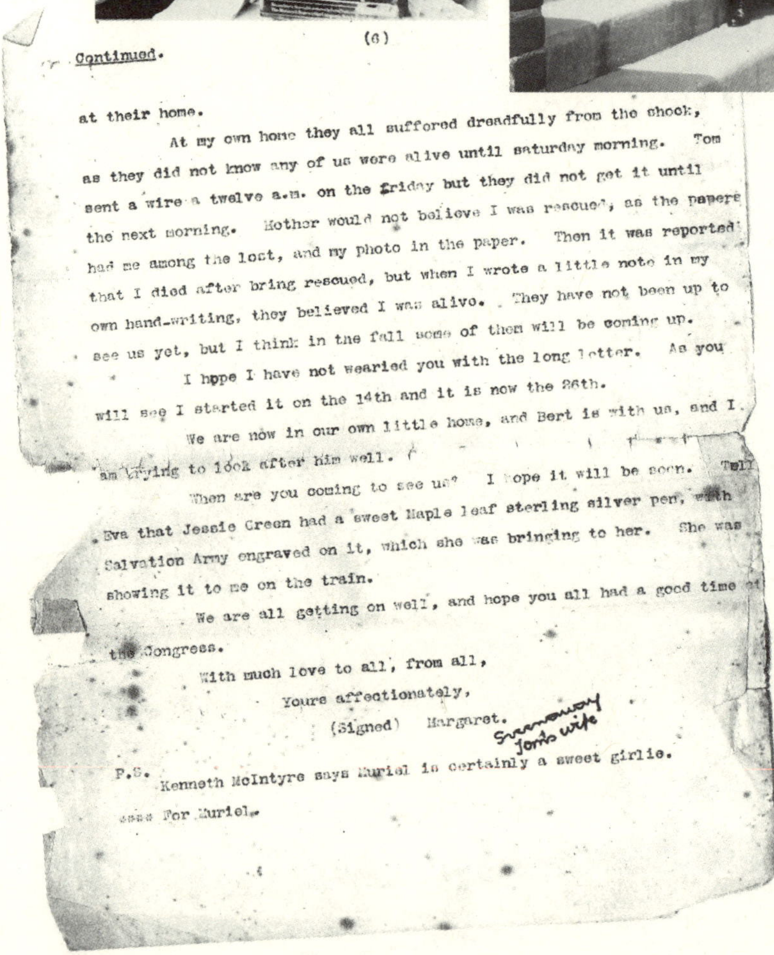

(6)

Continued.

at their home.

At my own home they all suffered dreadfully from the shock, as they did not know any of us were alive until saturday morning. Tom sent a wire a twelve a.m. on the friday but they did not get it until the next morning. Mother would not believe I was rescued, as the papers had me among the lost, and my photo in the paper. Then it was reported that I died after bring rescued, but when I wrote a little note in my own hand-writing, they believed I was alive. They have not been up to see us yet, but I think in the fall some of them will be coming up.

I hope I have not wearied you with the long letter. As you will see I started it on the 14th and it is now the 26th.

We are now in our own little home, and Bert is with us, and I am trying to look after him well.

When are you coming to see us? I hope it will be soon. Tell Eva that Jessie Green had a sweet Maple leaf sterling silver pen, with Salvation Army engraved on it, which she was bringing to her. She was showing it to me on the train.

We are all getting on well, and hope you all had a good time at the Congress.

With much love to all, from all,

Yours affectionately,

(Signed) Margaret. Greenaway Tom's wife

P.S. Kenneth McIntyre says Muriel is certainly a sweet girlie.

For Muriel.

CLOCKWISE FROM TOP LEFT: *Margaret Dalzell, shortly before her May 1914 marriage to Tom Greenaway and their trip to London on the* Empress; *Margaret and Tom Greenaway on the steps of their home in Hamilton, 1923; June 1914 letter from Margaret Greenaway to her in-laws* | *Courtesy of Denise Reynolds*

Dodd," Margaret replied.[42] She could hear some of the ship's officers shouting orders on the deck.

Margaret yelled at Tom to hurry and took off in a sprint along the corridor. But instead of going up the second-class stairs, she ran almost half the length of the ship toward the first-class stairs. She thought Tom was behind her. As she reached the stairs, the ship was listing so severely that she lost her hold and fell, rolling back against the corridor. Water was rushing down the corridor, but she managed to struggle to her feet and pull herself up on the deck. Just as she got there, the lights went out. She now knew that Tom had not followed her and thought he must be dead.

Rufus Spooner, a horn player with the Salvation Army band, had been promoted to captain three weeks earlier. He was sleeping on the bottom berth in a cabin shared with fellow band members Guido Whatmore, Stanley Bigland, and Alfred Keith when the shock of the collision woke him. Spooner threw on his pants and made his way to the deck with his cabinmates, passing open portholes where water was gushing in. He saw Margaret Greenaway standing at the railing. "I took hold of her and told her not to be afraid. We would be all right and we were in the hands of God. I told her not to move from where she was but stay right still and I would get down to the cabin and get some life preservers. It was easier said than done. After a search I found four and carried back and gave two of them to the two women standing near, then fastened one on Mrs. Greenaway, and one on myself."

"Tom will be all right," he told her. "Save yourself."[43] He directed her to stand on his feet and draped a blanket over the both of them for warmth. The listing of the ship forced them to climb through the railing and onto the side of the ship. Margaret lost sight of Spooner but found herself next to another Salvationist.

"As I stood there, I with my arms around bandsman Ernie Aldridge's neck, an explosion occurred right at my side, and we all

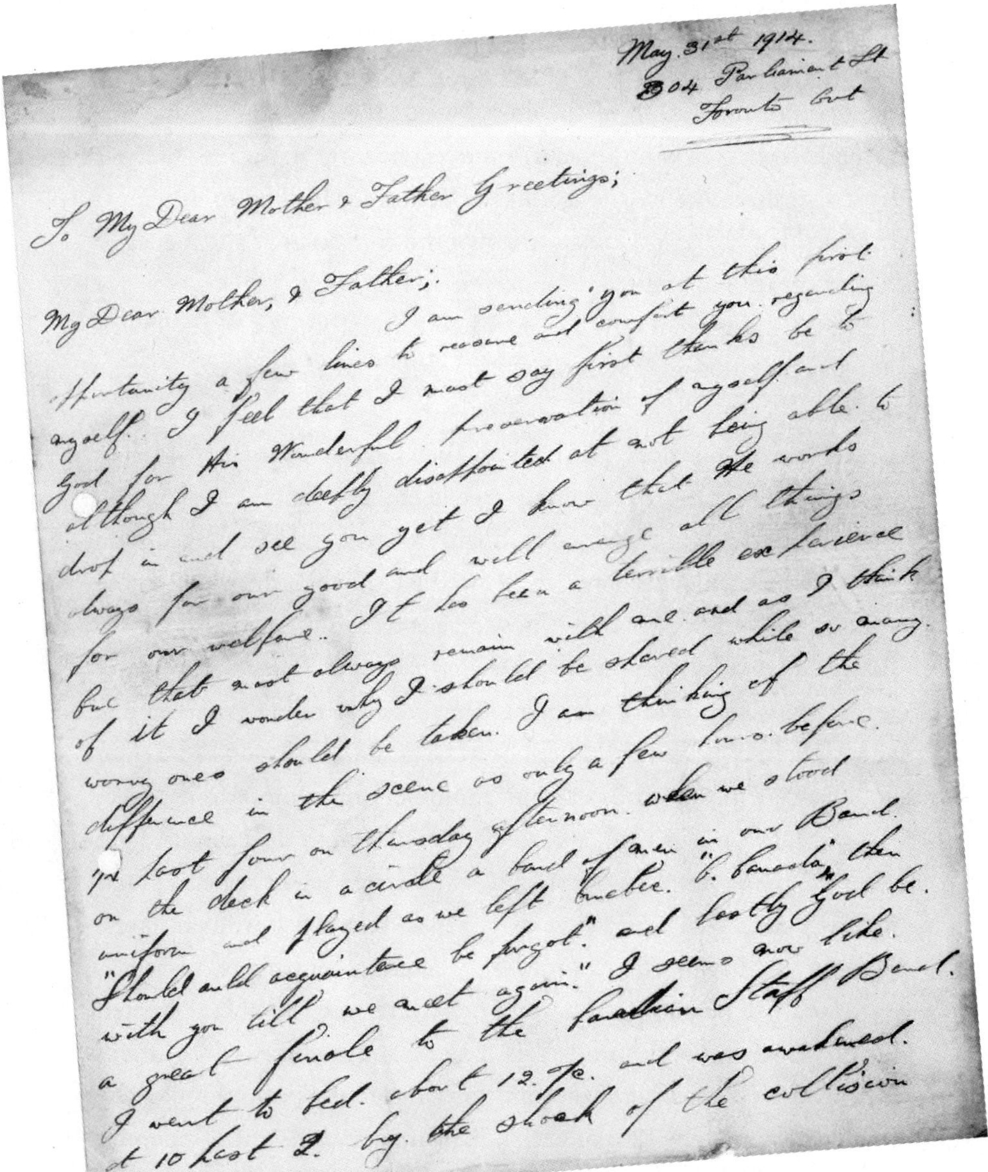

May 31st 1914.
304 Parliament St
Toronto Ont

To My Dear Mother & Father Greetings;

My Dear Mother, & Father;

I am sending you at this first opportunity a few lines to reassure and comfort you regarding myself. I feel that I must say first thanks be to God for His Wonderful preservation of myself and although I am deeply disappointed at not being able to drop in and see you yet I know that He works always for our good and will arrange all things for our welfare. It has been a terrible experience but that must always remain with me and as I think of it I wonder why I should be saved while so many worthy ones should be taken. I am thinking of the difference in the scene as only a few hours before ½ past four on Thursday afternoon when we stood on the deck in a circle a band of men in our Band uniform and played as we left Quebec. "O Canada" then "Should auld acquaintance be forgot" and lastly "God be with you till we meet again." It seems now like a great finale to the Canadian Staff Band. I went to bed about 12 p.c. and was awakened at 10 past 2. by the shock of the collision

Letter from Rufus Spooner to his parents, May 31, 1914 | Used by permission of the Salvation Army Canada and Bermuda Archives (Toronto, ON), photo S12 6D B1 F9

went into the water, and the *Empress* disappeared. I lost my grip of Aldridge, and just went down, down, down," said Margaret. "The water was filling me, and I was turning my wedding ring on my finger and thinking I had only been married a week. Then I just put my hands to my sides and asked Jesus to help me die easy, and I never knew anything more."[44]

When Margaret opened her eyes and lifted her head, she found that a deck chair was holding her up in the water. Just then a raft with two men on it floated nearby. One of the men was a big, burly Swede who held out a paddle to her and asked, "Are you alive?"

"I guess I am," she said. "Because the cut in my ankle and the burns are smarting me."

Margaret had no feeling from her waist down and little feeling in her arms, but she managed to catch hold of the paddle. The man pulled her through the dead bodies and wreckage and up into the boat. He told her not to be afraid. Margaret told him she'd lost her husband. He told her that he had lost his wife. "He stood me up and then the water began to come out of my mouth, eyes, and ears. The Swede opened his coat and buttoned me inside of it. That kept me warm, and I think it saved my life."[45]

Tom Greenaway hadn't realized the danger they were in. After Margaret woke him, he closed the porthole window, grabbed coats for his wife and himself, and struggled up the second-class stairs to the deck. When he got there, he couldn't find Margaret and thought she must be dead. He handed the coats to Nellie Green and her daughter, Jessie. As Tom tightened his hold on the rail, the ship's bow went down, water came sweeping up, and he was thrown into the water. When he came to the surface, the first thing he saw was the top of a round table. He wasn't a strong swimmer, so he clung to the table until a lifeboat from the *Empress* picked him up.

Harry and Nellie Green with their son, Ernie, and their daughter, Jessie. Ernie was the only member of the family to survive the tragedy. | Used by permission of the Salvation Army Canada and Bermuda Archives (Toronto, ON), photo 57233

THE BAND

Major Frank Morris had joined the Salvation Army in Winnipeg in 1891. He was sharing a second-class cabin with his younger brother, Arthur, as well as David McAmmond and Richard Turpin. He was lying awake in his bunk when he heard what sounded like two pans banged loudly together followed by a scraping sound. He woke his cabinmates, dressed quickly, and started for the upper deck. He thought he heard someone who sounded like Commissioner Rees singing a hymn, but the singing stopped when the ship started to sink. Morris could see the lights of the *Storstad* in the distance. He said to the people nearest him, "They don't seem to be doing anything. Let's call for help." And he shouted, "Help, help, help!" over and over as others joined in the chant.[46] Within a few minutes the *Storstad* launched its lifeboats.

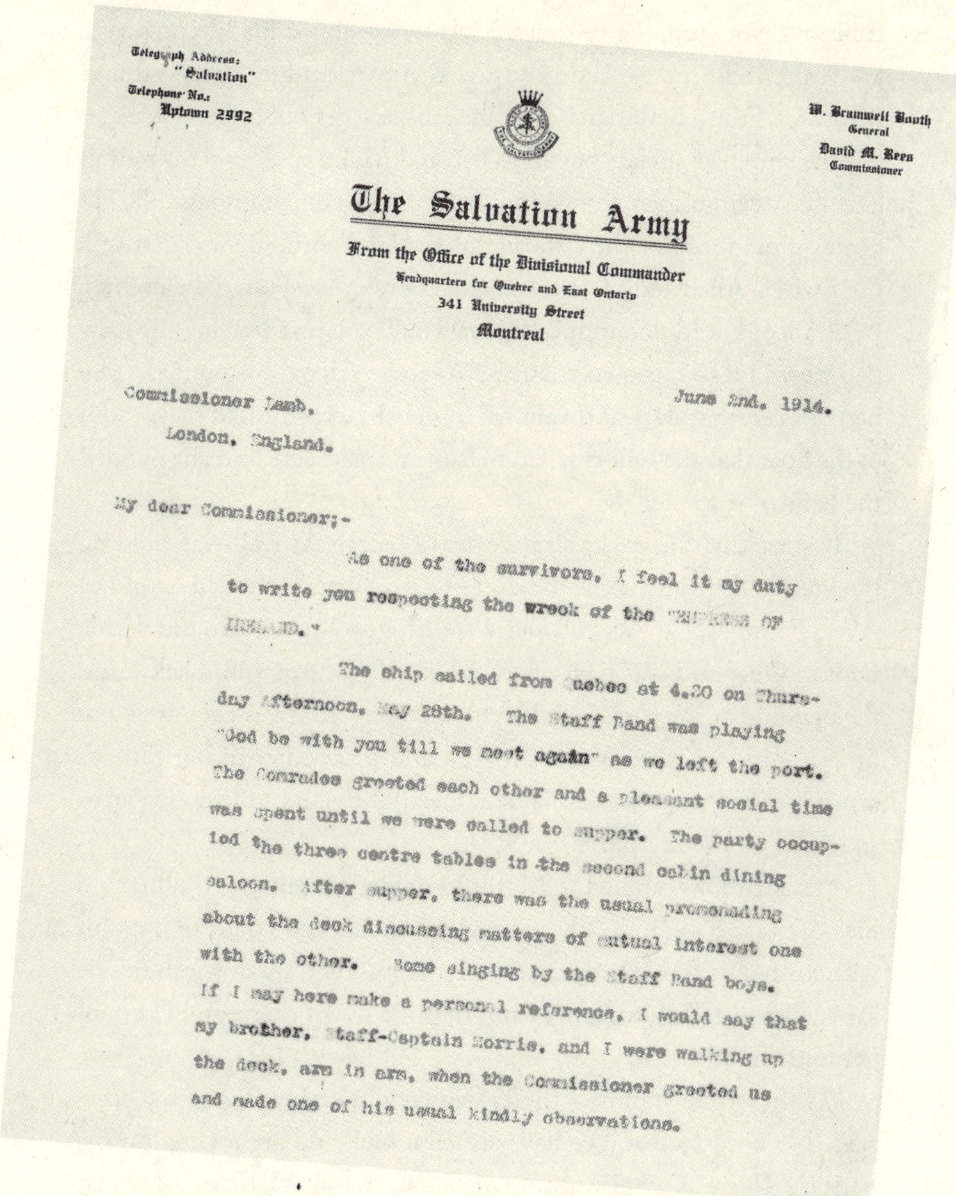
Telegraph Address: "Salvation"
Telephone No.: Uptown 2992

W. Bramwell Booth
General
David M. Rees
Commissioner

The Salvation Army

From the Office of the Divisional Commander
Headquarters for Quebec and East Ontario
341 University Street
Montreal

Commissioner Lamb,
London, England.

June 2nd. 1914.

My dear Commissioner;-

As one of the survivors, I feel it my duty to write you respecting the wreck of the "EMPRESS OF IRELAND."

The ship sailed from Quebec at 4.30 on Thursday Afternoon, May 28th. The Staff Band was playing "God be with you till we meet again" as we left the port. The Comrades greeted each other and a pleasant social time was spent until we were called to supper. The party occupied the three centre tables in the second cabin dining saloon. After supper, there was the usual promenading about the deck discussing matters of mutual interest one with the other. Some singing by the Staff Band boys. If I may here make a personal reference, I would say that my brother, Staff-Captain Morris, and I were walking up the deck, arm in arm, when the Commissioner greeted us and made one of his usual kindly observations.

Letter from Major Frank Morris to Commissioner Lamb, June 2, 1914 | Used by permission of the Salvation Army Canada and Bermuda Archives (Toronto, ON), photo M-7610

Ken McIntyre woke up scared. He felt the crash and the jar of the collision. Not stopping to dress, McIntyre grabbed his life preserver and told cabinmates Teddy Gray, Ernie Aldridge, and William Measures, "You'd better grab your lifebelts and get out of here quick!"[47]

The ship had already begun to list, and McIntyre found himself in a dense stream of people making the stairway almost impassable. He came across more of the bandsmen: Ernest Foord, George Attwell, their wives, Alice and Hattie, and the Foords' four-year-old daughter.

"[Alice] Foord said to me, 'Major, would you mind saving my baby and we will take our own chances?'" George Attwell recounted. "She had noticed that Mrs. Attwell had a lifebelt, which I had picked out of the boat that the sailors failed to launch. I said 'sure' and she handed the baby over to me."[48]

It struck McIntyre as strange that George Attwell was holding the Foords' little girl, so he took off his lifebelt and fastened it around Alice Foord while Attwell placed a broken lifebelt around Ernie Foord. "One cord was torn off, so I had to put it on him backwards, the opening at the back," McIntyre wrote in a letter. "I then took the little Foord girl from Major Attwell and placed her in her father's arms. I told Ernie to hold his daughter tightly and to keep his arms squeezed on the life preserver."[49]

Frank Brooks lurched to McIntyre's side and said he couldn't find his wife and daughter. "He was pale as death and could only point with his hands towards the hull of our ship. 'They are down there,' he kept repeating. 'My wife, my baby, they are down there, and I cannot get to them.'"[50]

As they were standing there, two crew members came by. "One said, 'No need to fear. We have struck a rock and are resting on the bottom.' This was wholly untrue of course," wrote McIntyre. "I would rather have been told that we had been in a collision." The Attwells went over the side of the ship together. "George Attwell many times has said that I saved his life by taking the little Foord girl from him and placing her into her father's arms," wrote McIntyre. "Actually, it was Mrs. Attwell who saved her husband's life. She had an inflated cushion. When they went down with the vessel, Mrs. Attwell clung to her husband's undershirt and brought him to the surface."[51]

Little Grace Hanagan woke up to a loud bang and thought a firecracker had gone off outside her window. The seven-year-old asked her father about the noise. He told her it was probably just the pilot boat leaving, but went out to the hallway to check. By the time the family got up to the deck, the list of the ship was so great that she was almost on her side. Grace sat on the high side of the rail in her pyjamas, and Salvation Army member Ernest Pugmire wrapped her inside his coat. Like many of the passengers, the Hanagans had left their lifebelts in the cabin in their haste to get to the deck. Grace held her parents' hands as they prayed and waited for the boat to go

Ted Hanagan with his wife, Edith, and their daughter, Grace | Used by permission of the Salvation Army Canada and Bermuda Archives (Toronto, ON)

down. A few Salvation Army members were singing "God Be with You Till We Meet Again," the same tune they'd sung when they set off from Quebec City with so much optimism the previous afternoon.

As the *Empress* sank, the Hanagans were tossed into the water. Grace wrapped her arms around her father's back, but they were quickly separated. Grace couldn't swim, and she went under twice before she was able to grab a piece of wood from the wreck. From there she watched as the luxury liner sank to the bottom of the river. "I saw a lifeboat, called for help and was lifted in. Then my first thought was for my mother and, not finding her there, I wanted to get out."[52] Freezing and in shock, Grace lost consciousness and woke up aboard the *Storstad*, wrapped in a blanket.

THE BARBOURS

Eight-year-old Florrie Barbour was in a cabin with her mother and younger sister. She remembered being woken up by an "awful bump" that threw her out of her bunk. The next thing she remembered was hearing screams in the dark as she was carried out of the second-class cabin by her uncle Bob. "Don't be frightened dear, I have got you," he told her. "I said, 'Have you got Mother and Evelyn?' I remember thinking how strange Uncle Bob's voice was when he said, 'God be willing darling, we will save everyone."[53]

Robert Crellin was still in his bare feet. He carried Florrie up the slanted corridor, slipping on the floor. She was shocked to hear him say, "Oh my God." When they reached the deck, she found her mother holding her sister, Evelyn. "I remember clinging to Uncle Bob and knew I would be safe as long as he had a hold of me. Thank God Uncle Bob was a big strong man. Just then I saw my mother reaching out for us, and Uncle Bob got a lifebelt to give to her, when someone else snatched it out of her hands. Then in the confusion she was pushed away from us, we heard her scream my sister's and my name, but we never saw her again."[54]

Crellin climbed down the ladder with Florrie on his back and jumped into the river. They were in the freezing water for what felt like an hour before they came across an overturned lifeboat from the *Empress*. Crellin managed to put Florrie on the boat while he clung to the side. Another man climbed aboard, and the three survivors drifted to a collapsible boat, which they managed to open and climb into. Soon they were fishing out other survivors from the river until they'd filled the boat with more than twenty people. Eventually, they were picked up by the *Lady Evelyn*.

LIKE RATS IN A TRAP

James Lennon woke up to the sound of water rushing into his cabin through the open porthole. He dashed out of his cabin to the corridor to find the stairs jammed with people desperately looking for a way out. The lights were out, but at the top of the stairs he could make out John Langley, the rancher from Canford, BC, he had been chatting to earlier in the smoking room.

After the collision woke him, Langley rushed out of the cabin without stopping to dress or look for a lifebelt. "I knew the way, so I got up to the top of the stairs without wasting a second. When I got to the top there were a few people there and the deck doors were locked. I tried them but so did everyone else and we couldn't stir them." Knowing that they were still in the St. Lawrence River with land on both sides, Langley wasn't too worried and thought they'd run ashore. Then the ship started to violently list at a steep angle, and Langley realized they were in danger. "I just felt sick, all churned up inside. There was no hope of getting out on deck and I thought we were penned up in there just to wait and be drowned without a single chance of helping ourselves."[55]

John Wise Langley | Langley family collection

Looking around, Langley saw a porthole that led out onto the deck and tried to squeeze himself through but couldn't get past his shoulders.* Then he saw James Lennon standing at the bottom of the stairs in his soaking-wet pyjamas. Noting that the man was of a smaller build, he suggested the other man try the porthole and if he got out, try opening the door on the outside. He helped Lennon through the porthole, but before Lennon could try to unlock the doors, the boat listed over, and he slid down the deck and into the river. Lennon couldn't swim but managed to grab the lid of a rope box and floated until he was saved.

Langley next helped a teenage boy through the porthole, then made another attempt to save himself. This time he put his arms over his head and squeezed himself through. "A steward came along just

* The porthole that Langley was attempting to squeeze through measured just 30.5 cm (12 in) in diameter.

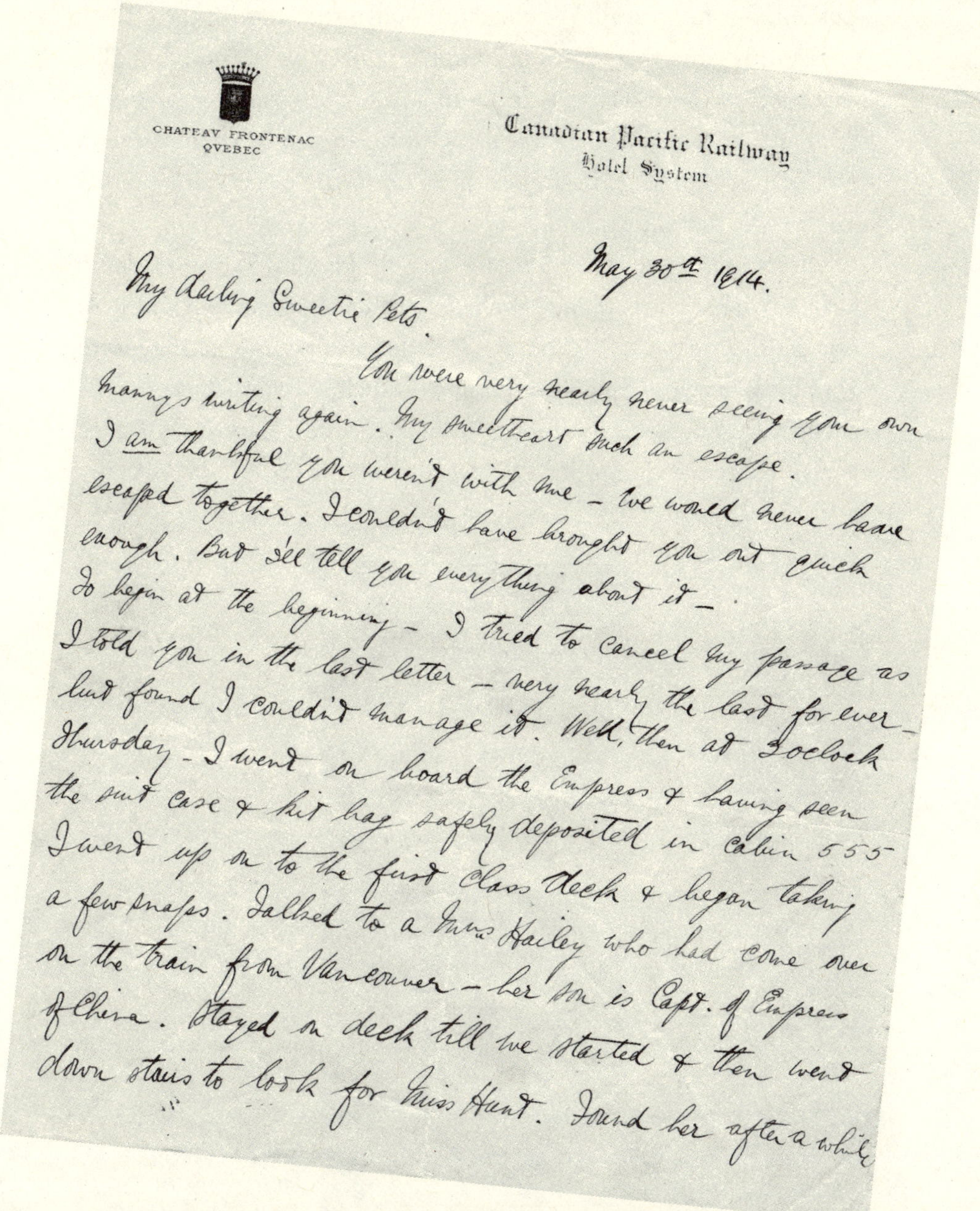

CHATEAU FRONTENAC
QUEBEC

Canadian Pacific Railway
Hotel System

May 30th 1914.

My darling Sweetie Pets.

You were very nearly never seeing your own Manny's writing again. My sweetheart such an escape. I am thankful you weren't with me — we would never have escaped together. I couldn't have brought you out quick enough. But I'll tell you everything about it —

To begin at the beginning — I tried to cancel my passage as I told you in the last letter — very nearly the last for ever — but found I couldn't manage it. Well, then at 3 o'clock Thursday — I went on board the Empress & having seen the suit case & kit bag safely deposited in Cabin 555 I went up on to the first class deck & began taking a few snaps. Talked to a Mrs Hailey who had come over on the train from Vancouver — her son is Capt. of Empress of China. Stayed on deck till we started & then went down stairs to look for Miss Hunt. Found her after a while

Letter from John Langley to his wife, Bessie, May 30, 1914 | Langley family collection

then and both of us pulled with all our might while those inside pushed. But to no avail. We could not budge that door."[56]

By this time the ship was completely over on its side. Langley managed to climb over the deck rail and found himself sitting next to an electrician from the crew. The electrician said he couldn't swim, but Langley could and said he'd hold on to the electrician's lifebelt and paddle him along.

Both men were sucked down into the vortex. "We went down with a swirl. It felt as though we had dived under a waterfall and were being driven down," said Langley.[57] After a minute or so they were shot back to the surface, with Langley still clutching the other man's lifebelt. They landed a few metres away from a steel lifeboat with three men already clinging to it. "I managed to secure an oar and with my

John Langley's pyjamas on display at the Canadian Museum of Immigration at Pier 21 in 2016 | Dan Conlin

friend the electrician and an engineer, we collected a few people floating about. Many people were drowned around us simply because we couldn't work the boat along quick enough."[58]

After a couple of hours, they were picked up by the *Eureka* and given a shot of "prewar very much over-proof rum."[59]

SURVIVORS PULLED FROM THE WATER

Gordon Davidson woke to the sound of rushing water. At first, he thought it was the crew flushing out the decks, but the noise was too loud. He turned on the electric light and was horrified to see water flowing into his cabin.

"Even then, I hardly realized what was wrong, but [Arthur] Stillman called that we were sinking and rushed out, and I followed in my nightshirt. By that time, the water was half filling the cabin," he said. "As I stepped into the passageway, a stream of water from the open porthole struck me between the shoulders and knocked me down. The water was spouting in there in a foot-wide stream that was 15 feet long. I scrambled on my hands and knees till I got beyond it. Then I climbed up two flights of stairs till I got to the saloon deck, where I braced myself against a door. The bow dipped under first, and she had listed so far that it was like a level floor when I ran down her side and dived off the keel."[60]

Davidson stripped off his nightshirt and swam away from the ship. The suction took him down, and when he came up, he swam into a frenzied crowd. "They tramped me under three times before I got through them. I swam on a little farther, but the water was fearfully cold, and I was out of practice swimming," he said.[61] Davidson was picked up by a lifeboat as he swam toward the *Storstad*.

Martin Gill had sat up late chatting to his five cabinmates but was still awake long after the others had fallen asleep. He heard the foghorn and then a "ferocious" bang. "I jumped out of bed and shouted to my cabinmates, 'Get out quick, get out quick. Something has happened.' I grabbed my pants and had one leg in when I was thrown right across the cabin. Apparently, the ship had gone over on its side."[62] Frightened by the sound of water rushing into the ship, Gill didn't take the time to finish dressing and left everything he owned in the cabin, except his gold watch, which was in the pocket of his pants. He was soon moving toward the upper deck in the dark, surrounded by a mass of humans.

Gill managed to get to the deck, where he saw two sailors trying to lower a lifeboat. He tried to help them push the lifeboat over the side,

Martin Gill on the right, 1915 | Courtesy of Mary McDermott

but it wasn't possible given the position of the ship and the weight of the lifeboat. Offering a silent thanks to his uncle, who had taught him to swim by throwing him into a river as a young boy and telling him to "keep up," Gill plunged into the water feet first. "As I did so, the keel of the ship touched me, leaving a slight mark along the side of my leg. I didn't know where I was until I was shot up again. I tried to get away as far as I could. Looking back over my shoulder, I saw a column of smoke rise into the air. I expected to be brought down any minute as the *Empress* was sinking fast. Still looking back, I saw the people as they stood motionless by the rails. They appeared utterly paralyzed and helpless."[63]

Gill swam toward a lifeboat, but it was already overcrowded, and one of the sailors yelled to him, "Keep up until we come back." The fog had lifted, and Gill could see the *Storstad* in the distance. He started swimming toward it. When he reached the boat, he found that his hands were so frozen he couldn't hold on to the rope ladder. "I had to work my way up on deck by gripping the rungs of the ladder with my elbows. It took some time before I regained the power of my hands. It was only then I got my pants on properly. Putting my hand into my pocket, I found my watch still there, the only thing I had left. It had stopped at five minutes after 2:00 a.m."[64] Gill kept his pants but gave up his singlet to a fellow survivor who was naked.

Theo Bartschi and his older brother, Christian, had fled their third-class cabin with their lifebelts, pushing through the water that was streaming through the open portholes to make their way up to the deck. The brothers climbed over the rail and dived into the water together. Theo cut his head open when it struck some debris from the wreck and badly bruised his knee. He swam to an empty lifeboat and found it half full of water. He helped four women and two men get into the lifeboat. He could see more people struggling with an upside-down lifeboat and managed to swim over to it and pull the

Theo and Chris Bartschi, circa 1914 | *Courtesy of Stettler Town and Country Museum* (AB)

two lifeboats together. "We slapped one another and beat our bodies to keep warm."[65] A little while later a lifeboat from the *Storstad* came along and towed them to the *Eureka*.

Twenty-two-year-old Christian Samuelson of Chicago was sharing a third-class cabin with two others from his hometown of Stavanger, Norway. When he felt the collision, he had the presence of mind to grab a lifebelt and head for the deck, leaving behind three suits, three gold watches, and some bracelets and rings he had bought as presents for his brothers and sisters. When he went into the water, he started swimming toward the collier. "I saw one of the *Storstad*'s boats coming in my direction. I yelled to them and one of the men replied, 'You're all right when you can shout like that!' The boat passed me and went away. Soon after that another boat from the *Storstad* came towards me and I was pulled on board. About twelve of us were saved in the second boat."[66] The boat was leaking badly, though, and they had to row quickly back to the *Storstad*. Samuelson was given a pillowcase to wear.

6. Everyone for Themselves

THERE WAS NO TIME to save the women and children first in the fourteen minutes it took the ship to sink. It was everyone for themselves.

Compared to the sinking of the *Titanic*, where only 24 percent of the crew survived, the *Empress of Ireland*'s crew had a much higher survival rate at 60 percent. The high crew survival rate was explored in the Inquiry, particularly as there was media speculation that some of the crew may have ignored passenger safety in their haste to save themselves.

This wasn't the case at all. Roughly half the crew were on night duty. Stokers and firemen worked in hot, dirty conditions and had access to ladders that would get them up to the deck quickly for breaks. Others knew the ship intimately, were used to rough seas, and were far better equipped than passengers to get around in the dark.

When the ship started to roll over and Kendall sounded the siren, it was a clear signal for everyone to look out for themselves, and many of the crew members either jumped into a lifeboat or grabbed an oar or a deck chair to float with as they jumped into the water.

The *Empress*'s passengers were at a big disadvantage, and their survival rate reflected this. Of the 1,056 passengers, only 220 or about one in five lived, and the vast majority of these were adult males.

A brass plaque was salvaged from the Empress, *2024 | Eve Lazarus*

At the time of the collision, most of the passengers were asleep in their berths. Those in steerage who stopped to dress likely drowned in their cabins. Those who did make it out of their cabins had not yet practised an emergency drill, were unfamiliar with the layout of the ship, and in many cases fled their cabins without their lifebelts. Those who made it to the boat deck found few available lifeboats.

First-class passengers had the best chance for survival, because the more you paid for your passage, the higher up in the ship you were, and those closest to the top deck had more time to swim away from the sinking ship or to get a seat in one of the few available lifeboats.

The eighty-seven passengers in first class were mostly a mix of Canadian and English businessmen, mothers and children returning to the UK to visit for the summer, and tourists returning home.*

---

* Of the 87 first-class passengers, 36 survived. Of the 255 second-class passengers, 48 survived. And in third class, only 136 passengers out of 714 survived.

THE IRVINGS

The most famous passengers on the ship were British actors Laurence Irving and his wife, Mabel Hackney.

The story that follows ran in newspapers around the world and is still being repeated in anniversary stories and books about the *Empress of Ireland*. It goes like this:

After the collision, the two celebrity passengers stepped out of their cabin in their sleepwear at about the same time that Frank Abbott, a forty-two-year-old commercial salesman from Toronto, appeared. Irving asked him, "Is the boat going down?" Abbott said he thought so. "Dearie," Irving said to his wife, "Hurry! There's no time to lose." Hackney began to cry. As Irving reached for a lifebelt, the boat suddenly lurched, and he was thrown against the door. Blood poured from a cut on his face, but he stayed calm and told his wife to "keep cool." He forced a lifebelt over her head, but Hackney wouldn't let go of him. Irving pushed her out the door and half-dragged, half-carried her up the stairs. "I asked if I could help," Abbott told a reporter. "Irving said, 'Look after yourself first, old man, but God bless you all the same."

Abbott went up on deck and dived into the river. He got hold of either a piece of timber from the wreckage or a deck chair (depending on the newspaper) and was able to stay afloat. He looked back at the ship and saw Irving kissing his wife. "As the ship went down, they were both clasped in each other's arms."

This story was published in various newspapers on May 31, 1914, and ran with headlines like "Irving and Wife Died in Each Other's Arms" along with the early first-hand accounts of traumatized survivors.* It's a great story. The problem is that, although many newspapers

* Laurence Irving's body was found two days after the wreck. He was floating face down on the west bank of the St. Lawrence River below Rimouski. His face was bruised beyond recognition; he was identified by a signet ring with the initials LI. His hand still held a shred of material possibly torn from his wife's nightgown. (Source: "Irving and Wife Died in Each Other's Arms," *Detroit Free Press*, May 31, 1914.)

A memorial plaque for Laurence Irving and Mabel Hackney was installed in the lobby of Winnipeg's Walker Theatre (now the Burton Cummings Theatre) in 1915 | *Courtesy of Payton Robinson*

ran the exact same account weeks and even decades later, I can't find any follow-up interviews with Abbott, and there is very little information about Abbott's family.* Several newspapers wrongly credited Clayton Burt, another first-class passenger from Toronto of around the same age, for the story.

Immediately following the Irving/Hackney article in the *Detroit Free Press* were a couple of paragraphs about the second-most famous passenger on the *Empress* that night. Although not nearly as romantic, his story was repeated just as often; it just wasn't true.

SIR HENRY SETON-KARR

Sir Henry Seton-Karr, a sixty-one-year-old lawyer, former member of parliament, and explorer, had just returned from a hunting trip in British Columbia. He had bagged a moose and was bringing its

* What we do know is that Abbott returned to Toronto to his wife, Edith, and their four-year-old daughter, Margery. He started Abbott Bros, a millinery wholesaling business with his brother, Arthur, in 1916. Abbott died in 1933, aged 61.

antlers back to England as a souvenir. After the collision, Seton-Karr and fellow Brit Murton Daniel Addison Darling, who was staying in the cabin opposite, bumped into each other in the passageway. "He had a lifebelt and he offered it to me. I refused it, but he said, 'Go on, man, take it and I will get another.' I told him to save himself, but he got angry and actually forced the belt over me. He then hurried along the corridor."[67]

Darling was horrified by the report. He told a reporter the next day that he and Seton-Karr had been together shortly after the collision, but both had lifebelts. Seton-Karr was already wearing his when they met and helped Darling tie on his own. Although the *Daily Telegraph* published a correction, the original story stuck.*

GEORGE BOGUE SMART

Another first-class passenger was George Bogue Smart, born in Brockville, Ontario, the chief inspector of British immigrant children since 1900.

Between 1906 and 1914, 918 orphans and abandoned children were transported to Canada on the *Empress of Ireland*. Many of these kids, known as British Home Children, whose average age was ten for girls and twelve for boys, ended up in abusive situations in Western Canada, where the boys would be used as cheap farm labour and the girls put to work in houses and in the fields.†

---

* Murton Darling joined the British Army and served as a captain in Gallipoli and France. He married Edith Thornton in 1917 in Yorkshire; after the war the couple immigrated to Victoria, BC, and had two children. Darling was the secretary treasurer of Deep End Cove Property Management for more than twenty years. He died in 1972, aged 86. (Source: obituary, *Victoria Times Colonist*, April 6, 1972.)

† The demand for British child workers also consistently exceeded supply. Between 1901 and 1915, more than 33,500 children immigrated to Canada from Britain while there were close to 300,000 applications for their services. Despite ongoing revelations of gross neglect and abuse, the government continued to allow child immigration and insist that it was, on the whole, a success. (Source: Ninette Kelley and Michael Trebilcock, *The Making of the Mosaic: A History of Canadian Immigration Policy* [Toronto: University of Toronto Press, 2010], 124.)

Between 1906 and 1914, 918 orphans and abandoned children were transported to Canada on the Empress of Ireland | © *Canada Post Corporation, 2010. Reproduced with permission*

It was two days before his fiftieth birthday, and Bogue Smart was on his way to England to bring back another group of children to Canada. Eleven British Home Children had been on the incoming voyage of the *Empress* the week before.

After the collision, Bogue Smart threw on a pair of pants and a coat and left his cabin but forgot to take a lifebelt. A deck chair kept him afloat until he was rescued by a lifeboat.*

TIRIA TOWNSHEND AND CLAYTON BURT

Seventeen-year-old Tiria Townshend of Blenheim, New Zealand, was awake in her berth when she heard the collision. She sprang out of bed, woke her aunt, Fanny Price, and they stopped only long enough to put on their coats. "When she had listed so much it was impossible to stand, I walked with my aunt down the port side right over the

* Bogue Smart retired in 1933. Under his watch, the immigration of unaccompanied children under 14 was stopped, and importing child labour was banned altogether by 1928, although small numbers of children continued to be sent to Canada throughout WWII. Bogue Smart died at his Ottawa home in 1947, aged 83. (Sources: "G. Bogue Smart," British Home Child Group International, accessed July 5, 2024, https://britishhomechild.com/g-bogue-smart/; obituary, *Ottawa Citizen*, March 24, 1947.)

portholes down onto the steel side of her, and I was standing on the side of her when she went down."[68]

They stayed by the rail until they were thrown into the water and carried down with the suction of the ship. Neither woman had a lifebelt, and when Townshend surfaced, her aunt had disappeared. Townshend was a strong swimmer, but her heavy coat dragged her down, and when she saw three men wearing lifebelts in the water beside her, she put her hand on the shoulder of one of them. He shoved her off, and she sank again. Remarkably, the young woman kept her cool, and when she fought her way back to the surface, she found herself next to a man whom she later learned was Clayton Burt.

Burt was the forty-year-old manager of the Russell Motor Car Company in Toronto, travelling to Europe on business. Originally from Massachusetts, Burt had moved his family to Toronto in 1913,

Seventeen-year-old Tiria Townshend from New Zealand was a strong swimmer. She managed to stay afloat until she was rescued by a lifeboat and taken to the Storstad. | *Bains News Service* LC-*B2-3079-6*

when he took over as factory manager. Whereas most cars produced in Canada were foreign designs, the Russell was a luxury vehicle designed and manufactured in Toronto and marketed as the "thoroughly Canadian car with Canadian materials, Canadian labour, and Canadian capital."[69] When Burt joined the company, Canada had entered an economic recession, and high-end car sales were struggling. Compounding the problem, the sleeve-valve engine in Russell's Silent Knight motor car had developed problems. Burt was travelling to Europe to look for alternatives.

The sound of dishes crashing on the floor of his stateroom woke Burt, and he rushed to the deck to investigate. Realizing the situation was serious, he returned to his room and threw on his blue suit, coat, and shoes and searched for a lifebelt. "I looked under the bed and in all corners of the room, I was not able to find one but found afterwards that they were located on top of the wardrobe," he wrote.[70] Once out on the deck another passenger rushed past him and dropped one of the lifebelts he was carrying. Burt picked it up, put it on, and dived headfirst into the water.

"It was a case of everybody for themselves and with everyone screaming and shouting for help it was very difficult to make much headway," he said. "Those who could swim were seriously handicapped by others trying to hold them down and it was very necessary to push them off in order to save yourself."[71]

Burt had managed to get hold of a suitcase floating by when Townshend saw him and asked him for help. "I asked him if he would give me the suitcase, and he said, 'Most certainly,'" Townshend said. "I kept myself afloat on that until I had recovered my breath sufficiently to speak properly. Then I said: 'I want you to help me off with this coat.' So, he pulled one arm, and I got out of the other."[72]

With the help of the suitcase and Burt's lifebelt, the two survivors managed to stay afloat until they were rescued and taken to the *Storstad*.

"The scenes on the deck of [the *Storstad*] are beyond the power of words to describe. I could never have conceived of anything so terrible," Townshend said. "People were brought on mad with hysteria or dying from their injuries. Some were maimed and mutilated to such a degree that it was only because our senses were dulled by our own sufferings that we were able to bear the sight."[73] Townshend was transferred to the *Lady Evelyn* wrapped in a curtain.

After surviving the sinking of the *Empress*, Burt refused to travel along the St. Lawrence River and took the White Star liner RMS *Baltic* out of New York to Liverpool. When war broke out, he set up a division of the Russell Motor Car Company to manufacture munitions. The car production side of the company continued to struggle and was sold to American manufacturer Willys–Overland Motors in 1916, with Burt staying on as general manager. By the end of the war, Burt had equipped six munitions factories in Canada and Buffalo, New York, and oversaw 8,500 workers.*

THE O'HARAS

Henry O'Hara, the head of a Toronto brokerage firm, was travelling with his wife, May, their eleven-year-old daughter, Helen, and their maid, Alice Brown. After the collision, Henry fastened a lifebelt around his wife, and they hurried to the stairway that led to the promenade deck. In the crowd, Henry and Helen were separated from May, who found her way to the deck and into the water. "I was picked up by a rowboat half full of water, which soon afterwards sank throwing all the occupants back into the sea," May O'Hara told a reporter.[74] A man helped her into a collapsible lifeboat, and she stayed there until

* In 1924, Burt was appointed vice president and general manager of Niles-Bement-Pond, the machine tool division of Pratt & Whitney later to become a huge player in the military and commercial aviation industry. Burt became president in 1930 and chair of the board in 1943. He died in October 1957, aged 82.

she was picked up by the *Eureka*. Henry, who didn't have a lifebelt, grabbed his daughter with one hand and slid down into the water. "He swam a little way holding me above water," said Helen. "Then a wave came along and washed me out of his arms, and that was the last I saw of my daddy." Helen had learned to swim at Haverhill College, and she made her way to a nearby rowboat, where a man was hanging on to the side. "I crawled up on his back and both he and I were pulled into the boat and later picked up."[75]

ETHEL GRUNDY PATON

Ethel Grundy Paton was in Stateroom 32 on the top deck. The collision woke her but wasn't violent enough to cause any real concern. She could hear people shouting, so she quickly got dressed, put on her jewellery, and went on deck to see what was going on. "Even then, I did not fear any serious consequences and returned to my stateroom, thinking that if the boat were going to sink it would take some time. In a few minutes, a man came to my stateroom and told me to put on my lifebelt if I wanted to be saved and go on deck. I asked if I had time to save my personal effects, and he replied, 'Not if you want to save your life.'"[76] The steward helped her put on the lifebelt and left. By that time, the deck was tilting quite near the water, and Paton was able to roll straight into a lifeboat, joining eighteen men and one woman.

THE GALLAGHERS

Immediately after they felt the crash, Cedric Aubrey Woolls Gallagher threw some pants over his pyjamas while his mother, Charlotte, put on her diamond necklace and rings and then her dressing gown. They went out onto the promenade deck, forgetting to grab their lifebelts. "There was a jumble of people crowded around the boats. They were foreigners, from steerage and ship's crew. They were all confused. Nobody seemed to be giving any orders. My mother and I tried to get into a lifeboat, but the crew drove us back. We went to the side and jumped. I had hold of Mother's hand," Cedric told a reporter. When they surfaced, Cedric managed to keep his mother afloat, but Charlotte became entangled in some ropes from the mast. "I tried to get her free but couldn't do it, and in a few minutes, she was dragged down under the water and torn away from my grasp. She was alive when she went under, and I swam around for a time, in the hope that in her struggles she would get free, and come to the surface, but I never saw her again."[77] Cedric swam until a lifeboat picked him up and took him to the *Storstad.* Charlotte's body was among the first to be picked up and was quickly identified with the help of her necklace.

FREDERICK GODSON

Cedric Gallagher wasn't the only first-class passenger to give the CPR some bad press. Twenty-six-year-old Frederick Godson, a Cambridge graduate from Worcestershire, England, studying mining and geology at Queen's University in Kingston, Ontario, was at the start of a round-the-world trip. Just as John Langley had at first believed, Godson told a reporter that passengers from second and third class died "like rats in a trap," because the doors to the exit were locked. He claimed that the crew had taken most of the lifebelts for themselves and that the few left on the promenade deck were tied so tightly with binder twine that they were difficult to free. He said that when he was eventually rescued by a lifeboat, it was less than half full but left for the *Storstad*, leaving dozens of struggling passengers to fend for themselves in the river.[78]

DR. GRANT

Dr. James Grant was thrown out of his bunk by the listing of the ship. He tried to turn on the lights, but the ship had already lost power. "I became very alarmed and tried to find my door. I got into cupboards and drawers but could not find the door in the darkness," he said. "The shrieking was deafening, and I could hear the water coming in the ship. I felt my time had come and I said my prayers." When he eventually found the door, the ship was almost turned over on her side; she was on such a steep angle that Grant couldn't walk. He grabbed hold of the carpet and pulled himself up, hand over hand. Just as he was within reach of the porthole, the carpet gave way, and he fell back down the passage. Instead of giving up, he wedged himself into a horizontal position with his feet against the opposite wall of the narrow corridor and wriggled himself all the way up to the porthole. Grant managed to get his head through, but his shoulders were stuck. He called for help, and a passenger pulled him through. "My shoulders and hips were deeply lacerated. For a moment I stood on the plates. I was able to make out the *Storstad* lights about a mile away and decided to swim to her and leave our boats to those who could not swim."[79] Grant stripped off his pyjamas and swam toward the collier.

In the end, only four of the forty lifeboats aboard the *Empress* could be released and used to rescue survivors from the river.

7. Heroes

CAPTAIN KENDALL STOOD ON the bridge, holding a megaphone in one hand and the rail with the other as water lapped around his feet. He'd already handed his lifebelt to a passenger, and he fully intended to go down with his ship. Instead, he was tossed into the water along with first assistant purser Ernest Hayes and sucked down into the vortex. When Kendall eventually resurfaced, the *Empress* was gone. A piece of wreckage bobbed up to the surface next to him, and the captain hung on to it.

As Kendall was preparing to go down with the ship, Charlie Spencer, a bellboy, dived into the river and resurfaced just in time to see one of the funnels topple over into the water, missing lifeboat no. 1 by a few centimetres. The people on the lifeboat weren't crushed, but just then a mast crashed down on another boat filled with about forty people, pulling them all underwater.

Kendall and young Spencer clung to the wreckage together. They were soon spotted by Hayes, who had been rescued by lifeboat no. 3. Kendall and Spencer were pulled into the lifeboat. The captain took command and began searching for survivors. When they'd filled the lifeboat to the point of sinking, they tied another ten people to the boat with ropes around their wrists and rowed to the collier. The fog had been so dense when the impact occurred that Kendall still did not know the name or nationality of the ship that had struck the *Empress*.

Kendall and six of his crew unloaded their bedraggled cargo and took off again to look for more survivors. They pulled seventy-three people from the water and kept searching until all that was left were frozen corpses.

STORSTAD TO THE RESCUE

Captain Andersen had tried to keep the *Storstad* wedged in the hole it had made in the *Empress* in order to give the crew time to lower the lifeboats so the passengers could leave the ship. But his efforts were futile, and he soon lost sight of the liner. At first, the Andersens thought the liner had just kept going and were shocked that its captain hadn't checked to see if the *Storstad* needed help. At that point, Andersen had no idea of the extent of the damage to his own vessel. Toftenes went to inspect the hold and see if they were going to sink.

Chief engineer Aaron Syvertsen was asleep in his bunk when the collision woke him. He hurriedly dressed and joined Captain

The Storstad *with damaged prow at the Port of Montreal, 1914 | Société d'Histoire du Bas-Canada (Beloeil, QC), Guy D'Astous collection*

Andersen and Anna on the deck. "I asked the captain what it was. He said it's a big boat that struck us. I ran right forward and looked at the damage. The bow was twisted in," he said. "We could not understand where the [*Empress*] had gone to. We never heard anything of it."[80]

Minutes later they heard screams and cries for help. Captain Andersen blew the ship's whistle several times but received no answer. He gave the order to proceed very slowly toward the sounds and to lower all the lifeboats.

The *Storstad*'s crew of thirty-six were not equipped to deal with a disaster of this magnitude, but they did what they could. Anna Andersen distributed the ship's stores of whisky, brandy, benedictine, and hot coffee to the frozen survivors as they came aboard the collier. Then she went about the ship quickly assembling as many clothes as she could from her own closet and those of the crew, as well as blankets, tablecloths, curtains, pillowcases—anything she could find to warm up the mostly naked survivors.

Annie Cook was the first woman to come aboard. "When she was brought to the cabin she ran to me, put her arms around my neck and said, 'God bless you, my angel. If you had not been here, we wouldn't have been saved,'" said Anna Andersen. "I put dry stockings and my fur coat on her and made her lie down on the berth."[81]

Marconi operator Ronald Ferguson had been saved by a deck chair that he'd grabbed on his way into the water. By the time he was picked up by a lifeboat from the *Empress*, he was naked. Most of the survivors lost what clothing they were wearing in the water or shed it to make swimming easier. When Ferguson reached the *Storstad*, Anna gave him her scarf, one of the only items she had left.

Anna was helping to clothe and warm up Alice Bales when she noticed Ethel Paton come on board. She couldn't help but notice that the woman was fully dressed, dry, and wearing lots of diamonds. Anna asked her how she had managed to dress and escape with all her jewellery. "I had lots of time," the socialite told her.[82]

Dr. Grant was exhausted, but he'd found a floating lifebelt and tied it around his neck and kept swimming. After a time, he was picked up by a *Storstad* lifeboat manned by three Norwegian sailors.

> I took an oar and we rowed quickly into the wreckage and filled our boat with those still floating. We then returned to the *Storstad* and it was a perilous climb, frozen as we were to mount that rope ladder. After getting on board, I rubbed myself and rolled up in a blanket until I collected myself, then I got up and opened a cupboard, at once there was a terrible rush for clothes, but I shouted that I was the doctor and to give me a pair of pants.[83]

The borrowed pants were much too large for Grant's small frame, so he kept them up with a piece of string. He first treated the women who were suffering from hypothermia and shock, giving them brandy and putting the most serious cases into berths. He fixed dislocated shoulders and broken arms and legs and treated open cuts and burns. He resuscitated those he could and covered those he couldn't.

Gordon Davidson had passed out in the lifeboat. When he came to, he found himself in the engine room of the *Storstad*, smeared with oil and coal dust and badly scraped up. "A big chap gave me an undershirt and an old torn pair of pants. It was a comfort to get something dry on."[84]

Ken McIntyre was dragged into a lifeboat by two husky Norwegian sailors. When they reached the *Storstad*, a sailor helped him up the rope ladder that led to the deck, and McIntyre made his way to the boiler room. A sailor handed McIntyre his own woollen undershirt; it hung to McIntyre's knees. "It was good to see friends and fellow survivors; but our concern was over the questions—who were saved? Who were lost?"[85]

Bodies are hoisted aboard the Lady Evelyn *from a lifeboat and taken to the temporary morgue in Rimouski, 1914* | *National Library and Archives of Quebec (Montreal, QC), 644388*

EUREKA AND *LADY EVELYN* TO THE RESCUE

At a little after three in the morning—just over an hour after the collision—the pilot boat *Eureka* arrived at the site of the sinking. The only thing left in the water to indicate that a ship had once been there was some wreckage and a few lifeboats still trying to collect survivors. Sixty-two-year-old Captain Jean-Baptiste Belanger, the same man who'd had a role in the arrest of Dr. Crippen four years earlier, arrived on the chaotic scene. He and the crew lowered the lifeboats and fished out thirty-two survivors from the St. Lawrence and picked up another 150 survivors from the lifeboats. The crew placed the dead bodies they'd recovered in the open stern and covered them with sheeting.

Once convinced there were no other survivors to be found, Captain Kendall returned to the *Storstad* and confronted Captain Andersen. "'Are you the captain of this ship?' He said: 'Yes.' I said: "You have sunk my ship.' I said: 'You were going full speed, and in that dense fog.' He said: 'I was not going full speed, you were going full speed.'" The angry exchange was interrupted by Captain Jean-Baptiste Pouliot of the *Lady Evelyn*, the second government steamer to arrive at the scene. "[Pouliot] came to me and said: 'Do not say anything; you had better go below.' With that I went off the bridge and went into his chart room. It was then I collapsed," said Kendall.[86]

Dr. Grant found Kendall suffering from shock and exposure.

> I was very concerned about him. His first words to me were "Doctor, there is only one thing I am sorry for and that is that they did not let me drown." I told him not to be foolish and that he had done everything any mortal man on a ship's bridge could have done. He would not permit me to remove his wet clothes and refused to take any brandy, saying he had never touched liquor in his life—which I learned to be the truth. He is a total abstainer.[87]

Kendall couldn't walk, and Grant had two other men help him aboard the *Lady Evelyn* to be taken to Rimouski along with about 350 other survivors.

Robert Crellin was in rough shape by the time he got aboard the steamer and was still clutching his charge, eight-year-old Florrie Barbour. Crellin still wore the trousers that he had swam in. He was amazed when he put his hand in his pocket and found his treasured watch, which he'd managed to grab on the way out of his cabin, and Florrie's little ring, which she had broken at the start of the trip and given to him to have repaired.*

Grant administered brandy to both patients, stripped Florrie down, and wrapped her in hot blankets.

Grant tended to as many injured passengers as he could. Seeing a woman passenger lying on the galley table with a broken leg, he pulled out a cutlery drawer and dumped its contents on the floor. He made a splint from the wood while a woman survivor from the Salvation Army handed him strips of fabric she had torn from a tablecloth. Even with this care, twenty-two people died between the crash site and the wharf.

The wharf at Rimouski became a triage station for the survivors. A freight shed at the end of the wharf normally used to store coal became a temporary morgue for the dead, who were carefully laid in rows and covered with what scanty clothing they were found in. The shed was quickly filled, and more buildings were found to house the massive number of dead.

---

* Historian Sébastien Hudon discovered the child's ring at the Site Historique Maritime de la Pointe-au-Père. Unfortunately all details concerning the ring's provenance were lost. "It is a child's ring in 22 karat gold," he told me. "The museum still had the original box for the ring, which matched the initials of the jeweller H. Samuel in England." Florrie mentioned the broken ring in her diary, and it's possible that she donated it when she was visiting Canada in 1964.

TOP: *handling the coffins at Rimouski* | Library of Congress (Washington, DC), LC-B2-3078-11 [P&P]; RIGHT: *Anastasia Ragoschin at the wharf in Rimouski. She lost her husband, Vladimir, and their eight-year-old son, Alexei, in the wreck.* | National Library and Archives of Quebec (Montreal, QC), 644388

HELP FROM RIMOUSKI

Horse-drawn carriages lined up near the pier to bring survivors into Rimouski a few kilometres away. With a population of a little over three thousand, the French Canadian town sprang into action. Villagers brought soup, bandages, and dry clothing to the survivors and took as many as possible into their own homes. Other survivors were taken to local hotels and convents, while the Sisters of Charity Hospice and the Hotel Alphonse Deon were converted into make-shift hospitals. Those with the most serious injuries were treated at the local hospital for everything from broken arms, fractured thighs, and burns to bruises and shock.

Every doctor in the area was called upon, and Dr. Grant continued to go from house to house, caring for the survivors. He was assisted by nineteen-year-old Grace Kohl of Montreal, who had spent less time in the water than many of the survivors. Although she didn't have medical training, she was able to offer some assistance and comfort to the survivors in Rimouski and later on the train to Quebec City.*

Still in shock, Captain Kendall limped into town, helped by his friends and fellow survivors Marion Sharp Adie and Doris Winifred Gaunt from Birmingham. He sent a telegram to his family in England saying that he was alive; he'd been found hanging on to a piece of wreckage.

Salvation Army officer Alfred Keith was taken to the Hôtel St-Germain for breakfast, still wearing a green embroidered woollen blanket from the *Storstad*.† Ernest Green was naked except for a towel around his waist.

---

* Grace Kohl married Richard Mather in 1916, and they had three daughters. She died in Montreal in 1976, aged 81.

† The Keith family later donated the blanket to the Salvation Army's George Railton Heritage Centre. The Salvation Army refers to the material as a tablecloth, but after inspecting the hand embroidery, I believe it's more likely to have come from the captain's bed.

Donna Millar displays the woollen blanket from the Storstad *given to Alfred Keith, now at the Salvation Heritage Centre in Toronto, 2023 | Eve Lazarus*

Theo Bartschi was brought to Rimouski aboard the *Eureka*. He'd searched for his brother on the steamer, but Christian wasn't among the survivors or the dead. Now Theo watched from the dock as the *Lady Evelyn* arrived with more survivors and dead bodies. He looked for his brother, but Christian was not among them. "Once at the dock at Rimouski, we went into the sheds and as our clothes were wet, we jumped around to keep warm. At half past six we were given some blankets and some clothes," he said.[88]

Theo was taken into town and given a place to stay. That afternoon, a doctor treated the gash on his head and bandaged up his injured knees.

Frank Brooks was reunited with his wife, Henrietta, in Rimouski, but the couple were shattered to later learn that the body of their young daughter, Dolly, had washed ashore at Métis-sur-Mer, over 30 kilometres (18 miles) below Father Point. She was found by thirteen-year-old Eileen Tuggy, who had been wandering along the beach not far from her home. Dolly's hands were clutching a small wallet,* and Eileen had placed a bouquet of forget-me-nots in Dolly's hand with a card attached. "Kindly accept my kindest and sincerest sympathy," she wrote. "May she rest in peace. If identified, I would like to know." Left with the body, there was also a wreath of lilies of the valley and another note saying, "As a token of respect from those who found her."[89]

Helen O'Hara and her mother were reunited in Rimouski. May O'Hara cabled her family in Toronto: "Helen and I saved; no trace of father."[90]

Little Grace Hanagan, the lone survivor of her family, received a new pair of shoes.

Gordon Davidson found Martin Gill, the young Irishman he had met on the train from Vancouver, in the galley of the *Lady Evelyn*.

Survivors from third class | *Library of Congress (Washington, DC), LC-B2-3079-7*

* The wallet is on display at the Site Historique Maritime de la Pointe-au-Père.

Later he saw James Lennon, who'd boarded the train in Winnipeg. "These two were the only acquaintances I had made on the rail trip who were saved. My roommate [Arthur Stillman] is not among the saved. Neither is a family named Law from Calgary—father, mother and six-year-old-boy … I did not see the wharf at Rimouski with some hundreds of dead bodies laid out on it. Thank goodness. It would haunt my sleep. But I have seen enough people who have lost relatives and friends to last me for a lifetime," said Davidson.

He and Gill were given blankets at the wharf in Rimouski before they headed into town.

> [My blanket] was a small one but it helped a lot in the cold gulf wind. The few wagons of clothes that came down were raided by a mob of men, many of whom had shoes on. Gill and I who were barefooted were afraid to venture among them. The cabs were busy carrying out the injured and those in a state of collapse. We went into the corner store there and after nearly an hour, I got an outfit of clothes. It was a weird-looking combination, but it was warm, I nearly collapsed when I was in the store. Then I went into a private house that had opened its doors and got a cup of tea and a little bread and butter.[91]

John Fowler, who had helped Eliza Willmot escape to the deck, had lost sight of her after she was taken aboard a lifeboat. They saw each other again in Rimouski. "She says that I saved her life and I was glad to have been able to help her what little I could," he said.[92]

SAVED AND ON THE WAY HOME

Annie Cook sent a telegram to her anxious husband and kids, saying, "Saved and on the way home." She and John Fowler were the only members of the Salvation Army's Vancouver contingent to survive. Fortunately, Annie was still wearing her nightie and the jacket that

Anna Andersen had given her aboard the *Storstad*, because it was several hours before the people supervising the rescue could find clothes to fit her tiny frame. She had walked barefoot from the landing at Rimouski to the hotel where she and the other survivors were billeted for the day.

There were only a handful of telephone lines available, and these were sought out by the media. Frank Morris, dressed in some chenille curtains from the *Storstad*, and Ken McIntyre, who wore a sailor's undershirt and a damp bedspread, tried to place a call to the Salvation Army, but the operator refused to take any message without payment. "They could see we were almost naked, but the money would have to be guaranteed. We tried for over an hour. Pleaded and threatened and finally got the manager. The manager refused unless we would pay $5.50," said Frank Morris. "Brigadier Rawling had been sitting up all night at Montreal and was asked over the phone at 9:00 a.m. if he would pay $5.50 to hear from Major Morris. He said he would pay $500—and this is how the first message got through to Montreal with the names of twenty-four survivors that I named to him."[93]

Morris and McIntyre were able to get some clothing in the village and returned to the wharf to try to identify some of their comrades from the more than two hundred who had been brought to shore. Morris's sister-in-law, Daisy, had decided to travel with her husband, Arthur, at the last minute, and because of that, she had been sleeping in a different cabin. She was one of the first of the bodies recovered.

Tom Greenaway was one of the first survivors to reach Rimouski. He was taken to a private house and soon joined by his brother, Bert, Ernie Pugmire, and Rufus Spooner. The men were given clothing and started searching for Tom's wife, Margaret, by going from house to house in the village. Margaret had woken up in a shed in Rimouski surrounded by the dead and dying. She was checked out by doctors, then taken to the Hôtel St-Germain in Rimouski. Tom finally found her there later that morning. She was in rough shape, but alive.

Two postcards of Rimouski, circa 1910 | Public domain

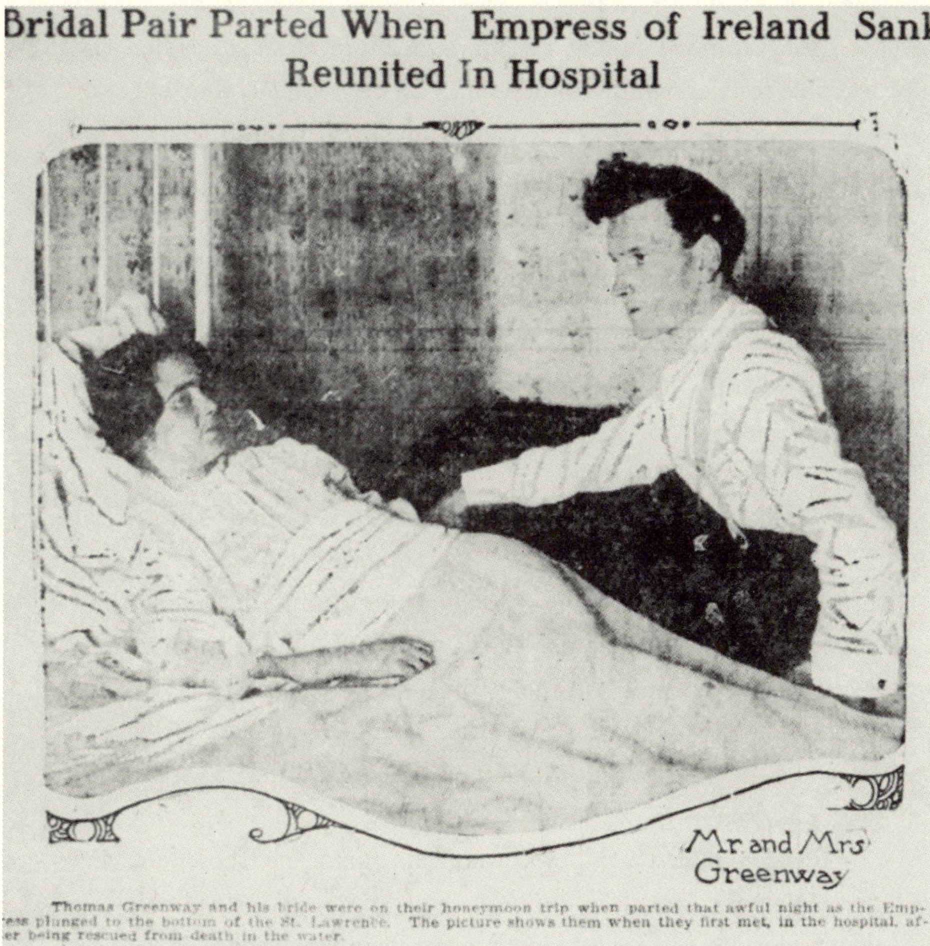

Bridal Pair Parted When Empress of Ireland Sank Reunited In Hospital

Thomas Greenway and his bride were on their honeymoon trip when parted that awful night as the Empress plunged to the bottom of the St. Lawrence. The picture shows them when they first met, in the hospital, after being rescued from death in the water.

South Bend News Times, *Indiana, June 5, 1914*

"You can imagine this joy. Bless him, he never ever looked quite so sweet to me. His hair was all in little curls and his face as white as death, but he was our boy just the same," Margaret wrote to her in-laws. "How I am alive is a mystery which we cannot solve. I was scalded on the arm, awfully bruised, and cut across the back of the ankle, and have been a little lame but it is getting better. Of course, we both feel the effects of the shock and I suppose will be a long time in getting over it."[94]

Ethel Grundy Paton was taken to the Hôtel Rimouski, where she was able to telegraph her brother, G.G. Grundy, general manager of the Temiscouata Railway. He came down to Rimouski to meet his sister and placed his private car at her disposal.*

TRAIN TO QUEBEC CITY

Thirty-seven of those rescued were too badly injured to travel and were kept at the hospital in Rimouski. The other 396 survivors were put on the train to Quebec City, which had been sent by the CPR along with medical staff.

Margaret and Tom Greenaway were taken to Grundy's private car and given full medical attention. Tom sent a wire to his family shortly before boarding the train, but they didn't get it until the next day, and they thought Margaret was dead. "Mother would not believe I was rescued as the papers had me among the lost and my photo in the paper. Then it was reported that I died after being rescued but when I wrote a little note in my own handwriting, they believed I was alive," wrote Margaret.[95]

The train pulled into Levis around 8:00 p.m., and those requiring immediate medical attention were taken by ambulance to the Jeffrey Hales Hospital in Quebec City. Among them was Euphemia Sanders Moir, the thirty-three-year-old daughter of a ship's captain, who had arrived in Montreal from Scotland five years before and worked as a maid before meeting barber Charles Moir and moving to Toronto. Sadly, she died shortly after being admitted to the hospital.

The remaining survivors continued on to Quebec City. And, even in the face of disaster, the class system ruled. Third-class passenger

* Ethel Paton was actively involved in the war effort, working with service men and veterans through the Canadian Red Cross, the Canadian Patriotic Society, and the Imperial Order of the Daughters of the Empire. She died at her home in Sherbrooke, Quebec, in 1956, aged 81. (Source: Dufferin County Museum, Ontario.)

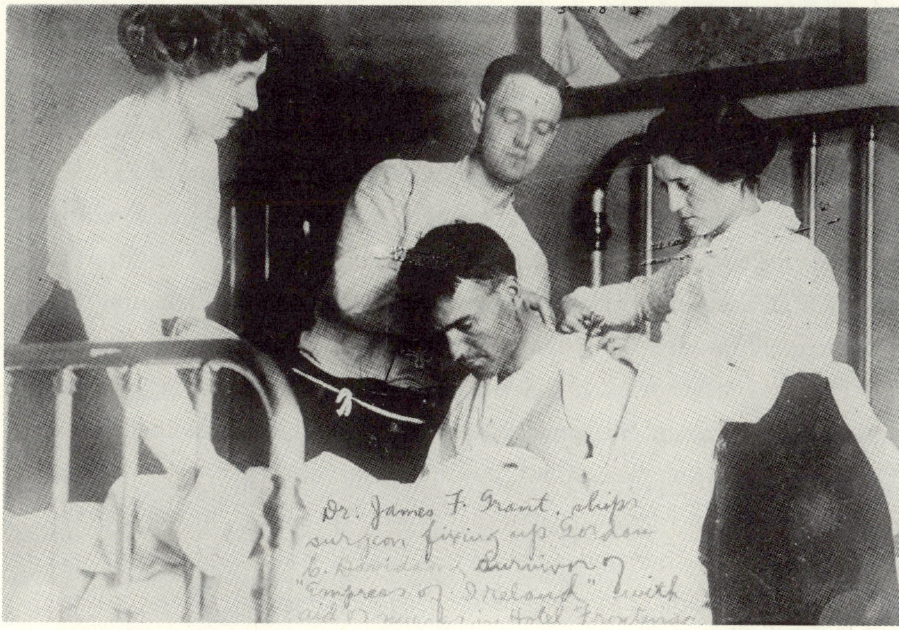

Dr. James Grant tending to Gordon Davidson at the Château Frontenac | Library of Congress (Washington, DC), LC-B2-3078-15

Martin Gill was taken to the SS *Alsatian*, which was berthed at the wharf, while Gordon Davidson was taken by car to the Canadian Pacific's luxury Château Frontenac, along with the other first- and second-class passengers.

"It took me almost three quarters of an hour to scrub off the oil and coal dust in a warm bath. Then the nurses bandaged up my abrasions. I got supper and went to bed," said Davidson. "Dr. Grant, who has been a regular hero, fixed me up again this morning. I am stiff and sore from my skin wounds, but I will be able to walk with something like comfort in a day or two."[96]

The train continued on to the Grand Trunk Railway's Bonaventure Station in Montreal, arriving on the morning of Saturday, May 30, with seventeen of the surviving Salvation Army members. They were greeted by a large party of Salvationists, who had brought bundles of clothing and other necessities.

The train also brought three coffins containing the first identified victims—all three were women. Nineteen-year-old Cedric Gallagher, described by a reporter as "tall, thin, almost weedy and wearing a badly fitted overcoat," was one of the first to disembark.[97] He had spent the night in the second baggage car from the engine, watching over the coffin that contained his mother, Charlotte. Now a group of men all dressed in black stepped forward and started unloading the three coffins. The other two victims were also first-class passengers: Frances Barlow of Montreal, whose husband, Dr. Alfred Barlow,* had also drowned, and Susanna Seybold of Ottawa. Her husband, Edward Seybold, a wholesaler from Ottawa, had survived.

The second-largest party of Salvationists on their way to the Congress, which included twenty-eight officers and the Peterborough band, were booked to travel on the *Alaunia*, departing May 30. Even though bandmaster William Peryer's mother, Jemima, had died on the *Empress*, as had many of the Salvationists' friends and colleagues, the group continued their trip. The *Alaunia* passed the *Storstad* as the collier completed her trip to Montreal. A few hours later, the ship passed close to the wreckage of the *Empress of Ireland*. The passengers and crew assembled on deck as the bandmaster dropped a wreath overboard and the company sang "Nearer, My God, to Thee." Shortly afterward, the *Alaunia* passed a lifeboat from the *Empress*, abandoned and floating in the river.

Captain Kendall was in a state of shock, barely coherent and possibly suicidal. Rather than travel to Quebec City with the rest of the passengers and crew, he was ordered to stay in Rimouski to testify at the Inquest, which was hastily pulled together and held in the town's schoolhouse. Kendall testified that the *Empress* was stopped dead in

---

* At the time of his death, Montreal-born Alfred Barlow was an author, a past president of the Canadian Mining Institution, and a lecturer in geology at McGill University. In 1916, a mountain located on the Continental Divide along the border of Alberta and British Columbia was named Mount Barlow in his honour.

The Peterborough Temple Bandsmen, travelling on the Alaunia, *passed this abandoned lifeboat from the* Empress *on their way to England the day after the sinking, May 30, 1914 | Used by permission of the Salvation Army Canada and Bermuda Archives (Toronto, ON), photo 66575*

the water, and not only had the *Storstad* caused the crash, but instead of keeping her bow inside the hole and effectively sealing it like a cork, the *Storstad* had pulled away, leaving the *Empress* to sink and her passengers and crew to drown. Kendall testified that the *Storstad* had stayed 2.4 kilometres (1.5 miles) away from the scene of the accident and that the *Empress*'s lifeboats had brought the majority of the survivors to the *Storstad*.[98]

In the rush to hold an inquest, no one from the *Storstad*—which had continued on to Montreal despite heavy damage to her bow—was available to answer these accusations. The Inquest was abandoned, and an Inquiry was scheduled for later in June in Quebec City to allow for further investigation. But when Kendall's version of events reached the newspapers, Captain Andersen was furious. That wasn't how it happened at all, he told his bosses at A.F. Klaverness & Co., and his shipping company released an official statement refuting Kendall's testimony.

New York Tribune

NEW YORK, SUNDAY, MAY 31, 1914.—SEVEN PARTS—72 PAGES.

PRICE FIVE CENTS

KENDALL BLAMES THE STORSTAD FOR BACKING AFTER IMPACT, THUS SHUTTING OFF ALL HOPE

CAPTAIN ANDERSON OF THE STORSTAD.

CHARGES STORSTAD LET PASSENGERS DIE

Prominent Montreal Lawyer Denounces "Odious Insouciance" of Crew and Captain of Collier—Thinks Explosion Killed Many on Unfortunate Empress.

Captain of Canadian Liner Empress of Ireland Testifies That His Vessel Was Rammed While Motionless.

DEATH LIST NOW 964; SAVED, 403

All on Doomed Ship Were Under Perfect Control, Reports Say, Officers and Men Doing Everything Possible, While Passengers Accepted Situation Without Fear or Panic.

Captain Kendall, who lost his ship and 964 lives in the St. Lawrence River Friday morning, only 403 passengers and crew, almost equally divided, surviving, blamed the disaster on the collier with which the Empress of Ireland was in collision when he appeared yesterday before the Coroner in Rimouski to tell his story.

"What was the cause of the collision?" he was asked.

"The Storstad running into the Empress, which was motionless," he replied, with emphasis.

Representatives of the collier maintained strict silence, except to say that charges placing the responsibility on their captain were probably unfounded. The collier proceeded slowly up the river to Quebec, where surly indifference was maintained, and then steamed on to Montreal.

BITTER ATTACK ON COLLIER.

This attitude, reported from Quebec by The Tribune's staff correspondent, received confirmation from the scene of the disaster. The French editor in Rimouski, publisher of the only paper there, sent The Tribune an interview with a prominent Montreal lawyer severely criticising Captain Anderson and the Storstad's crew for what he termed their "odious insouciance."

While the Empress of Ireland gave way before the onslaught of the sea against her unprotected amidships, and passengers and crew struggled in the water, the men of the collier remained indifferent and passive, the lawyer maintained. It was reported from another source that the Storstad withdrew to a point a mile and a half from the disaster and remained without headway while its victim disappeared, picking up those who succeeded in reaching its side; showing, however, even then a disposition to be put out by the delay in passing along upriver.

Quebec awaited the arrival of the Lady Grey, with 175 bodies. The city was stunned by the catastrophe, and its grief was silent but

I.W.W.'S IN TARRYTOWN JAIL

Woman and 11 Men Try to Orate in Rockefeller Town.

R. B. M'CLURE ENDS HIS LIFE BY SHOT

Mystery Surrounds Suicide of Publisher's Brother at Home.

COLONEL TO WAR ON BARNES AND MURPHY

'Sub-Bosses Must Go, Too,' He Says in Statement Ere He Sails Abroad.

WILL OPEN STATE FIGHT ON HIS RETURN

Condemns Wilson Administration for Making 'Pinch of Poverty' Felt in Nation.

TOP: *James Rankin testifying at the Inquest held in the schoolhouse in Rimouski, 1914* | *National Library and Archives of Quebec (Montreal, QC), 644388;* BOTTOM: New York Tribune, *May 31, 1914*

8. Identifying the Bodies

THE DAY AFTER HAL Beckett, his wife, and their eighteen-day-old daughter saw off their fellow Salvationists on their journey to London, he was back to work at the wharf. Two hundred immigrants under the Salvation Army's care were set to arrive, and they had to be met and cared for. At the sheds, a dock official called out to Beckett, "Heard about the *Empress*?"

"What about her?" he called back.

"She's lost!"

"Don't be silly, man," Beckett told him. "She only left here twelve hours ago. She's still in the river."

"She's lost, I tell you."

Sadly, the dock official was correct, and Beckett went about his work while snippets of news kept arriving throughout the day. By late afternoon, word was sent that a few survivors would reach Quebec City by that evening.

"We went over to meet them—a pathetic handful of the Army party that we had waved off twenty-four hours ago, with such enthusiasm," he said. "I grabbed the hands of one of the men survivors and said, 'Oh, it's good to see you. How did you manage to survive?' I shall never forget his answer. He said, 'I was not worthy to go over with the rest.' 'Are these all that are left?' Hal asked, again and again. 'These are all,' came the reply."[99]

Later, Beckett helped with the grisly work of identifying the bodies.

> People began to arrive as soon as it was made known that the first bodies had been recovered and brought to Quebec. We had to take these relatives in, and as they waited, try to calm them. When Mrs. Maidment's body was recovered, she was clasping a child in her arms, and the French Canadian authorities had written on the card "mere et enfant" (mother and child). When we claimed the body of Mrs. Maidment only, the French folk said, "No, this must be her child; no woman would show such anxiety for a child other than her own as she obviously struggled to save her life." Of course, it was not her child. Her daughter had remained in Canada.[100]

NEWS OF THE SINKING REACHES TORONTO

At 5:00 a.m. that morning (May 29), Staff Captain William Arnold of the Toronto Salvation Army was woken by the ringing of his phone. It was the editor of the *Toronto Globe*, who had received a dispatch from Rimouski with scant details about the sinking of the *Empress*. Arnold quickly got hold of other senior officers and headed for the Salvation Army Temple to contact relatives, friends, and co-workers. News came at 11:00 a.m. that everyone had survived the sinking, but by 2:30 p.m. those hopes were dashed after a much-awaited statement from Sir Thomas Shaughnessy, president of the CPR.

The Salvation Army members waited through the day and night. Eventually word reached them that out of the 161 members who had left for the Congress, only twenty-eight had survived. The Salvationists stood on the steps of the building and read out the names of the survivors.

Major Gideon Miller and Colonel W.J. Turner had already left Toronto and were on their way to Rimouski to identify the bodies

TOP: *victims from the* Empress of Ireland *are placed in coffins to be taken to Quebec City, 1914 | Library of Congress (Washington,* DC*),* LC*-B2-3339-10 [*P&P*];* BOTTOM: *the* Lady Grey *transported victims of the sinking from Rimouski to Quebec City | Library of Congress (Washington,* DC*), LC-B2-3079-5 [*P&P*]*

of as many of their comrades as possible. Once there, they were sent to a coal shed at the end of the wharf that had been converted into a morgue. They worked with an old lantern, searching the more than two hundred bodies lying in the makeshift morgue and were able to identify sixteen Salvationists. They marked each casket with a large red cross.

Also that morning, Captain Pouliot of the *Lady Evelyn* and Captain Belanger of the *Eureka* discharged their human cargo at Rimouski and headed back out to the crash site to search for more bodies. At low tide, the *Empress of Ireland* wasn't difficult to spot. Air bubbles were still coming up from the ship, and a huge oil slick covered the surface of the water. A small buoy with a Union Jack flag on top marked the site.

The crew picked up the *Empress of Ireland*'s logbook, which they found undamaged in a watertight metal box.

Another 134 bodies were recovered and taken back to Rimouski. Pouliot went back out in the steamer on Saturday and Sunday, staying out until dark each night, continuing to search for bodies.[101]

BODIES TAKEN TO QUEBEC CITY

The small town of Rimouski couldn't handle the large number of bodies coming in, and it was decided to send them to Quebec City. Early on the morning of Sunday, May 31, the *Lady Grey* arrived in Quebec City with 188 coffins lined up on her deck, accompanied by the British warship HMS *Essex*. Both ships flew their flags at half-mast. The *Essex* anchored a short distance away and sounded her bugle to signal the lowering of three lifeboats. Sailors from the *Essex* rowed them to the *Lady Grey* and quietly and respectfully began to unload the cargos, while the sailors who remained aboard the ship stood at attention. Church bells could be heard ringing in the distance.

More than ten thousand people gathered at the pier as sailors from the *Essex* carried the coffins on their shoulders from the ship to a freight shed at Pier 27 that had been converted into a makeshift morgue and draped in black cloth. They laid the coffins along three long counters. The officials in charge had underestimated the space needed for the coffins, and some had to be placed on the floor. Twenty-four small white caskets containing the bodies of children were placed along one side of the shed. Some of the coffins were quite elaborate, while others lacked handles and their wood was hastily stained. Others were just rough pine boxes. A crowd of people, including some survivors, relatives, and friends of the dead, waited in silence for permission to walk down the aisles to try to find and identify their loved ones.

Officials, CPR constables, and dozens of members of the press gathered outside the shed at Pier 27, along with many grieving family members and friends. Most of the surviving crew members of the *Empress* were waiting to identify former colleagues and friends. Many were visibly upset when they passed the body of chief officer Mansfield Steede, who had died while trying to free the lifeboats and save passenger lives. They stopped to pay tribute to a man they respected, and they keenly felt his loss.

Those bodies that had been in the water for several hours, hit by falling debris, sucked down into the vortex, or battered in the water were so bruised and swollen that it was difficult to recognize them, even for their loved ones. Those who could be identified had their names attached to the outsides of their coffins. A note on one coffin simply said "mother and child." The woman inside, who was found clutching her baby daughter, was later identified as twenty-eight-year-old Kathleen Hoad of Montreal. A note on another coffin read, "Anyone knowing Alex McDonald, purser, *Empress of Ireland*, please have a look at this body, so as to be sure that it is his."[102]

TOP: *sailors from the* HMS Essex *take children in coffins from the* Lady Grey *to Pier 27* | *Library of Congress (Washington,* DC*),* LC-B2-3079-1; BOTTOM: *sailors from the* HMS Essex *take coffins from the* Lady Grey *to Pier 27* | *National Library and Archives of Quebec (Montreal,* QC*), 644388*

Rescued members of the crew arrive at Quebec City, June 2, 1914 | American Press Association, Société d'Histoire du Bas-Canada (Beloeil, QC), Guy D'Astous collection

CPR constable Bailey, badge no. 151, was on duty at the morgue. The incident was deeply personal for him. Just that week he had seen off the Taverner family on the special train to Quebec City. He had lived with them for two years. James, a thirty-five-year-old stable worker, his wife, Clara (thirty-one), and their two children, Eva (seven), and Henry (eighteen months), had been returning home to England after five years in Montreal. When Bailey heard that the CPR was assigning security to the morgue, he volunteered.

"I wanted to be on hand when the bodies were brought up in order that I might identify them if they were found. I have looked and looked. Not one member of the family is here," he told a reporter. "They were so happy together during all the time that I lived with them. It was like saying goodbye to a brother and sister last Thursday. They had decided to return home to Eastham, London, to live. Mr. Taverner having been advised to do so on account of his health."[103]

SURVIVORS SEARCH FOR LOVED ONES

Twenty-two-year-old Richard Hedgecoe of Montreal came to search for the body of his sweetheart, Sarah "Nellie" Jones, a telephone operator with Bell Canada. They had planned to marry when they reached their family in England. The last time Hedgecoe saw Jones was on the deck, when he put his lifebelt around her. They were pulled down into the water by the suction, and only Hedgecoe surfaced.* When Hedgecoe found Jones's body in the shed, she was no longer wearing the sweater that she had been lost in, nor did she have the bag of money she had tied around her neck.

William Burrows of Galt, Ontario, was looking for the bodies of his wife, Charlotte, and their two children, ten-year-old William and eight-year-old May.† The Burrows had been taking an infant named Willie Leeks to live with his grandparents in England, after his mother had died in childbirth. Only Charlotte and Willie's bodies were recovered.

Egildo and Carolina Braga, who had been travelling in third class, searched for their son, Rino, among the corpses lined up for identification. He wasn't there. The couple had lost everything except for a leather belt Egildo had bought with his miner's savings and a gold chain.

Reporters took note when a woman wearing a long grey CPR coat entered the morgue. She was twenty-seven-year-old Fanny Evinson from Winnipeg, travelling to Liverpool for a holiday with her husband, Eli, and their baby boy, Julius. After the collision, Fanny had

---

* Richard Hedgecoe married Mary Kathleen and had two sons and a daughter. He died in Montreal in 1959, aged 67.

† William Burrows, a glass-packer, moved back to England and died in 1958, aged 78.

bundled up her baby, and she and her husband had fought their way to the deck. There was no time to look for lifebelts, and they were separated in the dark. The last thing she remembered was losing consciousness as the boat sank. She was picked up by a lifeboat, but the child was no longer in her arms.

Ignoring the people around her, Fanny walked straight over to the white coffins where the babies lay. She found Julius in the first one she looked in and fell to her knees, tears streaming down her face, making crooning sounds to her dead child. After a long time, Fanny left her baby and started to search for her husband. She went up and down the aisles three times, but Eli was not among the bodies so far recovered.

Just two days earlier, Charlotte Aldridge, known as Dot, and her three little children, six-year-old Bernard, four-year-old Hilda, and eight-week-old Dora, had walked their father to the streetcar stop at St. Clair Avenue and Dufferin Street in Toronto. Bernard had pulled along his father's luggage in his little toy wagon. The family had learned that Aldridge wouldn't be coming home again when a man knocked on the door and held up a newspaper. The headline read, "Empress of Ireland Sunk, All Lost." The newspaper was wrong, of course; there were survivors. Unfortunately, Ernest Aldridge, a thirty-year-old master carpenter and trombone player with the Salvation Army Staff Band, wasn't one of them.[104]

Hilma Taavettila lived in Fort William, Ontario, and had been travelling with her husband, Antti, and their seven-year-old son, Allan, to visit relatives in Helsinki. Hilma couldn't find her little boy among the children's caskets, but she was almost sure she had found her husband in casket 37. The man's face was badly scratched and swollen. She told one of the CPR constables that she had sewn one thousand dollars in each side of her husband's vest. The constable ripped the vest open with his knife. The money was found and Antti identified.*

---

* Hilma Taavettila returned to Fort William and married John Knuuttila, a Finnish-born widower and labourer, in December 1915. Hilma died in Thunder Bay in 1957.

Arvo Markkulla had left Negaunee, Michigan, with his father, Frans, an iron ore miner; his mother, Sofia; and his younger brothers, ten-year-old Eero and seven-year-old Aino; and his two-year-old sister, Tonia. The family had immigrated to the United States in 1910 and were visiting Finland. Arvo stopped by one of the children's coffins and broke down in tears. He'd found his baby sister. With the help of an immigration interpreter, he was able to identify his mother and one of his brothers. Arvo was less than two weeks shy of his fourteenth birthday. He was the only member of the family of six to survive.*

Seventeen-year-old Tiria Townshend was staying at the Château Frontenac until she could locate and identify her aunt Fanny among the hundreds of other bodies in the makeshift morgue. She found her aunt and was given Fanny's rings. When Townshend returned the next day, she was shocked to find that sailors from the *Empress* claimed the body was actually that of Elizabeth Leders, a forty-eight-year-old stewardess and member of the crew. Leders, whose husband, Charles, had died at sea eight years earlier, had a young daughter who was living with her mother-in-law in England. CPR officials were called in and shown the rings, and they confirmed the body was Fanny Price.[105]

Townshend and Price were at the beginning of a two-year trip around the world. Instead, Price was buried by the CPR at Mount Hermon Cemetery in Quebec City, and Townshend left for Vancouver, where she took the *Makura* back to New Zealand.†

John Delamont and his wife, son (Arthur), and daughter were four of the few passengers from third class who survived. They'd lost their son and brother, Leonard, and were staying in Quebec City in the hopes that his body would soon be recovered. In the three days

* Arvo Markkulla returned to Negaunee to live with his older brother, Einar, and later moved to Chicago, where he died in 1968.

† Tiria Townshend graduated as a nurse in 1921 and married Thomas White in 1926. They had a son and two daughters. She died in 1956 and is buried in Whangārei, New Zealand.

that they stayed there, John Delamont made five trips through the temporary morgue, searching for his eldest son.

In a letter to his older sister in Moose Jaw, Arthur Delamont tells her that he and his father identified the body of Salvation Army band member Charles Wilkes and are having his body sent on to Moose Jaw. He goes on to say the family is staying in Quebec City for a few days to try and locate the body of their brother Leonard (Len) and that they have lost everything but their nightshirts. "We have not given up hope of Len yet, although he must be gone. We came back from the wharf just now and out of 250 bodies, Len is not there. As soon as we can, we shall go to Toronto, for of course, we are not going on. We have lost everything ... Your loving brother, Arthur."[106]

Archie Brown arrived in Rimouski barefoot and wearing a blanket and a woman's dress. He was taken to receive medical attention to Quebec City, where he wrote to his family in Moose Jaw. "I've just had a doctor examine me, and he says I have contracted a slight attack of pleurisy. Gee! I'm sore from head to foot! Just now I am alone, I don't know where the folks are, and as far as poor Charlie and Len are concerned, we don't know where they are or whether they are saved."[107]

TWO FATHERS CLAIM THE SAME BABY

Tracey Archer had been travelling with his wife, Ruth, and their young son. They had left their six-month-old baby, Gordon, with friends in Regina, Saskatchewan, while they visited Ruth's dying mother in Nova Scotia and continued on to visit Archer's mother in London. In the morgue, Archer got into an argument with Frederick Cullen, who wasn't aboard the *Empress* but had lost his wife, Maude, and his young son and daughter. Only Jennie Blyth, the family's twenty-six-year-old Scottish nanny, survived the sinking. An older son, eight-year-old Arthur Frederick (Freddie), had stayed with friends on a farm for the summer.

Earlier that day, Cullen, a candy buyer with the T. Eaton Company in Toronto, had the heartbreaking task of identifying his six-year-old daughter, Isobel Maud, in casket 116. He thought he had found Albert, his twenty-eight-month-old son, in casket 118, but Archer was also certain the body was that of his son, Alfred. Both fathers said their boys had heavy eyebrows and a lot of hair for children of that age. Archer, though, was less convinced. Alfred Archer had been five months younger than Albert Cullen, and another little boy in casket 135 also looked very much like Alfred.

In the end, officials had Jennie Blyth, the Cullens' nanny, brought over from the Château Frontenac.* She had known the child better than his father, and she had been holding little Albert when the ship went down. A CPR constable carried the cold little body over to the window, where Blyth could see the boy more clearly in the light. Blyth and the two fathers viewed the body from every angle, opening his eyelids to check the colour of his eyes and opening his mouth. Blyth saw the little milk tooth her charge had recently cut, and he was identified as Albert Cullen.

FAMILIES TRAVEL FROM THE WEST IN SEARCH OF LOVED ONES

Several men travelled from British Columbia to identify their wives and children. Vancouver Police constable James Duffy was able to identify the body of his wife, Mary Ann. He sent a wire back to his boss, Chief Malcolm McLennan, with the sad news.

Frank Hepburn arrived from Vancouver, searching for his wife, Mary Katherine; their two children, three-year-old Barbara and nine-month-old Owen; and their friend, Eleanor Hunt. Hepburn, a mining engineer, told a reporter before he left Vancouver that he

* Little is known about Jennie Blyth, but it's likely that she remained unwed, moved to Vancouver, and died there in 1967 as Jeanie Pattison Blyth, aged 79.

The Salvation Army band with Commissioner Rees and Colonel Maidment before they embarked on the Empress of Ireland, *1914. Those marked* X *were rescued | Used by permission of the Salvation Army Canada and Bermuda Archives (Toronto,* ON*), photo 84887*

held no hope for their survival, because their cabin had been right at the point where the *Storstad* struck. He had the task of identifying his tiny daughter and fifty-four-year-old Eleanor Hunt. His wife and son were lost.

All day and through the night, rain splattered down on the metal roof of the shed. By 9:00 p.m., only a few more who had arrived on the late trains came to the morgue in hopes of identifying their relatives, colleagues, and friends. Shortly before midnight, Constable Bailey helped to replace the lids on the coffins before settling down for the night to guard the bodies and the rings and other valuables they were wearing that could help identify them.

Captain Henry Kendall, still in poor health, continued on to Montreal. He checked into the Place Viger hotel, refusing to answer any questions put to him by the press, and asked the switchboard operator to disconnect the telephone in his room. Then he left strict instructions not to be disturbed.

THE FIRST SURVIVORS ARRIVE IN TORONTO

The first survivors to arrive at Toronto's Union Station on May 30 included Salvationists Ernest Pugmire, Rufus Spooner, Ernest Green—who had lost both parents and his sister, Jessie—Annie Cook, and Alice Bales.* Pugmire had made sure that little Grace Hanagan boarded the rescue train safely, and she was looked after along the way by Hattie Attwell.† Grace was expecting to meet her parents in Toronto, not aware yet that they were dead. "An *Empress* officer on [the *Storstad*] was very kind. I asked him for my mother, and he promised to find her," said Grace. "I clung to his promise for months but, as time went on, I wondered why she didn't come. My father's body was found, and I saw him at the undertaker's parlour and realized he had passed away. But where was my mother?"[108]

The survivors were greeted by a packed crowd. The Salvationists wore white arm bands instead of the customary black, showing that their dead had "been promoted to glory."‡

TWO SURVIVORS RETURN TO VANCOUVER

John Fowler and Annie Cook, both members of the Salvation Army, continued on to Vancouver by train and were met by their families and more than 150 Salvation Army members, who lined the platform

---

* Rufus Spooner's sweetheart, Margaret Wright, greeted him at Union Station. They were married on September 1, 1915, and had a son and a daughter. Spooner became a colonel with the Salvation Army and died in Toronto in 1961, aged 72. Alice Bales returned to Yorkshire, England, and married Henry Shaw in 1917. They had three children, and Bales died in 1972, aged 78. Ernest Green had prayed to god that if he survived, he would enter the Salvation Army training college to become an officer. He eventually became a corps commander, and his daughter was a lieutenant colonel at the time of his death in 1972, aged 80. (Sources: "Three Times Lucky," *Ottawa Citizen*, April 27, 1998; "Ernest Green, 80 of Salvation Army," *Toronto Star*, November 15, 1972.)

† George and Hattie Attwell spent the rest of their lives in Toronto, where George worked in the Salvation Army's printing department. Hattie died in 1950, aged 83, and George died in 1961, aged 90.

‡ In the Salvation Army, "promoted to glory" means going to heaven and a better life.

Vancouver Survivors Welcomed Home

Families of Band-Sergeant Fowler and Mrs. George E. Cook Meet Their Loved Ones.

Again Tell the Story of Their Wonderful Escape from Death

Still harboring memories of their awful experiences in the Empress of Ireland catastrophe, Mr. John Fowler, 1221 Eighteenth avenue east, Salvation Army bandsman and C. P. R. employee, together with Mrs. George E. Cook of the Salvation Army, living at 4755 Commercial street, South Vancouver, returned to Vancouver and their families last night.

Their stories differ in several respects from the stories they were reported to have given to newspaper at Rimouski. They both say that the errors which crept in were doubtless caused by the haste with which the reporters gathered their news then.

This morning, in their own homes, surrounded by their families, they gave personal stories to The World and these stories substantiate the stories of horror and grief at that awful catastrophe.

Mr. Fowler left Vancouver with the intension of not only attending the Salvation Army convention in London, but also with the hope of improving his health. He said this morning that the events through which he had passed had sapped much of his vitality and he was really in a much worse condition than when he left his home.

He Was Ill

The fact of his illness was borne out by his sickness on the boat.

"I have crossed the Atlantic five times," he said this morning, "and I did not expect to be sick this time. I never was seasick before. We were only on the St. Lawrence, and I was sick then.

Out of the Jaws of Death

MRS. GEO. COOK,
survivor of Empress of Ireland, her little daughter Irma and her mother, Mrs. Rampling, Lowestoft, Eng.

Vancouver Daily World, *June 5, 1914*

to greet them. Upon seeing her husband, George, her two sons, aged five and twenty-one, and her eleven-year-old daughter, Cook fell to her knees and hugged the two youngest children.*

Fowler followed Cook onto the platform. He was thrilled to see his wife, Lena, and their three children. He could barely walk, and Salvation Army bandsmen lifted him up on their shoulders and

* Annie Cook lived the rest of her life in Vancouver, serving the Salvation Army. She died in 1964, aged 93.

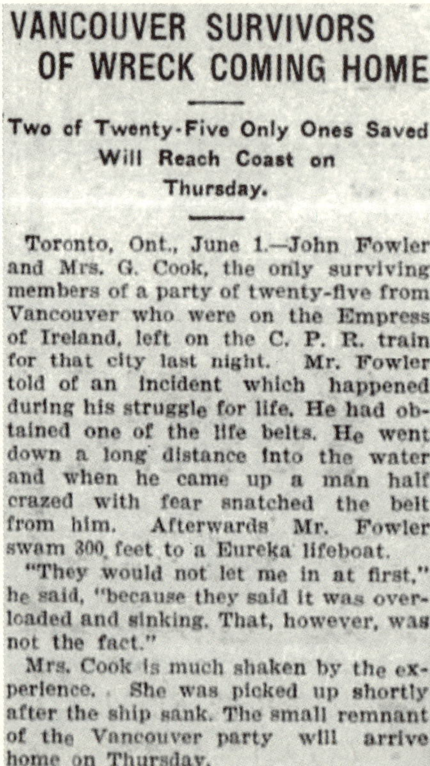

VANCOUVER SURVIVORS OF WRECK COMING HOME

Two of Twenty-Five Only Ones Saved Will Reach Coast on Thursday.

Toronto, Ont., June 1.—John Fowler and Mrs. G. Cook, the only surviving members of a party of twenty-five from Vancouver who were on the Empress of Ireland, left on the C. P. R. train for that city last night. Mr. Fowler told of an incident which happened during his struggle for life. He had obtained one of the life belts. He went down a long distance into the water and when he came up a man half crazed with fear snatched the belt from him. Afterwards Mr. Fowler swam 300 feet to a Eureka lifeboat.

"They would not let me in at first," he said, "because they said it was overloaded and sinking. That, however, was not the fact."

Mrs. Cook is much shaken by the experience. She was picked up shortly after the ship sank. The small remnant of the Vancouver party will arrive home on Thursday.

CLOCKWISE FROM TOP LEFT: Victoria Daily Times, *June 1, 1914; the Fowlers' house, still standing at 1221 East 18th Avenue in Vancouver, 2024* | *Eve Lazarus; monument erected by the* CPR *at Point-au-Père after the sinking of the* Empress of Ireland | *Library and Archives Canada (Ottawa,* ON*)*

carried him to a waiting car. A few hundred people had gathered on Cordova Street, near the entrance to the train depot, and as the two cars carrying the survivors passed by, every hat was raised as a token of respect and sympathy.

Bodies continued to be recovered. Most were women and children, and the majority were from third class. Those who couldn't be identified were photographed, tagged, and buried either at the Catholic cemetery in Rimouski or on a plot of land near Pointe-au-Père paid for by the CPR.

9. Burying the Dead

JOHN LANGLEY'S NAME WAS not on the first list of saved survivors. A telegram was sent to his family in Merritt, BC, saying, "Regret J.W. Langley not amongst list of saved. Send relatives to identify body." Shortly afterward, Langley's wife, Bessie, received a telegram from him saying, "My address will be care of CPR till Thursday."[109] Then he wrote his wife a letter on Château Frontenac stationery: "My Darling Sweetie Pets: Such an escape. I am thankful you weren't with me. We would never have escaped together. I couldn't have brought you out quickly enough." He told Bessie that he had lost his ring in the water and the only thing he'd managed to save were the purple

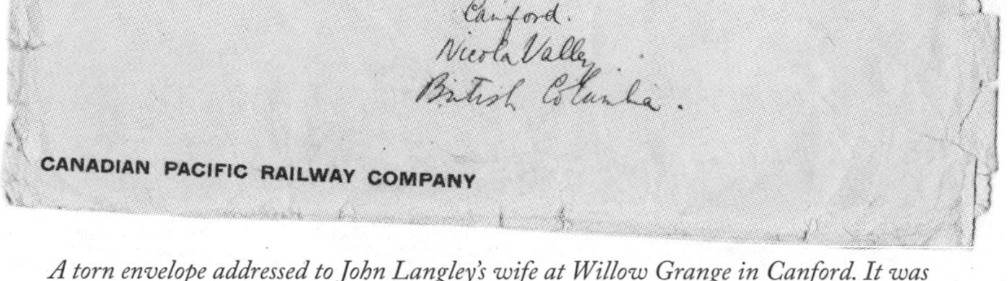

A torn envelope addressed to John Langley's wife at Willow Grange in Canford. It was sent to her by the CPR. | Langley family collection

Funeral held at the Anglican church, June 1914 | *National Library and Archives of Quebec (Montreal, QC), 644388*

striped pyjamas he was wearing. The CPR had paid for a new grey suit, a Burberry coat, and a suitcase full of clothes and toiletries. He wrote that the Château Frontenac was the finest hotel he'd ever seen. "Poor Miss Hunt is gone and Mrs. Hepburn with the little bubbas. Think of that poor man when he got the news that all his family were gone. He must be nearly mad. Curiously, there was a Miss Langley onboard from Vancouver. I was going to find out who she was, but now she's gone."[110]

While Canadians were still reeling from the shock of the *Titanic* disaster two years earlier, that tragedy wasn't felt with anything like the same force as the wreck of the *Empress of Ireland*. Within a week of the shipwreck, funerals were being held across Canada to bury the dead.

FUNERAL FOR THE CREW

On June 4, 1914, twelve members of the crew, all from Liverpool, were buried in Quebec City. The service was attended by thousands, including the premier of the province, cabinet members, the lieutenant governor of Quebec, officers from the HMS *Essex*, marines, military and naval officers, police, representatives of the CPR, and survivors of the shipwreck.

Captain Kendall took the train from Montreal to attend the funeral of his crew. He was still in poor health and had to be assisted in and out of the church. There were two funeral services: a requiem mass for the Catholic crew members and a funeral service for the Protestants. After the services, twelve hearses were followed by Captains Kendall and John Walsh, marine superintendent of the CPR, and the survivors until they were divided again—the Catholics to Saint Patrick's Cemetery and the Protestants to Mount Hermon Cemetery. The bodies were buried in large single lots paid for by the CPR. Later that same day, a much smaller funeral was held for Sir Henry Seton-Karr at Mount Hermon, attended only by a couple of close friends and representatives of the CPR.

Many of the bodies recovered later were so badly mutilated that they were never identified. Sixty-eight unidentified people, classified as "unknown," are buried in a mass grave near the Pointe-au-Père lighthouse, in sight of the shipwreck. Others are buried at Saint-Germain-de-Rimouski Cemetery in Rimouski; Mount Hermon Cemetery, Saint Patrick's Cemetery, and the Beth Israel Jewish Cemetery in Quebec City; and Mount Pleasant Cemetery in Toronto.

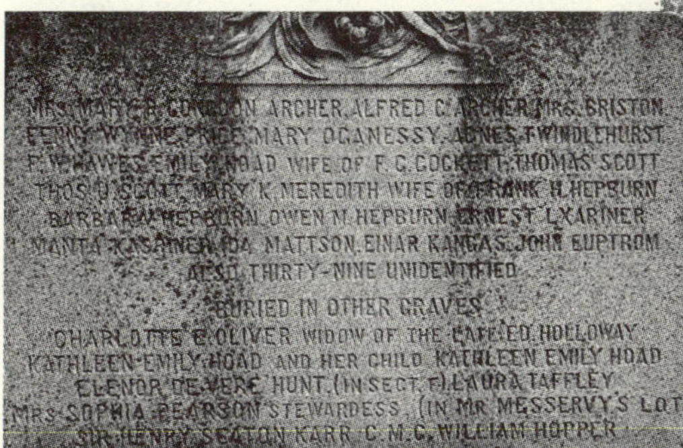

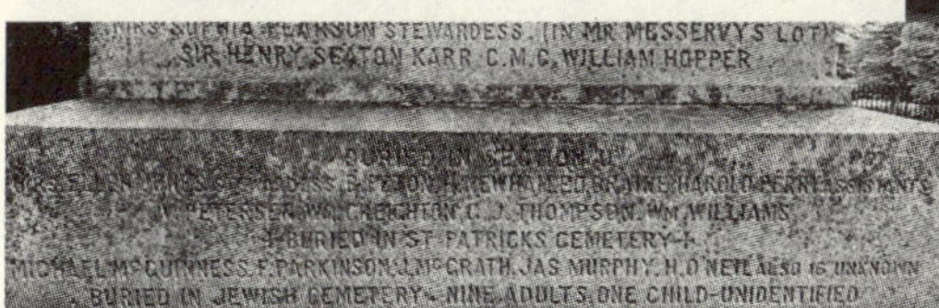

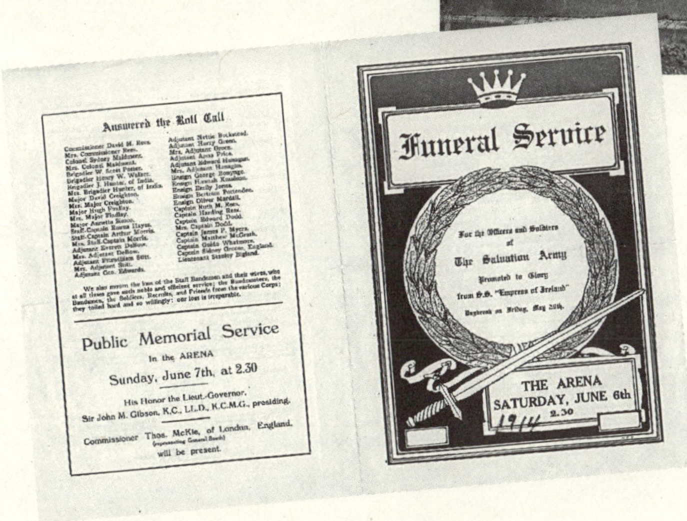

Answered the Roll Call

Commissioner David M. Rees.
Mrs. Commissioner Rees.
Colonel Sydney Maidment.
Mrs. Colonel Maidment.
Brigadier W. Scott Potter.
Brigadier Henry W. Walker.
Brigadier J. Hunter, of India.
Mrs. Brigadier Hunter, of India.
Major David Creighton.
Mrs. Major Creighton.
Major Hugh Findlay.
Mrs. Major Findlay.
Major Annetta Simco.
Staff-Captain Rowena Hayes.
Staff-Captain Arthur Morris.
Mrs. Staff-Captain Morris.
Adjutant Evrett DeBow.
Mrs. Adjutant DeBow.
Adjutant Fitzwilliam Stitt.
Mrs. Adjutant Stitt.
Adjutant Geo. Edwards.
Adjutant Nettie Bucksteed.
Adjutant Harry Green.
Mrs. Adjutant Green.
Adjutant Anna Price.
Adjutant Edward Hanagan.
Mrs. Adjutant Hanagan.
Ensign George Bonynge.
Ensign Hannah Knudson.
Ensign Emily Jones.
Ensign Bertram Pattenden.
Ensign Oliver Mardall.
Captain Ruth M. Rees.
Captain Harding Rees.
Captain Edward Dodd.
Mrs. Captain Dodd.
Captain James P. Myers.
Captain Matthew McGrath.
Captain Guido Whatmore.
Captain Sidney Green, England.
Lieutenant Stanley Bigland.

We also mourn the loss of the Staff Bandsmen and their wives, who at all times gave such noble and efficient service; the Bandmasters, the Bandsmen, the Soldiers, Recruits, and Friends from the various Corps; they toiled hard and so willingly; our loss is irreparable.

Public Memorial Service

In the ARENA

Sunday, June 7th, at 2.30

His Honor the Lieut.-Governor,
Sir John M. Gibson, K.C., LL.D., K.C.M.G., presiding.

Commissioner Thos. McKie, of London, England.
(representing General Booth)
will be present.

Funeral Service

For the Officers and Soldiers
of
The Salvation Army
Promoted to Glory
from S.S. "Empress of Ireland"
Daybreak on Friday, May 29th.

THE ARENA
SATURDAY, JUNE 6th
2.30
1914

TOP: CPR *memorial at Mount Hermon Cemetery, Quebec City, 2024* | *Eve Lazarus;*
BOTTOM: *funeral service program, June 1914* | *Used by permission of the Salvation Army Canada and Bermuda Archives (Toronto,* ON*), photo S26 3E B1 F10*

SALVATIONISTS PROMOTED TO GLORY

On Saturday, June 6, 1914, the Salvation Army organized a massive funeral at the Mutual Street Arena in Toronto—the only venue large enough to hold a crowd of close to eight thousand. The Canadian leadership had been decimated, friends were lost, and families were destroyed. The crowd stretched back along Dundas Street, down Dalhousie Street, and along Shuter Street.

TOP: *funeral procession for the victims of the* Empress of Ireland *wreck;* BOTTOM: Empress of Ireland *memorial service at the Mutual Street Arena in Toronto, June 6, 1914* | *Used by permission of the Salvation Army Canada and Bermuda Archives (Toronto, ON), photos 82520, 1010 & 1011*

Salvation Army memorial at Mount Pleasant Cemetery, Toronto, 2023 | *Eve Lazarus*

The deaths of Colonel Sydney Maidment and his wife, Harriet, were also a huge loss for the Norwegian community, as Sydney had been deputy leader of the Salvation Army in Norway from 1905 to 1908, and the couple were well liked. The Maidments had left their five younger children at home in Toronto under the care of their eldest daughter, who was twenty. All six were now orphans. Five members of the Rees family were wiped out: Commissioner David Rees and his wife, Ruth, and their three oldest children. Their fourteen-year-old son and twelve-year-old daughter had stayed with their adult son, William, who was married and living in Calgary.

Sixteen caskets, including the small white coffin of little Alice Foord, were lined up in three rows at the centre of the arena, with space for people to pass by them. One hundred children dressed in white robes sang "Home Beyond the Tide." At the centre of the arena, the name of each victim was engraved on a silver plate; under each name was the word *promoted*.

Major Frank Morris spoke at the service. "I am here to testify that my comrades knew how to live, and thanks be to God, they knew how to die."[III] The Salvation Army members had selflessly risked their lives to help others reach the deck, often giving up their lifebelts, and in so doing, in many cases giving up their lives.

Over the following weeks, the bodies of another six Salvationists were recovered and buried with their comrades in the plot at Mount Pleasant Cemetery.

The Salvation Army held a memorial service at the Royal Albert Hall in London on Friday, June 5, 1914. Since almost all of the *Empress*'s crew and many of her passengers were British, more than fifteen thousand people attended.

Ken McIntyre arrived in London on Saturday, June 13, 1914, the first day of the Congress. He had sailed over on White Star's *Baltic* two days earlier. McIntyre was the only survivor of the *Empress* to attend the Congress[*] until fellow band members James Johnston and the Delamonts had a change of heart and arrived later in the month.

---

* Ken McIntyre died in Cleveland, Ohio, in 1960, aged 71.

SERVICES ACROSS THE COUNTRY

Every province of Canada and almost every major city had one resident or more among the lost, and services were held across the country.

Quebec

Of the more than forty passengers from the province of Quebec, only eight people survived: Louis-Aldéï Gosselin, George Henderson, Lionel Kent, Grace Kohl, Ethel Paton, Josephine Schongut, Bernard Weinrauch, and Richard Hedgecoe.

Camille Verniers, a piano repairer, had immigrated with his wife, Edmée-Marie, to Saguenay in 1909. They had been taking their children back to Belgium to meet their grandparents for the first time. The entire family of eight was wiped out in the wreck.

GELOOFD ZIJ JESUS-CHRISTUS. AMEN !

†

GODVRUCHTIG AANDENKEN

VAN MIJNHEER

CAMILLE-JOSEPH-MARIA VERNIERS,

geboren te St-Nikolaas, den 27 Augustus 1879;

VAN ZIJN ECHTGENOOTE

Mevrouw CAMILLE VERNIERS,

geboren EDMÉE-MARIE MUNAUT,

te Cornay (Frankrijk), den 18 Januari 1873;

EN VAN HUN KINDEREN

JEAN (9 jaar); **LOUIS** (8 jaar); **EDOUARD** (7 jaar); **RENÉE** (5 jaar); **MARIE-MARGUERITE** (4 jaar) en **JOSEPH** (9 maand);

Allen den 29 Mei 1914, bij de ramp van den „Empress of Ireland", *in den St-Lorensstroom (Canada) omgekomen.*

Wij zijn reizigers op deze wereld, onze dagen vlieden voorbij als een schaduw... Wij hebben hier geene blijvende woonplaats, maar zoeken de toekomende. I. PARAL 29. 15. — HEBR. 13. 14.

In de oogen der onzinnigen schenen zij te sterven, en werd hun overlijden als een ramp beschouwd... doch zij zijn in vrede... Een weinig hebben zij geleden, doch een groot geluk is hun wedervaren, omdat God hen zijner waardig bevonden heeft. WIJSHEID 3. 2. 5.

Lieve Moeder, Broeders, Zusters, Bloedverwanten, weest niet bedroefd gelijk degenen die geene hoop hebben; allen die in Jesus ontslapen zijn, zullen met Hem verrijzen. THES. 4. 11. 12. Weest niet bekommerd om ons lichaam; enkel vragen wij u dat gij ons indachtig wezet aan het altaar, gij vooral, mijn Broeders, priesters des Heeren, overal waar gij u bevindt. S. AUG.

Laat de kleinen tot Mij komen, want voor dezulken is het rijk der hemelen. MARC. 10. 14.

Barmhartige Heer Jesus, geef hun de eeuwige rust. *(300 dagen aflaat iedere maal.)*

DRUKK. STRYBOL-VERCRUYSSEN.

The funeral announcement for the Verniers family of Quebec. Camille and Edmée-Marie and their six children, all under ten, were killed in the wreck. | Société d'Histoire du Bas-Canada (Beloeil, QC), Guy D'Astous collection

Ontario

Kate Parker, thirty-one, was excited that her father, William Russell, her two sisters, Sarah and Mary, her brother-in-law, Peter Kerr, and her five nieces and nephews, aged between two and thirteen, were returning to Scotland to live. Kate was still holding the letter that Mary had written from their home in London, Ontario, dated May 21, 1914, when a reporter from the Glasgow *Daily Record* knocked on her door. He told her that all nine of her family members were dead.[112]

Toronto alone lost more than 160 lives in the wreck. Major Frank Morris, head of the Salvation Army in London, Ontario, was the only one to survive out of the twenty-three people who'd left from that city.

Photos in the *Brantford Daily Expositor* showed the devastating loss to that town, which is situated roughly halfway between Toronto and London, Ontario. Of the two dozen passengers who had left Brantford, only Philip Lawler and his fifteen-year-old son, Herbert, returned. Herbert's mother, Ellen Lawler, who was captured in a photo with her husband, was lost. There was a photo of Lena White in her nurse's uniform, also lost. Another photo shows twenty-one-year-old Gertie Longley, her husband, Leonard, and their two-year-old daughter, Miriam, standing in their garden shortly before their trip. All three died. Annie Tarry and her two children, ten-year-old Hilda and eight-year-old Albert Junior, had been travelling to England for a family visit, while Annie's husband, Albert, a bootmaker, stayed home to work. Shortly after a photo of the family was taken, Albert lost his entire family in the wreck.[113]

The impact of the wreck on Western Canadians was brutal.

The Prairies

More than forty people booked through the CPR's office in Winnipeg. Only Robert Cunningham, Walter Erzinger, Fanny Evinson, Cedric Gallagher, Hannes and Tilly Peturson, and James Lennon survived.*

James Dandy, a forty-seven-year-old hardware store owner from Pierson, Manitoba, brought home his friend Christopher Halliday, fifty-two, in a box. Halliday had emigrated from Scotland fifteen years before and was the town's postmaster. Dandy never recovered from the wreck and died eighteen months later.[114]

Of the more than thirty people who booked out of towns and cities across Saskatchewan, only a few survived. These included Per "Peter" Johnson Rask, a farmer and father of seven who lived in Broadview. He had been returning to Sweden for the first time since immigrating to Canada in 1893. The first newspaper reports did not mention him as one of the survivors. "For some reason my father's name was not there, yet we knew he must have been on the *Empress*," said his daughter, Annie. "On Monday, June 1, around 11:30 p.m. there was a knock at the door. None of us could have been asleep because it seemed to me that we all jumped out of bed to rush down to answer it. Our late caller was from the CPR and in his hand, he had a telegram from my father sent from North Bay, saying he was on his way home and would arrive in Broadview on Wednesday, June 3. I shall not even try to describe our feelings."[115]

Rask couldn't swim, but before going to bed that night he had read the instructions on how to put on a lifebelt properly, and he had remembered to take the lifebelt from his cabin. Once in the water,

---

* James Lennon was on his way home to Ireland to marry Nannie Magdalen. After the sinking, he continued on his journey, returning to New York the following October. Nannie followed on August 14, 1916, and they were married the next day. They had a daughter in 1918 and spent the rest of their lives in New York. James died in 1967, aged 84. Hannes Peturson, 26, was a Winnipeg real estate agent when he and his wife, Tilly, booked passage on the *Empress of Ireland*. They were considering a permanent move to Iceland; instead, they returned to Winnipeg after the sinking and had a daughter. Hannes died in Winnipeg in 1961, aged 73. Tilly moved to Vancouver and died ten years later, aged 83.

Robert Cunningham with the 1915–16 University of Manitoba football team | Courtesy of University of Manitoba Archives & Special Collections (Winnipeg, MB)

he clung to a piece of wreckage and stayed afloat until he was picked up by a rescue boat. At the train station he was told he'd have a train ticket home to Broadview courtesy of the CPR, but he'd lost all of his clothes and his money in the wreck. A sympathetic survivor passed around his hat and collected twenty-five dollars for Rask.[116]

Miraculously, four of the five Delamonts from Moose Jaw, as well as Archie Brown, survived. The town grieved the losses of twenty-five-year-old Leonard Delamont and twenty-two-year-old Charles Wilkes, two young men who had contributed so much in their short lives.

Leonard Delamont had run a harness business in Moose Jaw and had played in the Salvation Army band since the age of seven. He had organized the first Army band in Moose Jaw and was their band-master, and he was married with a small child. His body was never recovered.

Funeral in Lethbridge for Salvation Army brigadier John Hunter and his son, Stewart, July 13, 1914. John's wife, Jessie, and their daughter, Grace, were also lost in the tragedy. | *Société d'Histoire du Bas-Canada (Beloeil, QC), Guy D'Astous collection*

Thousands of locals turned out for the funeral of Charles Wilkes. Wilkes had lost both parents as a teenager. His father was killed by a runaway horse team, and his mother died in a railway crossing accident. When Wilkes moved to Moose Jaw from Hereford, England, Leonard Delamont had talked him into joining the Army band. Wilkes played cornet and trombone and worked at the Alex Macdonald Company, a wholesale grocer.

Alberta

After he reached Quebec City, Theo Bartschi spent ten nights recovering at the Neptune Inn, too sick to leave his bed. When he was well enough, he caught the train back to Alberta. Of the more than fifty people who were booked on the *Empress of Ireland* from Alberta, Bartschi was the only one (beside Tom Smart) who returned.

The Mardalls' house at 3347 West 8th Avenue in Vancouver, 2024 | *Eve Lazarus*

British Columbia

The people of Vancouver, especially those in the Salvation Army, deeply felt the loss of William Wakefield, twenty-five-year-old deputy bandmaster, and Oliver Mardall, a thirty-one-year-old ensign and a well-known and popular social worker. The *Province* newspaper and the citizens of Vancouver opened their hearts and wallets to Oliver Mardall's widow, Isabelle, who was left with four children under the age of seven, a rental house in Kitsilano, and a Salvation Army pension of less than five dollars a week. Attorney general William Bowser, who would become premier in 1915, had known Oliver personally from his work with prisoners and contributed fifty dollars to the fund.*

* Over $1,300 CAD in 2024.

The Salvation Army held a memorial service on July 24, 1914, and erected a brass plaque at the Army Hall in East Vancouver bearing the names of Major N. Simco, Ensign O. Mardall, Deputy Bandmaster Wakefield, Dorothea Axten, and Leonard Axten, Dorothea's four-year-old son. The following week, the Mardall family at least had some resolution when Oliver's body was recovered from the wreck.

There were also near misses. Vancouver Police Department inspector John Jackson and his wife had booked passage on the *Empress* as the start of a four-month trip back to England. But due to Jackson's responsibilities with the Jack Kong murder trial, they rebooked on a later sailing.

PASSENGERS AND CREW CONTINUE TO ENGLAND

Not surprisingly, dozens of survivors decided against continuing their journeys on other liners and instead travelled back to their respective homes. Many had lost loved ones, and most were just too traumatized or scared to continue.

Others had little choice but to go on.

Gordon Davidson sailed on the *Empress of Britain*, which left Quebec City on June 11, 1914. Davidson, who had been travelling to London on a research grant for his PhD, lost all his precious research materials in the wreck.*

> I can get back nearly all of my money because it was in traveller's cheques. The CPR is giving me a good outfit of clothes, besides keeping me free of charge. But I have lost my notes for my thesis, in fact what I had gathered on the fur trade in the last two years. I shall have

* Davidson returned to Canada a year later on the SS *Metagama*. His book, *The North West Company*, based on his doctorate work, was published in 1918 and was so well received that it was republished in 1967.

> to trust a good deal to my memory to find the information again. However, I shall go on over to England and put in my year of study. And I pray to God that I may never be in a shipwreck again.[117]

The *Alsatian* sailed on June 4, carrying 169 *Empress* survivors, including 122 crew members. There were also nine bodies coming back for burial: chief officer Mansfield Steede, two other crew members, and six passengers, including Wallace Leonard Palmer, associate editor of the *Financial News*, and his wife, Ethel. When the ship docked in Liverpool, the survivors must have looked like a motley group, wearing a bizarre mix of clothing and shouting and singing and waving their hats in the air. Charlie Spencer, the young bellboy who had been plucked from the St. Lawrence River alongside Captain Kendall, came running into the waiting room dressed in odd garments and wearing a straw Panama hat. His family were there to meet him; his mother, father, sister, and brother greeted and hugged him. "There's nothing to cry for," Charlie said, but the tears were streaming down his own cheeks as well.[118]

MARTIN GILL

Martin Gill returned to Ireland via Glasgow, Scotland, on the *Corsican* along with several other survivors from third class. He had immigrated to Canada as a seventeen-year-old in 1907 and worked mostly as a miner in BC.

While I was trying to find out more about Gill, I came across a comment from his granddaughter, Mary McDermott, that she'd left on a message board more than twenty years before. It included her email address, so I crossed my fingers and fired off an introduction. She phoned me a few days later.

Mary is a nun with the Presentation of the Blessed Virgin Mary in Ireland. Her grandfather, she told me, had returned to Ireland

Martin Gill outside his house in the West of Ireland, 1966 | Courtesy of Mary McDermott

after the sinking, staying for just over a year. During that time, he met eighteen-year-old Bridget O'Gara. Gill then returned to North America with Bridget's brother and worked in Idaho and Montana. Following his father's death from the influenza pandemic in 1919, Gill returned to Ireland and took over the small family farm in West Ireland. He married Bridget, and they had a daughter.

Mary's parents stayed on the farm, and she lived with her grandparents until she turned eighteen and joined the religious order. "My grandmother said that even though it was six years after [the sinking] when they married, there were times when he jumped out of bed with the fright. Almost as if he was living through the trauma again. So, I would say it had a huge effect on him in that way."

Mary told me she had travelled to Quebec for the first time in 1991. "I had always wanted to go there and honour my granddad. Rimouski has been a name in my memory since I was about four or five years old." She visited the museum at Pointe-au-Père; that was the first time she realized the full extent of the tragedy and how lucky her grandfather had been to survive it. "They showed a film, and it had Grace Hanagan speaking. I was literally just stuck to the chair after it had finished, because it had such an effect on me. It was the first time that I had really grieved my grandfather," she said.

Mary was twenty-two when her grandfather died in 1969. She says her grandfather's stories of Canadian places and wildlife shaped her life. "I remember him telling me how cold it was. How cold the wind was off the St. Lawrence." Gill rarely spoke of the tragedy when Mary was growing up, but when he turned seventy-five in 1964, he told his story to Mary's mother.

"You were asking what sort of things I remember about him. Certainly, his sense of adventure. He had a good old sense of humour. He was marvellous at mathematics. He would do any problem in his head at night without a pencil or paper or anything. He was absolutely brilliant."

Mary still has the gold pocket watch that Gill had in the pocket of his pants when he was rescued from the *Empress* in 1914. "It stopped when he entered the water. It has his initials on the back."

10. Salvaging the Wreck

BACK IN RIMOUSKI, THE salvage operation was in full swing. The Yankee Salvage Association was headed up by William Wotherspoon, who was hired by the CPR to recover bodies from the wreck. They were joined in the search by divers from the HMS *Essex*.

Wilfred Whitehead of the *Essex* was sent down to find out what direction the *Empress* was lying in. "I went down and examined the plates, and the plates told me which was forward, and which was aft, and I travelled along in that direction. They could see my bubbles, and could note the place I went down and note the direction of the bubbles, and that would give them the direction she was lying in."[119]

It was difficult and dangerous work carried out in brutal conditions. The most a diver could manage in one trip was a simple task such as opening a door. Divers were known as "hard hats" because their helmets, which were made from copper and heavy glass, weighed 25 kilograms (55 pounds) each. Heavy equipment restricted mobility. A canvas diving suit, including lead belts and boots, brought the weight of the entire ensemble to over 90 kilograms (200 pounds).

Each diver had a handler on the surface attached to the other end of their lifeline. The handler monitored their air supply and the lifeline. Working in the treacherous St. Lawrence River, the hard hats faced little to no visibility, near-freezing water, and violent shifting currents. Decompression sickness (the bends) was always a threat, but for a diver, a simple mistake could be deadly. In a worst-case scenario, if a diver fell and their air hose was severed, the negative pressure caused by the severed hose could vacuum the diver's body up into their helmet, squeezing them to death.

On June 21, 1914, Edward Cossaboom, a diver from New Brunswick, was working with two of the hard hats from the *Essex*. They were working off an old schooner called the *Marie Josephine*, which they'd moored above the sunken liner. Cossaboom had already made two dives that morning and brought up two bodies. On the third dive of the day, Cossaboom lost his footing and slipped off the wreck's hull, plummeting to the river bottom more than 40 metres (130 feet) below the surface. A diver from the *Essex* was able to bring Cossaboom to the surface and take him to the decompression chamber, but he died thirty minutes later. The salvage operators decided it was too risky to attempt to recover any more bodies, and operations were suspended.

FAMILIES WAIT FOR NEWS

While the salvage operations were going ahead in Rimouski, the Inquiry into the accident was proceeding in Quebec City. Many of the victims' families were staying there, hoping for news.

Frederick Cullen, who had lost his wife, Maude, and his two small children, returned to Toronto. Meanwhile, Maude's twenty-six-year-old brother, Charlie Young, travelled from Fernie, BC, in the hopes that he could find and identify his sister's body. He booked a room at the Neptune Hotel in Quebec City. Young telegrammed his brother-in-law, Cullen, to inform him that Young would stay in Quebec City while there was still some hope of finding the bodies. Two bodies, he said, had just been recovered but were so badly decomposed that they were unrecognizable. Another woman's body was picked up nearly 100 kilometres (60 miles) from the scene of the accident. She was identified by her rings, one of which had the initials AR. Young asked Cullen to send descriptions of the clothing and jewellery that his wife might have been wearing.

On June 23, Young learned of Cossaboom's death and the decision to suspend recovery operations. He wrote to Cullen on Neptune Hotel letterhead: "Dear Fred: The death of one of the divers has put a complete stop to the work. Have been talking to several of the CPR officials today and they seem to be all of one mind. That there will be nothing more done for some time to come, if at all. The salvage expert was on the stand at the Inquiry this morning and stated that it would be impossible to raise the *Empress* ... If anything turns up to change the prospect, I shall wire you. Charlie."[120]

William Wotherspoon told the CPR that the search for bodies would resume if the CPR paid for improved communication devices, new helmets that would offer divers more freedom of movement, an underwater telephone, and underwater lamps. The CPR agreed, and the new gear arrived from England on the *Empress of Britain* on July 2. While the ship stopped just outside Rimouski to unload mail and to pick up a river pilot, divers came aboard to familiarize themselves with the ship's layout, which was identical to the *Empress of Ireland*'s. Each diver was assigned a section of the ship to explore, taking note of obstructions and openings.

Now with better equipment and a sense of direction, the divers resumed the gruesome business of recovering bloated and disfigured bodies. One by one, bodies were hooked up to lines and pulled to the surface. Wotherspoon told reporters that the divers would search the decks and companionways where he believed most of the bodies would be found. It was too dangerous, he said, for divers to search the cabins, and so, for those who had been unable to leave their cabins, they would be in their final resting places.

The brother of prominent Montreal businessman Henry Lyman was the first family member to arrive in Rimouski. He was taken to meet Wotherspoon aboard the *Marie Josephine* at the wreck site.

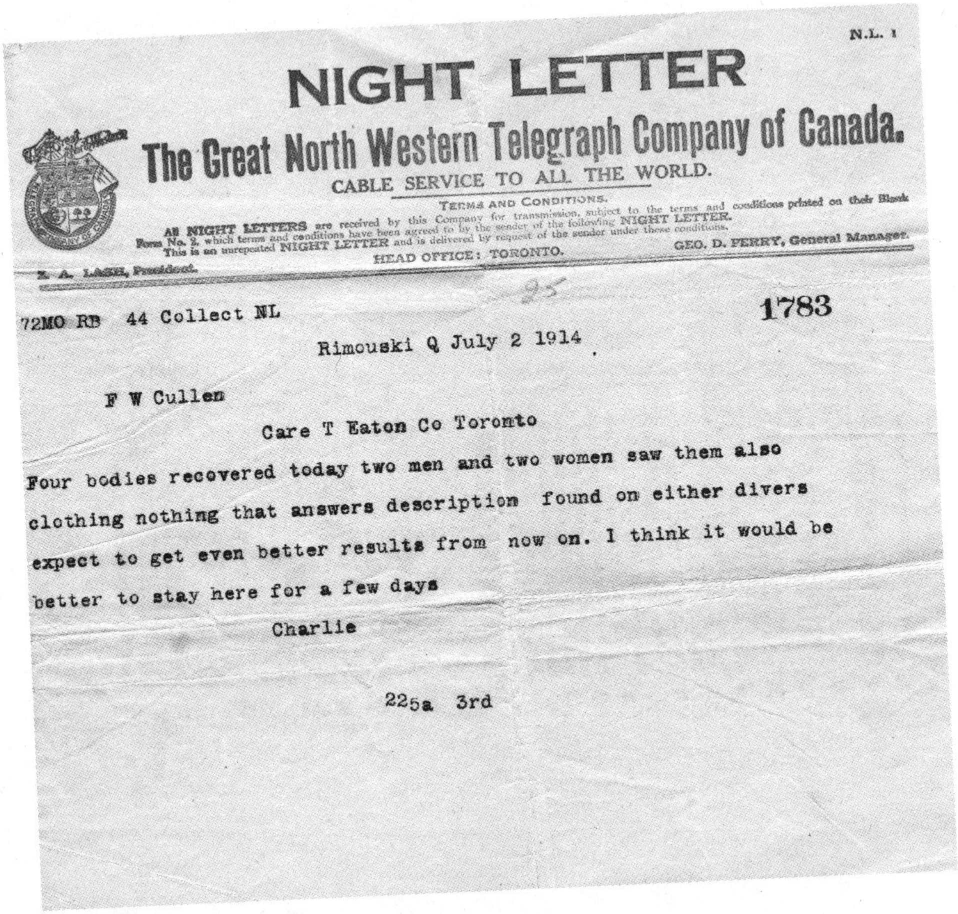

N.L. 1

NIGHT LETTER

The Great North Western Telegraph Company of Canada.

CABLE SERVICE TO ALL THE WORLD.

TERMS AND CONDITIONS.

All NIGHT LETTERS are received by this Company for transmission, subject to the terms and conditions printed on their Blank Form No. 2, which terms and conditions have been agreed to by the sender of the following NIGHT LETTER. This is an unrepeated NIGHT LETTER and is delivered by request of the sender under these conditions.

HEAD OFFICE: TORONTO.

GEO. D. PERRY, General Manager.

Z. A. LASH, President.

95

72MO RB 44 Collect NL 1783

Rimouski Q July 2 1914

F W Cullen

Care T Eaton Co Toronto

Four bodies recovered today two men and two women saw them also clothing nothing that answers description found on either divers expect to get even better results from now on. I think it would be better to stay here for a few days

Charlie

225a 3rd

Telegram from Charlie Young to his brother-in-law, Frederick Cullen | Shepherd Archival Collection, Canadian Museum of History (Gatineau, QC), 2013-H0009.38

On the ship's plan, he showed Wotherspoon the staterooms where his brother and sister-in-law, Florence, had been staying. Lyman left a description of the jewellery thirty-seven-year-old Florence would likely have been wearing.

That night, Charlie Young arrived in Rimouski with John Clark from Vancouver, who was looking for his wife, Ellen, and their twenty-four-year-old son, Stephen. They were joined by John Silman of Broadview, Saskatchewan, who was looking for his friend Christopher

Edwards, and Martin Tolander, a farmer from Warner, Alberta, who was looking for his wife, Emma.

Young telegrammed Cullen that a woman's body had been recovered that day. She was wearing a blue kimono, a skirt, and black woollen stockings, but no jewellery that might identify her. "Almost positive body found not Maude," he said. The following day, he telegrammed again: "Four bodies recovered today. Two men and two women. Saw them. Nothing that answers description found on either. Divers expect to get even better results from now on. I think it would be better to stay here for a few days. Charlie."*[121]

Richard Fisher came from Chicago to try to identify his mother, Margaret, and his twenty-one-year-old brother, Wilf, who had been headed to England for a family reunion. "The divers have got fifteen bodies so far and the tugboat as a rule comes into port between 3:00 and 5:00 p.m.," he wrote to his sister, Greta, on July 7. "Yesterday afternoon I helped to bury two bodies. One was an old man about sixty and the other a young woman about twenty-five. There was only four of us that could speak English, the rest was all French. The American consul read the services."[122]

DELEGATES RETURN HOME

On July 9, the first of the Canadian delegates from the Salvation Army Congress were returning home on the *Calgarian*. It had been a rough journey, and fog slowed the ship's progress. With the disaster of the *Empress* fresh in their minds, many of the passengers slept in their clothes. As the ship reached the spot where the *Empress of Ireland* had sunk, the Peterborough band launched into "Nearer, My God, to Thee." Many of the passengers joined in to sing the hymn. As

* Maude Cullen's body was never recovered. Charlie Young returned to Fernie, BC. In January 1916, he enlisted with the 103rd Battalion. He died in August 1917 with the rank of sergeant, aged 29.

the song finished, two female Salvationists from Winnipeg stepped to the side of the boat and dropped a wreath into the St. Lawrence River where many of their friends were entombed below. A short distance away, they could see the *Marie Josephine*, where the salvage team were working. The passengers would find out later that the crew was retrieving the body of Commissioner David Rees. The Salvationists believed that their leader had been called up from his ocean grave by their tribute. He was buried with his wife and children at Mount Pleasant Cemetery.[123]

The salvage operation continued to recover bodies, but most of the third-class passengers were buried too deeply inside the wreck to be safely extracted. The CPR turned its focus to recovering 212 silver bars and the ship's safe.

THE SHIP'S VALUABLES

Because the CPR was concerned about litigation from passengers who had put their valuables in the ship's safe, the safe had to be brought to the surface unopened and undamaged. The problem was that it was the size of a shower stall and weighed several hundred pounds.

The divers created a hole in the ship, and the safe was brought to the surface on August 19, 1914. It was taken to Quebec City by the *Lady Evelyn* and brought to the Bank of Montreal. Two days later, the safe was opened in front of a crowd of officials, media, and lawyers. The modest contents recovered from the safe showed just how outlandish insurance claims had been.

As well as the silver ingots, the divers were able to bring up 318 bags of mail. The salvaged mail, comprising thousands of letters, parcels, and registered documents, was brought to the Rimouski railway station, which at the time of the sinking was managed by Desire Pare, who lived upstairs with his family. One hundred years later, Pare's grandson, Pierre Pare, said that each piece of mail had to be dried out.

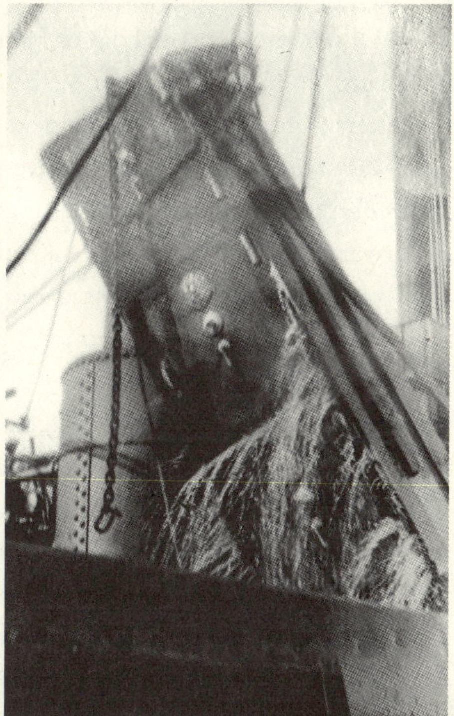

CLOCKWISE FROM TOP LEFT: *Ralph Stratton Blydenburgh with some of the silver ingots salvaged from the* Empress *in August 1914; the safe from the* Empress *being brought up by the Yankee Salvage Association, August 1914; diving crew of* the Empress *salvage operations aboard the* Marie Josephine, *summer 1914* | *David Saint-Pierre collection*

This his grandmother Anna did by hanging the mail from clotheslines she strung up in the basement of the station. After they were dried, the letters were forwarded to the dead-letter office in Ottawa, where each was stamped "recovered by divers from wreck of SS *Empress of Ireland.*" If the address was legible, it was either returned to the sender or forwarded to the intended recipient. Pare says his father, Andre, who was twelve at the time, used the stamps that had fallen off the mail to start his stamp collection.[124]

In January 1915, Bert Elderton, a homesteader who had immigrated to Swift Current, Saskatchewan, from England in 1904, received a large envelope marked "OHMS" (On His Majesty's Service). The package was the return of the love letter and the birthday card he had sent to his fiancée, Marie Louise, in England the previous May, along with a five-cent coin. The coin had been the last of his money left until his expected crop was hauled to market. The gum on the flaps of the envelope and the stamp had disappeared, but the contents of the letter were quite readable, except for parts where the ink had run. Elderton married Marie Louise in Croydon, England, the following January.

On August 7, 1914, divers recovered the bodies of twelve men, including third officer Charles Moore, who had been on the bridge when the accident occurred. The salvage operations continued until September 16. Although there were still hundreds of bodies left inside the wreck, divers had recovered around 175 of them.

11. The Inquiry

> This is a very great shock to the confidence which people were beginning to feel in the floating capacity of these large passenger ships and to their belief that no collision, no matter how severe, could have the effect of sinking a ship of the size and equipment of the *Empress* in such a short space of time.
>
> —*Empress of Ireland* Wreck Commissioner's Inquiry

THE *STORSTAD* DOCKED AT the Dominion Coal Company wharf in Montreal just after 2:00 p.m. on Sunday, May 31, 1914. Her bow was battered, and there was a rip in the port side just above the water line. Her steel anchor was badly twisted, and a Norwegian flag flew at half-mast. A reporter from the *Toronto Daily Star* slipped on board with an acting deputy sheriff, and minutes later they were nailing up a warrant of arrest to the *Storstad*'s main mast.

"The ship is seized," the deputy told Captain Andersen.

"The ship is seized?" said Andersen. "By whose authority do you come aboard my ship and arrest it?"

"By the authority of the British Empire," answered the deputy.[125]

The warrant had been taken out by the registrar of the Quebec Admiralty Court on behalf of the Canadian Pacific Railway. The CPR

The Storstad *after her collision with the* Empress of Ireland | *McCord Stewart Museum (Montreal, QC),* VIEW-*14183*

The Storstad *en route to Montreal in May 1914, showing her damaged prow | McCord Stewart Museum (Montreal, QC), M2011.64.2.5.19*

was claiming $2 million of losses and damages against the *Storstad*'s owners, Norway-based A.F. Klaverness & Co.

A formal inquiry into the accident was still over two weeks away, but already the media was blaming the Norwegians with headlines such as "Big Liner Rammed and Sent to Bottom by Collier" and "Collier's Anchor Tore Through Liner's Steel Like Giant Can-Opener."[126] There were unfounded allegations that the Norwegians maintained their monopoly for carrying coal on the St. Lawrence River through excessive speed and cutting corners.

The crew of the *Storstad* received a further blow when two of her sailors were arrested in Montreal attempting to cash one thousand dollars' worth of traveller's cheques from first-class passenger Lionel Kent of Montreal.* Kent, manager of the Energite Explosive Company, said he had hidden the traveller's cheques in his shirt and thought they were lost sometime between his escaping the *Empress* and being brought aboard the *Storstad*.† Manuel Chute of Honolulu

* Over $26,000 CAD in 2024.

† Lionel Kent continued his business trip later that year. He died in Montreal in 1945, aged 62.

was arrested at the Merchants Bank of Canada while trying to cash one of Kent's cheques. His shipmate, Carmel Sperritti from Malta, was arrested aboard the *Storstad* when police found a further $950 in cheques and $41 in cash hidden in his bunk.

Worried that grieving relatives would try to harm the "foreigners," the police gave protection to the crew of the *Storstad*.

NINE DAYS OF TESTIMONY

The pages of the official Wreck Commissioner's Inquiry take up more than half a banker's box on my desk. The hearing kicked off on June 16, 1914, asked several thousand questions, and heard nine days of testimony from sixty-one witnesses—twenty-four officers and crew of the *Empress* and twelve of the *Storstad*; five passengers from the *Empress*; and twenty other individuals, including divers, marconi operators, naval architects, and the crew and officers of other ships. Captain James Murray, the Quebec harbourmaster and previous captain of the *Empress of Ireland*, was also called to testify.

The owners and crew of both ships blamed each other for what was the worst shipping disaster in the history of Canada. Each commander said that his ship was stopped at the time of collision. Each said the other vessel changed its course and was going too fast. Each said he sighted the other ship before the fog descended. Each interpreted the exchange of whistle blows differently. Their stories didn't correspond at all.

Lord Mersey (John Charles Bigham), a London-based retired barrister and judge, conducted the Inquiry. He had presided over the *Titanic* investigation in 1912 and would preside over the Inquiry into the sinking of the *Lusitania* in May 1915.

Right from the start, there was pressure on Lord Mersey to find someone to blame for the disaster, and the public did not want that to be a British/Canadian passenger ship.

Captain Kendall made four separate appearances at the Inquiry and answered hundreds of questions. He and his senior officers maintained that the *Storstad* signalled one way and then changed to a different course. They argued that first officer Alfred Toftenes should have woken his captain as soon as fog descended and that he instead changed the course of the *Storstad*, placing it directly in the path of the *Empress*.

The Norwegians were at a language disadvantage and were either supplied with an interpreter or, if one wasn't available, were forced to plod along in broken English. Captain Andersen and his senior officers argued that the *Empress* was not stopped in the water but rather, was going too fast, and that was evident by the damage done to the *Storstad*. They argued that the *Empress* had steering problems and that she had not followed the normal right of way and had changed course.

Toftenes admitted that he had tried to change the *Storstad*'s course when he noticed that the current was carrying the collier toward the shore. He'd ordered Jacob Saxe to port the wheel to the right minutes before the collision. When the ship failed to respond, Saxe took hold of the wheel and turned it hard right. The Norwegians claimed that they had been going so slowly the ship did not alter its course.

"The two stories are irreconcilable," said Lord Mersey. "The question of who is to blame resolves itself into a simple issue—namely, which of the two ships changed her course during the fog."[127]

Edward Newcombe, the Canadian deputy minister of justice, said that both sides had made bad decisions. "I am suggesting that there was an improper use of the port helm by the *Storstad*, and an improper reversing and stopping on the part of the *Empress*," he told Lord Mersey. "I am suggesting negligence on both sides. Certainly, the accident could not have happened if the *Empress* had not taken this extraordinary course of reversing and stopping almost in the track of the approaching *Storstad*."[128]

New York Tribune

NEW YORK, SATURDAY, MAY 30, 1914. PRICE ONE CENT

954 DROWNED IN STEAMSHIP CRASH; EMPRESS OF IRELAND SINKS IN FOG; GOES TO BOTTOM IN FIFTEEN MINUTES

THE EMPRESS OF IRELAND, CAPTAIN KENDALL AND SCENE OF DISASTER.

Canadian Pacific Liner, Struck by Collier in St. Lawrence River at Daybreak—Laurence Irving Among the Missing.

MANY SURVIVORS TELL THE STORY

Blow Cleaves Ship Almost in Twain and Boiler Explosion Ends All—433 Saved, Mostly from Second Cabin and Crew—S. O. S. Brings Vessels Too Late.

SON SAFE AFTER ALL

J. P. MORGAN OFFERS TO FACE N. H. QUIZ

"I SAVED MYSELF," SAYS LITTLE GIRL

SHIP'S SURGEON TELLS OF CRASH

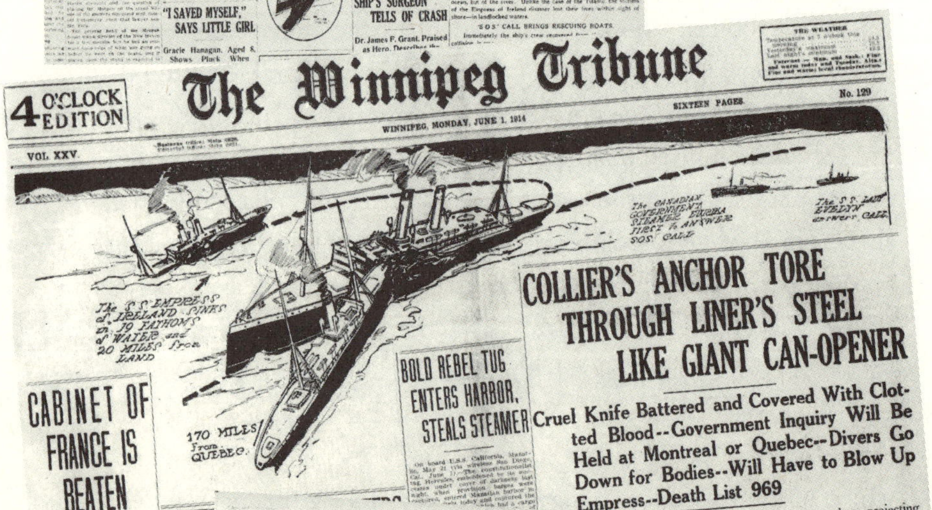

The Winnipeg Tribune

4 O'CLOCK EDITION

VOL. XXV. WINNIPEG, MONDAY, JUNE 1, 1914 SIXTEEN PAGES No. 129

COLLIER'S ANCHOR TORE THROUGH LINER'S STEEL LIKE GIANT CAN-OPENER

Cruel Knife Battered and Covered With Clotted Blood--Government Inquiry Will Be Held at Montreal or Quebec--Divers Go Down for Bodies--Will Have to Blow Up Empress--Death List 969

CABINET OF FRANCE IS BEATEN

Three Years Military Service Agitation Causes Change in Power of Republic

BOLD REBEL TUG ENTERS HARBOR, STEALS STEAMER

HUNDREDS DROWN WHEN LINER SINKS

4 O'CLOCK EDITION

The Winnipeg Tribune

VOL. XXV. WINNIPEG, FRIDAY, MAY 29, 1914 TWENTY PAGES No. 127

C.P.R. EMPRESS RAMMED BY COAL BOAT IN FOG; REPORTS CONFLICTING

TOP TO BOTTOM: New York Tribune, *May 30, 1914;* Winnipeg Tribune, *June 1, 1914;* Winnipeg Tribune, *May 29, 1914 | Winnipeg Tribune Archives, University of Manitoba Archives & Special Collections*

THE CAPTAINS SHOULD HAVE SHARED BLAME

More than a century later, mariners, historians, and divers are still dissecting the testimonies of both captains and the crew members and other witnesses from that day. Animations and documentaries have been created attempting to illustrate both points of view. Some believe that the *Empress* was blameless, and some think there was a conspiracy by the powerful CPR to deflect blame onto a foreign ship. Reading through the pages of the Inquiry, it seems to me that both commanding officers made mistakes they would not have in the absence of fog. If both captains had only held their courses and their speeds, they would have comfortably passed each other.

But the Inquiry needed a villain, and it was decided, somewhat reluctantly, that it would be Alfred Toftenes, the thirty-three-year-old second-in-command of the *Storstad*. The commissioners believed that when Toftenes changed the *Storstad*'s course, he had caused the collision. They criticized him for not waking his captain when fog descended and decided that he had misjudged the course of the *Empress* prior to the fog. The introduction to the Inquiry's summary is instructive:

> We regret to have to impute blame to anyone in connection to this lamentable disaster, and we should not do so if we felt that any reasonable alternative was left to us. We can, however, come to no other conclusion than that Mr. Toftenes was wrong and negligent in keeping the navigation of the vessel in his own hands, and in failing to call the captain when he saw the fog coming up.[129]

Captain Kendall didn't get off completely, though. The commissioners criticized his decision to stop the *Empress* in the fog. They didn't believe that the *Empress* was stopped dead in the water at the time of the accident, as Kendall claimed.

A lot of time was spent discussing why the *Empress* had sunk so rapidly; if it had been kept afloat longer, many more passenger and crew lives could have been saved. Why, asked Newcombe, did Captain Kendall not order the closing of the watertight doors when he said that he was stopped in the fog for over five minutes? Newcombe then read from the CPR's own rulebook: "The commander will see that all times in foggy weather or in falling snow hands are stationed to close instantly all watertight doors which are not already closed."[130]

RAPID SINKING COULD HAVE BEEN AVOIDED

The open porthole windows in some of the cabins and passageways also contributed to the rapid sinking of the *Empress*, said Newcombe. The rule was that once at sea, all portholes must remain closed. But this rule was often ignored, especially on a warm night in fine weather. It was most likely thought to be an unnecessary precaution, since they were still on the St. Lawrence River.

Wilfred Whitehead, a diver from the HMS *Essex*, testified that he had been asked to look for open portholes in the wreck. In the parts of the ship that were accessible to him, he had found evidence of only one. "I saw a piece of blue cotton sticking out of the porthole, and the porthole jammed home tight on top of it," he said.[131]

Several passengers, including John Fowler, Tom Greenaway, James Lennon, and Philip Lawler, told of closing the portholes in their cabins to stop water flowing in. Gordon Davidson, Bert Greenaway, and Rufus Spooner all mentioned water flooding in through open portholes in the passageways. Frank Harrison, a second-class steward, acknowledged that sometimes passengers refused to close their portholes; if this was the case, Harrison left a note for the night watchman. On the night of the sinking, Harrison's shift had ended at 10:00 p.m., and some of the portholes in the passageways were open.

Another issue for Newcombe was why the decks leading from the second-class lounge were locked, as Frederick Godson and John Langley claimed. "The doors are never locked. There is no need to lock the doors, there is no reason," Kendall told Newcombe. He said it was quite possible that the doors had jammed when the ship began to list; if doors had been shut at the time of the collision, they would be difficult to open afterward. "When a collision occurs and a ship gets on her side as much as this ship has done, the strain becomes so great on the decks that the doors of cabins as well as companionways are likely to be jammed."[132]

At first, Langley believed that the doors were locked to stop those in second class from mingling with the higher-paying passengers, and shortly before the salvage operations were underway, he sent a telegram to John Douglas Hazen, minister of marine and fisheries, requesting that divers examine the door he'd been unable to open. The evidence at the Inquiry convinced him otherwise, because in an article he wrote for the *Merritt Herald*, he said, "Evidently the twisting strain caused by the ship turning over had so warped the frame as to make the door immovable."[133]

NORWEGIANS FELT WRONGED

On June 29, 1914, the Norwegians conducted their own investigation at the Norwegian Consulate General in Montreal. The only witnesses who appeared at that inquiry were crew members of the *Storstad*. Norwegian journalist and filmmaker Kjetil Saugestad found a transcript at the National Archives in Oslo while researching his documentary *Good Ship, Bad Ship* in 2012. Saugestad says that the *Storstad* crew were interviewed by the Norwegian Consul and two Norwegian captains familiar with navigating the St. Lawrence River. Their statements were then sent to Emil Wettergren, the maritime inspector for Southern Norway, along with the findings from the Canadian Inquiry.

Wettergren released his report the following October. "He found that the *Storstad* had the normal right of way, and that the *Empress* should have turned to give way to the *Storstad* and was to blame for the collision," says Saugestad. "He also agreed with the Canadians that Toftenes should have alerted the captain earlier about the fog but did not believe that his mistake contributed to the collision."

The *Storstad* was auctioned off for $175,000 CAD and bought back by her original owners, A.F. Klaverness & Co. The results of the Canadian and the Norwegian Inquiries were sent to the Exchequer Court of Canada for a final decision. The *Storstad* was found at fault, and the owner's liability was limited to $175,000, the value of the ship.

While researching his documentary, Saugestad visited Captain Andersen's former home in Arendal, Norway. The current owner had discovered an old box of papers in the attic belonging to Andersen. Among the papers was an accounts ledger confirming that after the accident, the *Storstad* was repaired and the same officers and crew returned to work to finish the contract with the Dominion Coal Company.

"The tragedy appears all the more terrible since it is due to the blunders of men," wrote a reporter on June 1, 1914. "It was not a case of two vessels, unaware of each other's existence, colliding in fog. They collided because they were aware of each other. Each took a precaution that would have prevented accident if the other had taken none."[134]

12. Myth Busting

THE SURVIVORS HAD BARELY reached Rimouski when news of the wreck reached the world media. Initially, there was much confusion. The first reports said that the *Empress* had collided with the SS *Hannover*, a German passenger liner sailing from Rotterdam (that had actually arrived at the wreck site about an hour after the sinking), and that both ships had sunk.

Several newspapers reported that all passengers and crew were safe. In later editions some survivors were reported as lost, and others who had died were reported as saved. Some passengers who changed travel plans at the last minute must have been surprised to read that they were missing.

A little over twelve hours after the *Empress* went down, reporters from the *Toronto Daily Star* and the *Montreal Star* were on a chartered train on their way to meet the train carrying survivors and get their first-hand stories. Half the reporters continued on to Rimouski, while the other half joined the survivors on the train to Quebec City. Reporters aggressively pumped the survivors for information, and by the time they reached Quebec City, every survivor who could throw light on the accident had been interviewed. This gave the reporters a head start over all the other media.

The amount of information that went out around the world in such a short period of time is truly astounding. Reporters recorded their interviews in shorthand and used typewriters and telephones. With the invention of Google still nearly a hundred years away, fact checking was labour intensive and down to harried staffers. The result was that newspapers that reported on the sinking were packed full of dense, often repetitive copy, with no bylines and few photos and broken up by sidebars, subtitles, and the odd graphic.

When the *Toronto Daily Star* rolled off the presses on Saturday, May 30, 1914—one day after the wreck—there were a staggering seventy-six column inches of first-hand coverage of the *Empress* wreck. "Rarely has any large story been out so quickly and so completely. There were no days of waiting, as happened in the *Titanic* disaster. All the information on the subject, cause of collision, inquest, experiences of the survivors and collateral data were available within forty-eight hours after the *Empress* went down, and by noon Monday two New York and Boston correspondents were ready to pull out."[135]

Much of this frantic reporting had come from traumatized survivors. Many had just lost children or spouses or parents and were themselves in need of medical attention, and so, not surprisingly, some of the information was wrong. Although many survivors attempted to correct misinformation in later interviews, most of the world's press continued to replay the more sensational (and incorrect) original reports.

MORRIS DID NOT SWIM WITH REES ON HIS BACK

It wasn't enough just to have survived the tragedy—the media also needed stories of heroism and superhuman feats. The survival story attributed by reporters to Frank Morris, the thirty-nine-year-old Salvation Army divisional commander from London, Ontario, was mystifying. It appears to have originated with a *Montreal Star* reporter who travelled with the survivors on the train from Rimouski to Quebec City. Ensign Ernest Pugmire supposedly told the reporter that he had seen Commissioner David Rees running back to get his wife.* Major Frank Morris, he said, had been blown overboard in an explosion, severely scalding his arm. Morris then tried to save Commissioner Rees by carrying him on his back in the water until his strength gave out.

The *Montreal Gazette* went even further, quoting an unnamed Salvation Army source: "Without hesitation [Morris] swam to the assistance of his aged and almost exhausted chief and raised him on his shoulder. Buffeted by the swell, and braving the freezing waves, he swam on nobly, trying to bear his charge to a resting place. In spite of his gallant efforts, however, the task proved too great, and the major felt the commissioner slip from his supporting body."[136]

Morris was not blown overboard in an explosion, and he did not scald his arm. He dived over the side when the ship began to sink and was sucked down with it. After he surfaced, he swam toward the *Storstad* and was picked up by one of the collier's lifeboats.

But newspapers around the world ran the wildly embellished story. Only the *Calgary Herald* published the correct version on June 12, 1914, with the headline "Did Not Swim with Rees on His Back. Major Frank Morris of Salvation Army Denies Report Circulated." Morris said that, immediately after the collision, he remembered seeing Commissioner Rees holding his wife's arm as they struggled up the stairs with two of their children. "I took the commissioner by the arm to assist him and Mrs. Rees up the stairs now at a very dangerous angle due to the great list of the ship. Commissioner Rees whispered so the ladies wouldn't hear, 'Major what is the matter: what has happened?' I quickly whispered, 'There has been a collision. Commissioner we are sinking,' and urged him along. He nodded his head in a matter-of-fact way, as though he perfectly understood the situation."[137]

---

* National Commander Ernest Pugmire of the Salvation Army died from a heart attack on June 24, 1953, aged 65.

Then Morris lost his footing and fell, hurting his left shoulder. It was the last time he saw the commissioner.*

LAWLER'S WIFE DID NOT SLIP FROM HIS ARMS

Philip Lawler was travelling on the *Empress* with his wife, Ellen, and fifteen-year-old Herbert, the youngest of their three sons. Philip was an iron worker at Massey-Harris Moulding in Brantford, Ontario, and the family were Salvationists heading to the Congress. Ellen planned to combine the trip with a visit to her aging and ailing parents. According to a newspaper story, Herbert had told his parents that he didn't want to go on the trip because he was afraid. It's hard to say whether Herbert really had a premonition or it was made up by a reporter, because when it came to the Lawler family, reporters got a few facts wrong.

An early version of the story that first appeared on May 29, 1914, in various papers around the world reported that "Lawler with his wife and son were unable to stand on the sloping deck and slipped overboard. Lawler had his wife in his arms, but she slipped from his grasp and was drowned." This was followed up over the next few days with increasingly elaborate details.

The *St. Louis Post Dispatch* was one of several newspapers that changed the report into a quote by Philip. "I managed to grasp my wife, at the same time helping my boy Herbert to reach the surface of the water safely. Somehow my wife slipped from my hands, and when I looked around for her, she was under. As Herbert could swim, I dived under for my wife, but could not get her."[138]

---

* Frank Morris helped to establish the Salvation Army in Dawson, Yukon, during the Klondike gold rush in the late 1890s. He was put in charge of the Army's work in BC and acquired much of the Army's real estate holdings in the Greater Vancouver area. In April 1924, Morris, now a lieutenant colonel, accepted a promotion to resident secretary for Salvation Army emigration affairs in Montreal. While on a farewell tour in Regina, he had a stroke and died, aged 50.

The Lawlers' hometown newspaper, the *Brantford Daily Expositor*, had an even more exciting story that ran under the headline "Mr. Lawler Had to Fight for Life of His Young Son." "I had to fight to keep the lifebelt on my boy," he declared. "They rushed at him and tried to tear it off. I had to fight them, and I did it with my fists."[139]

When Philip Lawler arrived back in Brantford, he was eager to tell his real story—one that wasn't nearly as heroic or romantic as the newspaper versions.

Philip had not watched his wife of twenty-seven years slip from his grasp and slide into the icy water, like a scene from the *Titanic* movie. He hadn't even seen her. Philip and Herbert were sharing a cabin with two other Salvation Army men in the centre of the ship, while Ellen was sharing a cabin with Lena White on the port side. They had all retired to their cabins at around 10:00 p.m. A few hours later a loud noise woke him. "I went to the deck immediately slipping on my trousers as I went and telling the boy to follow me. We reached the deck without any trouble and there we saw that the *Empress* was listing to port." They rushed back down the stairs to look for Ellen and Lena, but all the portholes were open, water was pouring in, and they couldn't get to the cabin. They made their way onto the deck and into the water and started swimming toward the *Storstad*.

"After we had been swimming for a while, Herbert asked me to let him go, as we were both tiring, but I held on to him. A man came along and tried to get on top of Herbert, but I struck him with my fist and forced him to let go. It was a case of a man wanting to get safety for himself, even at someone else's expense."[140] Lawler and his son were in the water for about thirty minutes before they were picked up by a lifeboat from the *Empress*—the same one that had rescued Captain Kendall.

PASSENGERS WERE NOT HACKED TO DEATH

At the same time as these stirring accounts of survival were running in newspapers around the world, so were rumours of cowardly and dangerous behaviour like this one from the *Vancouver Daily News Advertiser.*

> Women were trampled underfoot it is claimed in the mad rush for the stairs. The primeval instinct to save themselves swayed all, and screaming in their panic, they fought to save themselves; like tigers snared, they leaped and scratched and bit their way to the front. There at the foot of the stairs was an impasse. The crowd had jammed. Here knives came out and men hacked at the human wall that held them back as though it were a door of wood.[141]

NO DOUBT NUMBER WERE DEAD BEFORE ENTERING WATER

Undertaker Confirms Report That Many Bodies Bear Knife Wounds.

TORONTO, June 2.—A special to a local paper this morning says that the undertakers preparing bodies at Quebec have found some with wounds of such a nature that it leads to the opinion that in the forehold of the doomed liner an inferno of ferocious

Saskatoon Daily Star, *June 2, 1914*

Fuelling the rumours of knife-wielding maniacs were stories like this one in the *Saskatoon Daily Star*.

> Undertakers preparing bodies at Quebec have found some with wounds of such a nature that it leads to the opinion that in the forehold of the doomed liner an inferno of ferocious passions raged as men strove to fight their way to safety … With knives, they drove through the terror-stricken mass like a pack of demons, thrusting and cutting to make channels to the exits.[142]

The story quoted Norman Craig, a Toronto undertaker who was assisting with the embalming of the bodies in Quebec. He supposedly told the reporter: "There is no doubt that nearly all were killed by injuries received before they were cast into the water."[143]

Philip Lawler said reports that he had been cut in the head because of a fight "with a swarm of knife-armed and maddened foreigners in his bid to reach freedom," as was claimed in the initial newspaper story, were not true. The only physical marks he received were the scrapes on his legs as he was dragged into the lifeboat.

"I heard that knife wounds were found on the dead bodies, but I did not see any knives used, nor did I see any bodies with such wounds on them." What he did see, though, was truly awful. "When we were going down the starboard side of the ship we saw two men trying to get out of the portholes. Only the tops of their heads were visible as they could not get even their heads through. I do not know how they even managed to get their heads up to the portholes, as the boat was on its side at the time."*[144]

* Less than four months after surviving the wreck, Philip Lawler moved his family to Flint, Michigan. In 1918, he remarried and worked as an inspector in a car factory. He died in 1943, aged 88. Herbert Lawler, now a tool and die maker and married with a baby daughter, was issued a US draft card in September 1918. Under medical condition, it says, "weak heart, nervous," which is not surprising, as he'd endured the sinking of the *Empress* just four years earlier. The war ended before Herbert was called up to fight, and his twin daughters were born in 1922. Herbert died in 1992, aged 94. He is buried in Yucca Valley, California.

FOWLER DID NOT FIGHT TO THE DEATH IN THE RIVER

Stories of passenger violence in the St. Lawrence were also attributed to Vancouver-based CPR car inspector and Salvation Army band sergeant John Fowler. Fowler's supposed survival story ran in dozens of newspapers around the world. "Bodies cold and clammy bumped into me, but I could not think of that in my dreadful battle for life. Once a big, husky man threw his arms around me while we were still underwater, and I had to fight to break the clench of his grip. Oh, it was dreadful, that mad battle against an unseen foe amidst those corpses and that wreckage beneath the waters of the St. Lawrence."[145]

No, said Fowler when he was interviewed in his Vancouver home, he did not fight to the death with another man, and he did not see a headlong rush for the lifeboats or any "foreigners" carrying knives. "I saw one man staggering about with a heavy valise. But he soon let that go and turned his attention to saving his life. I never saw him again."[146]

CAPTAIN KENDALL WAS NOT CURSED

According to various stories in books, documentaries, and newspapers about the *Empress* over the last century or so, when Dr. Hawley Harvey Crippen was arrested aboard the *Montrose* in July 1910, he had some final words for Captain Kendall, the man responsible for his capture. This is one of my favourite versions, which appeared in the *Windsor Star*:

> It was in those very waters where the *Empress of Ireland* went down that Kendall handed the wretched doctor, till then unaware that his disguise had been penetrated, over to the tender mercies of the Scotland Yard Inspector Dew and the officers of the police force of the province of Quebec. "You will suffer for this treachery, Sir," the

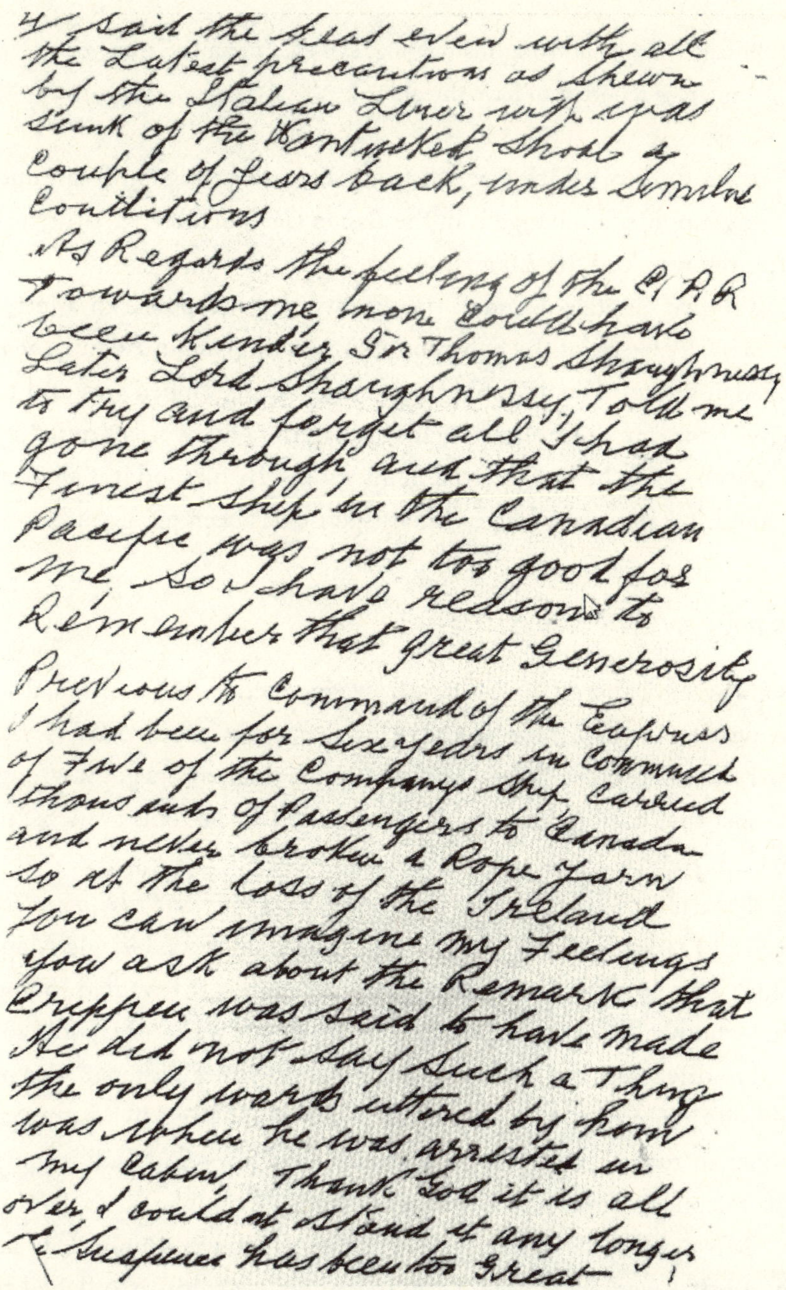
4 said the Seas even with all
the Latest precautions as Shewn
by the Italian Liner with was
Sunk of the Nantucket Shoal a
Couple of Years back, under Similar
Conditions
As Regards the feeling of the C.P.R.
Towards me none could have
been Kinder Sir Thomas Shaughnessy
Later Lord Shaughnessy, Told me
to try and forget all I had
gone through and that the
Finest ship in the Canadian
Pacific was not too good for
me, So I have reason to
Remember that Great Generosity
Previous to Command of the Empress
I had been for Six years in Command
of Five of the Companys Ship carried
thousands of Passengers to Canada
and never broken a Rope Yarn
so at the loss of the Ireland
You can imagine my Feelings
you ask about the Remark that
Crippen was said to have made
He did not say such a Thing
the only words uttered by him
was when he was arrested in
my cabin, Thank God it is all
over, I couldnt stand it any longer,
the Suspense has been too Great

Letter from Captain Kendall to Mr. Wally Court of the Salvation Army in England, about a remark Dr. Crippen was have supposed to have made to him, August 14, 1963 | Used by permission of the Salvation Army Canada and Bermuda Archives (Toronto, ON)

> enraged Crippen, fixing his bulging, evil eyes upon the trim young captain, is reported to have threatened.[147]

It's a fun story—it's just not true. The earliest version I can find of this supposed exchange is in the *Boston Globe* of May 30, 1914, just after the wreck of the *Empress*.

I'll give Captain Kendall the last word. In response to a letter from Wally Court of the Salvation Army in England in August 1963, Kendall wrote, "You ask about the remark that Crippen was said to have made. He did not say such a thing. The only words uttered by him were when he was arrested in my cabin. 'Thank God it is all over, I couldn't stand it any longer. The suspense has been too great.'"[148]

WHAT WENT WRONG?

So, why have these fake or grossly exaggerated stories continued to be written up in anniversary articles and books about the *Empress* over the last century? Well, it's not so much that writers got it wrong, it's just that until quite recently, we didn't have the tools available to make it right.

I started to research my first book, *At Home with History: The Secrets of Greater Vancouver's Heritage Homes*, in 2004. Google Maps didn't exist, and BC Assessment wasn't yet online. If I wanted to find out whether an original house from 1910, say, was still standing, I had to drive over and check it out for myself. Street addresses weren't online then either. If I wanted to know who'd been living in that house in 1910, I had to go to Vancouver Archives and look it up in the telephone directory.

Most of my days were spent at the Vancouver Public Library (VPL). If I wanted to read a newspaper article from 1910, I had to search the microfilm. This was a long and painful experience. First you had to locate the right film in the filing cabinets and find an available working machine. Next you took the reel of old and often fragile film out of its box, threaded it onto the microfilm reader's spindle, fed it through a roller and then under the glass, and hooked it up to another spindle on the other side of the machine. Once you got that working, you could scroll through each page of the newspaper—and you had to look through everything. The image quality was often poor and hard to read, and newspapers of the time were jam-packed with articles and few pictures. When you got to the end of the reel and wanted to see a new date or a different newspaper, you had to start the whole process over again. Not only was it time consuming, it was also expensive. Each page cost twenty cents to print; you'd feed the change into the machine and hope that it worked. If it was a long article, you often had to blow up each section, and the cost could quickly add up.

Thanks to Newspapers.com, what in the past would have taken me a trip downtown and hours of time now takes a few minutes on my home computer or phone. I can search multiple newspapers, go straight to the article I want, and find dozens more that I wouldn't have known to look for.

In researching this book, it was relatively easy for me to find the origin story—the one that was wrong. Still, not everything is digitized, so in many cases I contacted the archives near to where an *Empress* survivor had lived, and when I was lucky, they sent me copies of articles from local papers in which the survivor was interviewed or occasionally wrote their own account. Many of the later articles contradicted the early reports that were printed immediately after the collision and taken from interviews with emotionally and physically damaged survivors. But sometimes reports from well-respected newspapers are all that we researchers have to go by, so it's easy to see how one wrong story can be perpetuated over time.

When I started researching Gordon Davidson in 2017, newspapers such as the *Province*, the *Vancouver Sun*, and the *Calgary Herald* weren't yet online. So, it was back to the VPL and spooling through microfilm for me. It wasn't until the newspapers were added to Newspapers.com in 2022 that I was able to find out everything about Davidson and his alleged swim to shore.

DAVIDSON DID NOT SWIM TO SHORE

When Gordon Davidson reached Quebec City, he saw that early newspaper reports had listed him among the missing. He immediately sent telegrams to his father in Union, Ontario, and his friend and colleague, Professor Frederick Teggart at the University of California, Berkeley, letting them know that he was safe. His father contacted Gordon's brother, James, in Vancouver. James then gave an interview to the *Province*, and somehow the story of Gordon Davidson's survival got blown out of proportion. The story, which appeared in the Vancouver *Province* on June 1, 1914, ran with the headline "He Swam Ashore as *Empress* Sank."

"If the report that he swam ashore is correct, he performed a really wonderful feat," wrote the reporter. "From the meagre particulars of Mr. Davidson's escape received by his brother here, his experiences may be pictured. The boat sinking with its hundreds of passengers pitched into the water all struggling for life; the frantic attempt to seize the boats or to secure a piece of wreckage on which to float to safety, can be imagined."[149]

The story goes on to say that, after seeing the lifeboats were filled to capacity, Davidson kept swimming until he was too far out for rescue and instead decided to swim to shore. It ends with the reporter noting that Davidson was a strong swimmer and had managed to find a lifebelt.

The following day, the *Berkeley Daily Gazette* added its own spin: "Fighting his way through wreckage and floating bodies, Davidson struck out for the distant shore. A lifeboat passed near him, but he was not seen. He swam on alone through the night. It was after hours of struggle, kept alive in the cold water, only by his physical efforts that he reached the shore."[150]

None of it happened. It was all one reporter's wild speculation. And even though Davidson tried to correct the information himself, that one reporter's version from two days after the shipwreck is the one repeated and embellished in newspaper articles, in books, and even in his own obituary. In one book written ninety years after the shipwreck, the author says he can imagine Davidson's remarkable four-mile swim to shore in his pyjamas and lifebelt, in temperatures that killed most people in minutes, then his finding the Catholic church at Sainte-Luce and knocking on the rectory door.

We know from the letter that Davidson wrote to his parents on May 30, 1914, that he was naked when he went into the water. We also know that he was not wearing a lifebelt.

> Fortunately, I came to two men floating side by side with lifebelts on. One was dead, floating with his face underwater. The other was on his back. He was a frail little fellow and chilled through. I caught hold of the dead man's lifebelt with my left hand, rested my right arm over the little man's lifebelt and caught hold of a bit of wreckage with my right hand. I swam with my feet then, pushing this mass ahead of me. I now sighted two or three lifeboats. The first was full and rowed past. The second passed us at a distance and the others were farther away and picking up people. So, I turned and started for the collier. I had reached about a couple of hundred yards from her when a lifeboat came up. I was exhausted and fainted as they pulled me over the side.[151]

AS JOURNAL.

, JUNE 2, 1914 ESTABLISHED 1859.

LOCAL BOY TELLS A GRAPHIC STORY OF FIGHT WITH DEATH WHEN EMPRESS WENT DOWN

UNION BOY WHO FOUGHT BRAVELY

GORDON DAVIDSON

Whose story of his successful fight for life in the Empress Disaster is the most graphic of any which have yet been published.

Gordon Davidson in Letter to His Parents at Union Says He was Awakened in His Berth by Inrush by Water Through Porthole—Knocked Down When He Stepped Into Passageway.

SUCTION OF SINKING BOAT CARRIED HIM DOWN 20 FEET;

Two Lifeboats Passed Him by as He Swam, Supported by Lifebelt on Dead Passenger and Bit of Wreckage—Storstad was Quarter of a Mile Off—Fainted as He was Pulled Into Lifeboat—When He Ceme to was in Engine Room of Collier Smeared With Oil and Coal Dust.

Chateau Frontenac, Quebec,
Saturday, May 30, 1914

Dear Folks at Home,—

It certainly is good to be alive, when so many poor people went down in the Empress of Ireland yesterday without a single chance for their lives. It was an awful affair. I was in room 524 which is on the starboard side on the main deck. It was an outside room, i.e., it had a porthole which the cabin steward had closed the evening before when I went to bed about ten o'clock. There was a young business man, Stillman, of Calgary, in the berth above.

... 2.30 a.m. She cut deeply, clear to the engine room, some of the crew told me later. I did not hear the collision but was awakened by a rush of water which I thought at first was the cre... too loud and I turned on the elec... my cabin from the passageway and... hardly realized what was wrong b... and rushed out. I followed in my... half filling the cabin.

KNOCKED DOWN ...

As I stepped into the passage...

THREW OFF NIGHTS...

I threw off my nightshirt and ... away when the boat sank. The ... twenty feet. When I came up I s...

CITY'S BANKING CREATES A STIR IN COMMITTEE

Mayor Johnson is Blamed for the Awkward Position That Has Developed

ONE MEMBER SUGGESTS A LONDON ARRANGEMENT

At the last meeting of the finance committee of the city council a motion was passed after considerable discussion and wrangling following Treasurer Perry's report of banking conditions as a result of the withdrawal of the Hydro-Electric ac...

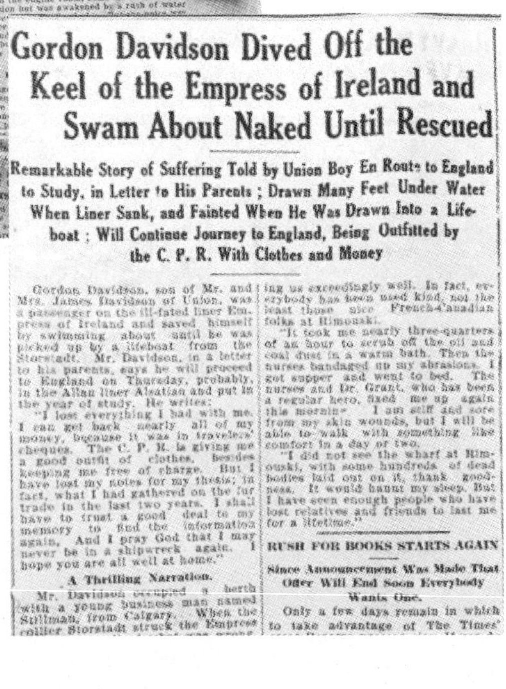

Gordon Davidson Dived Off the Keel of the Empress of Ireland and Swam About Naked Until Rescued

Remarkable Story of Suffering Told by Union Boy En Route to England to Study, in Letter to His Parents; Drawn Many Feet Under Water When Liner Sank, and Fainted When He Was Drawn Into a Lifeboat; Will Continue Journey to England, Being Outfitted by the C. P. R. With Clothes and Money

Gordon Davidson, son of Mr. and Mrs. James Davidson of Union, was a passenger on the ill-fated liner Empress of Ireland and saved himself by swimming about until he was picked up by a lifeboat from the Storstadt. Mr. Davidson, in a letter to his parents, says he will proceed to England on Thursday, probably, in the Allan liner Alsatian and put in the year of study. He writes:

"I lost everything I had with me. I can get back nearly all of my money, because it was in travelers' cheques. The C. P. R. is giving me a good outfit of clothes, besides keeping me free of charge. But I have lost my notes for my thesis; in fact, what I had gathered on the fur trade in the last two years. I shall have to trust a good deal to my memory to find the information again. And I pray God that I may never be in a shipwreck again. I hope you are all well at home."

A Thrilling Narration.

Mr. Davidson occupied a berth with a young business man named Stillman, from Calgary. When the collier Storstadt struck the Empress ...

... ing us exceedingly well. In fact, everybody has been used kind, not the least those nice French-Canadian folks at Rimouski.

"It took me nearly three-quarters of an hour to scrub off the oil and coal dust in a warm bath. Then the nurses bandaged up my abrasions. I got supper and went to bed. The nurses and Dr. Grant, who has been a regular hero, fixed me up again this morning. I am stiff and sore from my skin wounds, but I will be able to walk with something like comfort in a day or two.

"I did not see the wharf at Rimouski, with some hundreds of dead bodies laid out on it, thank goodness. It would haunt my sleep. But I have seen enough people who have lost relatives and friends to last me for a lifetime."

RUSH FOR BOOKS STARTS AGAIN

Since Announcement Was Made That Offer Will End Soon Everybody Wants One.

Only a few days remain in which to take advantage of The Times' ...

TOP: St. Thomas Journal, *June 2, 1914 | Courtesy of Margaret Patmore;* BOTTOM: St. Thomas Daily Times, *June 3, 1914 | Courtesy of Elgin County Archives (St. Thomas, ON)*

THE REAL SURVIVAL STORY

When Hugh Verrier hired me to research Gordon Davidson and the story of his miraculous swim, the first thing I did was put together a family tree. Gordon had not had children, but his older brother, James, had three, and that seemed like a good place to start.

James Davidson had been a physics professor at the University of British Columbia. He retired in 1939 and moved to La Jolla Beach, California. His obituary gave me the name of his daughter, Janet Davidson Curtis. Janet had died in 2014 at the age of ninety-eight, and her obituary gave me the name of her daughter, Margaret Patmore, and her stepson, Harold Curtis. While there were no listings for Margaret in the La Jolla area, I found Harold in Yucaipa, California. Harold gave me Margaret's email.

Margaret, who goes by Peggy, lives in Madrid, Spain. Not only is she the keeper of the Davidson family history, she had Gordon's actual survival account of that horrible night in May 1914, in the form of a century-old torn-up newspaper clipping. The problem was that the name of the newspaper that it was printed in was mostly torn out and only identified as "—as Journal." The headline was "Local Boy Tells a Graphic Story of Fight with Death When Empress Went Down."

With the help of my friend Tom Carter, a Vancouver artist and historian, we were able to track the article to the *St. Thomas Journal*, a newspaper that had merged with the *St. Thomas Daily Times* in 1918 to become the *St. Thomas Times-Journal*, which still publishes. Unfortunately, none of its early issues had been digitized. Gina Dewaele at the Elgin County Archives found Gordon's letter printed in full in the *St. Thomas Journal* of June 2, 1914, and in the *St. Thomas Daily Times* the next day.

And, just over two years after Gordon Davidson survived the sinking of the *Empress*, he would once again be forced to fight for his life, this time on a muddy field at the Western Front.

Just four weeks after the tragedy claimed front-page headlines around the world, the *Empress of Ireland* abruptly disappeared from the newspapers. On June 28, 1914, Austrian archduke Franz Ferdinand and his wife, Sophia, were shot dead in Bosnia. By the following month, much of the world was at war. And many of those young men who had narrowly escaped death on the *Empress* would soon face an even bigger threat: four years of unprecedented carnage, slaughter, and destruction.

13. Survivors in World War I

CANADIANS SANG AND MARCHED in the streets at the declaration of war in early August 1914. Those who opposed the war mostly stayed silent. In October 1914, less than five months after the sinking of the *Empress of Ireland*, the first Canadian contingent sailed for England with over thirty thousand volunteers.

When I started writing this book, my intention was to talk about the impact that such a large loss of life from the *Empress of Ireland* shipwreck had on Canada. I soon realized that I couldn't properly separate the *Empress* tragedy from the war that followed on its heels. Over a thousand people died that night, many of them women and children, but this pales in comparison to the massive loss of life that would follow a few short months later. Between 1914 and 1918, over 650,000 Canadians and Newfoundlanders* served in the war, and over 66,000 did not come home. Another 172,000 Canadians were wounded, and many, like Gordon Davidson, bore the scars—both physical and mental. It's not so surprising, then, that the *Empress* quickly faded from the headlines and was left out of most history books.

On June 13, 1916, the same week that he earned his doctorate and exactly two years and two weeks after he survived the sinking of

* Newfoundland was a separate dominion from Canada at the time.

the *Empress*, Gordon Davidson enlisted as a private with the 196th (Western Universities) Battalion at Vancouver, BC.

GORDON DAVIDSON

On October 26, 1917, Lieutenant Gordon Davidson was part of the Canadian offensive at the Battle of Passchendaele. For the next seven days, he was under heavy enemy fire and fighting for his life on a muddy battlefield in northwest Belgium. Early on the morning of November 2, he led an attack on two enemy outposts. He shot the sentry before he could raise an alarm and captured a German pillbox while being pounded with machine-gun fire and exploding artillery shells.*

> We were outnumbered and cut down by the bombs and bullets. A German stick bomb broke at my heels and put a bit in my right calf and another in my left thigh. A few minutes later I was hit by a bit of shrapnel in the face, and it knocked me down. I thought my cheek was blown off for a second. We struck there until there was only four men with me. There is a hole in the middle of the upper lip and another just in front of the right ear. I do not know which way the scrap of metal was going but anyway it took off the teeth from the right side of the upper jaw, except the two back molars, pulped the gums and splintered the bone.[152]

Four days later, Davidson was recovering in a London hospital when the Canadian Corps captured the ridge near the ruined village of Passchendaele, leaving nearly sixteen thousand Canadians dead or wounded.

---

* A pillbox is a bunker constructed of concrete reinforced with steel with holes through which to fire machine guns.

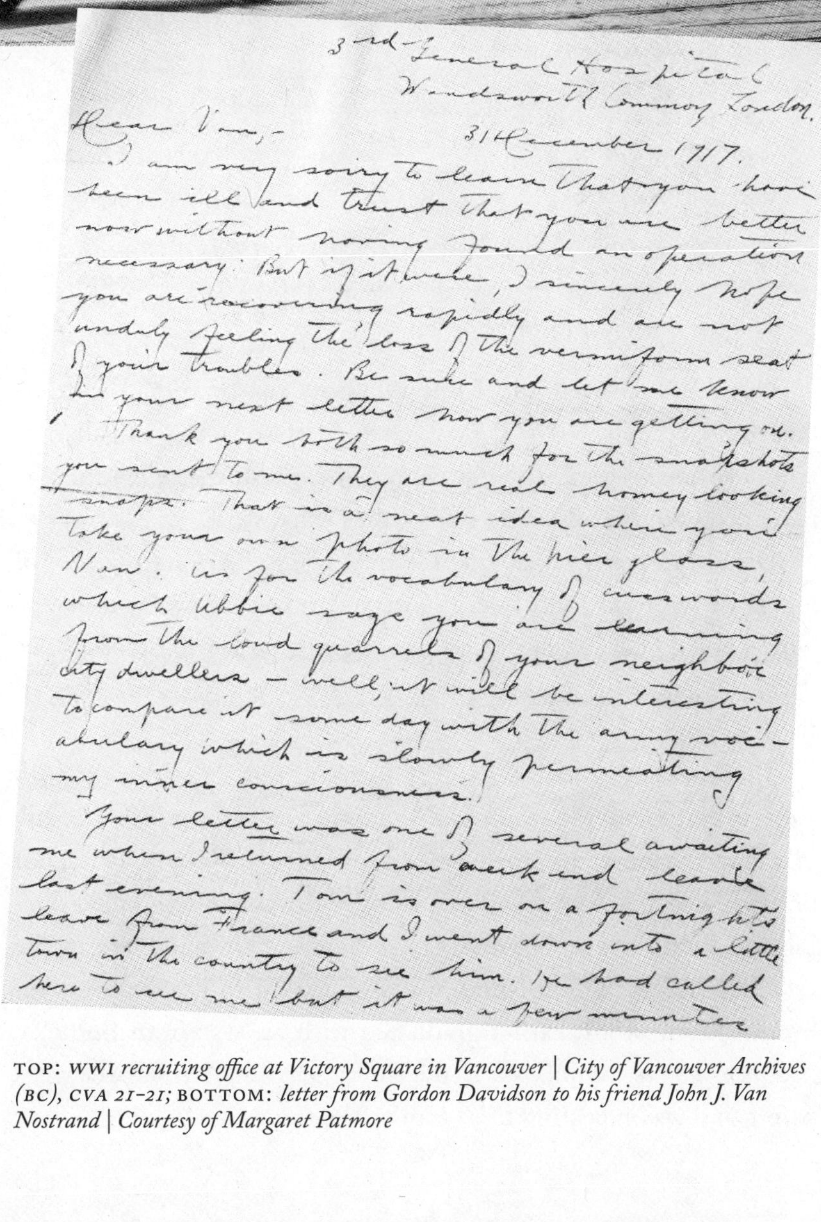

3rd General Hospital
Wandsworth Common, London.

Dear Van,- 31 December 1917.

I am very sorry to learn that you have been ill and trust that you are better now without having found an operation necessary. But if it were, I sincerely hope you are recovering rapidly and are not unduly feeling the loss of the vermiform seat of your troubles. Be sure and let me know in your next letter how you are getting on.

Thank you both so much for the snapshots you sent to me. They are real homey looking snaps. That is a neat idea where you take your own photo in the pier glass, Van. As for the vocabulary of cuss words which Abbie says you are learning from the loud quarrels of your neighbor city dwellers – well, it will be interesting to compare it some day with the army vocabulary which is slowly permeating my inner consciousness.

Your letter was one of several awaiting me when I returned from week end leave last evening. Tom is over on a fortnight's leave from France and I went down into a little town in the country to see him. He had called here to see me but it was a few minutes

TOP: *WWI recruiting office at Victory Square in Vancouver | City of Vancouver Archives (BC), CVA 21-21;* BOTTOM: *letter from Gordon Davidson to his friend John J. Van Nostrand | Courtesy of Margaret Patmore*

Gordon Davidson, August 8, 1918 | Courtesy of Margaret Patmore

Davidson received the Military Cross for bravery. The military gazette of February 4, 1918, cited, "For conspicuous gallantry and devotion to duty. Though wounded early in the operations he remained with the attacking troops until exhausted."[153]

Davidson's wartime experiences are recounted through a series of letters he wrote to John J. Van Nostrand, a history professor at the University of Pennsylvania who was a friend from Davidson's Berkeley days. The letters belong to Davidson's descendant, Margaret "Peggy" Patmore, and they are riveting.

The first letter is dated April 1, 1917, and was sent from the 19th Reserve Battalion. Davidson told "Van" that he had made lieutenant. His commission came weeks after learning that Ken, his youngest brother, who had just graduated from high school, was killed during the Battle of the Somme. Gordon, now first lieutenant in the 1st Canadian Mounted Rifles, was shipped off to France. Another brother, Tom, who'd earlier graduated with an MSC from Berkeley, had received his commission to the Royal Garrison Artillery the week before and was expecting to be sent to the front.

Gordon wrote to Van Nostrand on New Year's Eve, 1917, telling him that the hospital had held a dance, and Tom and his fiancée, Connie, attended. "He is looking very well. You would know him at once although he is greying a bit which is inexcusable in one of his years," he wrote. "Connie is a good looker and a jolly girl with a bit of determination of her own. Watch your eye, Tom! She is a brown haired, bluish eyed lass with a certain ability for music and a quite decent ability with the needle and the cooking utensils. Tom is going to attend a four-week course at an artillery school in France."[154]

Two months later, Tom was dead. Gordon recovered enough to teach machine gunnery to soldiers at Bramshott Camp.

When Gordon Davidson was demobilized in March 1919, he had served the military for two years and 249 days, with sixteen of those months spent overseas in England and France.

CHARLES LINDSAY CLAUDE BOWES-LYON

One of the first survivors from the *Empress* to enlist and then die in the war was twenty-nine-year-old Charles Lindsay Claude Bowes-Lyon. The eldest son of the Earl of Strathmore and an Eton-educated civil engineer, Bowes-Lyon enlisted as a lieutenant with the Black Watch Royal Highlanders at the outbreak of war. He served through the battles of the Marne and the Aisne and was killed in action at Ypres on October 23, 1914. He is buried in the churchyard at Boezinge, Belgium.

ROBERT CRELLIN

Robert Crellin arrived in England in the middle of June 1914 and barely had time to recuperate and grieve his friends before England was at war. He enlisted with the Royal Army Medical Corps, and by November 1915 he was in France. Most soldiers' personnel records from World War I are digitized and available to search and download through the Library and Archives Canada website. The records for British Army soldiers are held at the National Archives in London. Unfortunately, only about 40 percent of the records still exist; the rest were destroyed in a bombing raid in 1940. Crellin's records were among those lost, and so our knowledge of his war years is spotty. There are a couple of references, including Florrie Barbour's memoir, that say Crellin was held in a German prisoner-of-war camp toward the end of the war, but I was unable to confirm this.

The 1919 Medal and Award Rolls lists Crellin as a sergeant with the Royal Army Medical Corps and a recipient of both the Victory Medal and the British War Medal.

At the beginning of the war, thousands of Canadians showed up at their local recruiting stations in an unprecedented burst of patriotic fervour. Many had strong emotional ties to Great Britain. Of the first contingent, 70 percent were British-born, although many had lived in Canada for years and considered themselves Canadian.

CEDRIC GALLAGHER

Montreal-born Cedric Gallagher's life was full of promise when he set off on the *Empress of Ireland* with his mother in May 1914. The nineteen-year-old had been accepted into McGill University's medical school, and the three-month tour of Europe was a gift from his parents. Instead, his trip came to a crushing end when his mother drowned.

Gallagher started medical school that fall, as his mother had wished, but he didn't finish the first year. He enlisted with the Canadian Army Medical Corps as Private 356 on February 18, 1915, and by that summer, he was in France. In August 1916, Gallagher was back in Canada on special leave to attend his father's funeral and arrange for the care of his now-orphaned eight-year-old sister, Evelyn.

While in Canada, Gallagher was found medically unfit for further service and discharged from the army on October 31, 1916. Clearly he didn't agree, because he joined the UK Air Force the following June as a provisional lieutenant. On September 21, 1918, he married Marion Chapman of Winnipeg in the Young Methodist Church and was named his sister's legal guardian. The couple lived in Winnipeg after the war, had two children, and moved to Montreal in 1938. Cedric Gallagher died in 1954, aged fifty-nine.

LEFT: *Cedric Gallagher's marriage announcement to Marion Chapman in the* Winnipeg Tribune, *September 21, 1918 | Winnipeg Tribune Archives, University of Manitoba Archives & Special Collections;* ABOVE: *Cedric Gallagher, circa 1918 | Courtesy of Shelagh Mahoney*

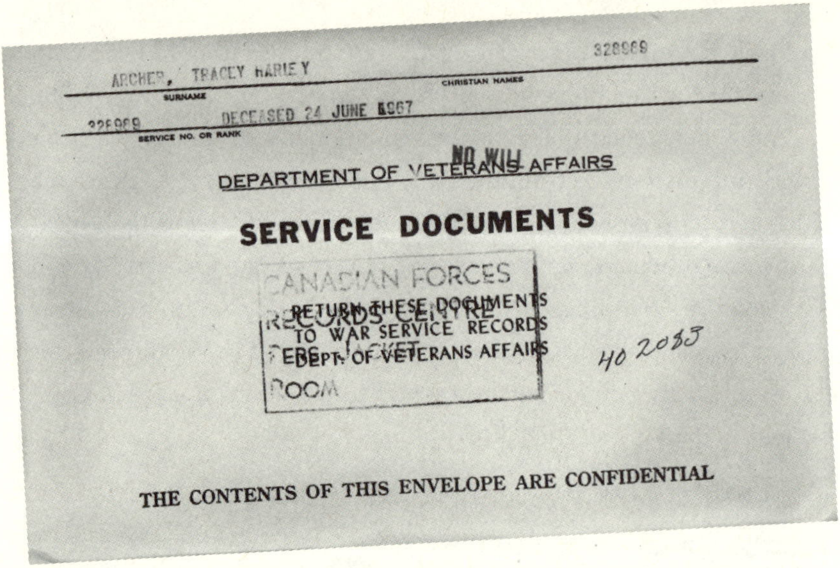
328989
ARCHER, TRACEY HARLEY
SURNAME CHRISTIAN NAMES
328989 DECEASED 24 JUNE 1967
SERVICE NO. OR RANK
NO WILL
DEPARTMENT OF VETERANS AFFAIRS
SERVICE DOCUMENTS
CANADIAN FORCES
RECORDS CENTRE
ROOM
RETURN THESE DOCUMENTS
TO WAR SERVICE RECORDS
DEPT. OF VETERANS AFFAIRS
40 2083
THE CONTENTS OF THIS ENVELOPE ARE CONFIDENTIAL

Attestation papers of Tracey Harley Archer | 328989 © Government of Canada. Reproduced with permission of Library and Archives Canada (2024). Library and Archives Canada / Canadian Expeditionary Force (CEF) / Acc. 1992-93/166, Box 210-30

TRACEY ARCHER

Tracey Archer of Regina, Saskatchewan, had suffered the loss of his wife and son in the sinking of the *Empress*. In May 1916, he enlisted as a driver with the 14th Brigade Canadian Field Artillery. He shipped out to France in August of the following year.

Archer was shot in the head on September 17, 1918, and spent the next six weeks in hospital. His medical examination record says that he had experienced nervousness and likely "shell shock" for a few months after the injury but was "feeling completely normal" for the two months prior to his discharge in March 1919, when he was considered "healthy."

He married Gladys Ross, a twenty-five-year-old teacher, in 1923, and they had two children.* In 1998, Archer's son, Douglas, wrote to

* Archer retired from his position as secretary and treasurer for the City of Regina and moved to Vancouver in 1937. He died at the Shaughnessy Military Hospital in 1967, aged 86.

American author David Zeni: "The ship has always held a special place in my life because, had it not been for the tragedy of its sinking, neither my sister nor I would have been born," he said. "Our father never spoke of the sinking, and my sister and I knew instinctively not to ask him anything about it. All we knew we learned from our mother and what she knew was quite limited."[155]

For the first two years of war, Canadians rushed to enlist for reasons that ran the gamut from patriotism to adventure to employment to peer pressure. But not everyone was welcome. Racism ran deep, and most visible minorities were rejected, as was anyone under eighteen or over forty-five. Strict medical exams filtered out those with poor eyesight, flat feet, or bad teeth.

WWI recruitment posters | Archives of Ontario (Toronto, ON), War Poster Collection, 1915, 10016181 and 10016175

Victorious Canadians celebrating after Vimy Ridge, circa 1918 | Archives of Ontario (Toronto, ON), War Poster Collection, C224-0-0-9-41

ARCHIE BROWN

Archie Brown was one of the rare third-class *Empress* survivors travelling to England as a member of the Salvation Army Staff Band. Born in Glasgow, Scotland, in 1890, he had immigrated to Canada, and in 1911 was boarding with the Delamonts in Moose Jaw, Saskatchewan, and working for the CPR.

Brown enlisted in June 1916. Standing at just five foot three, he barely squeaked in at the minimum height requirement. He only got as far as the Niagara Camp in Ontario before being discharged as medically unfit because of complications with appendicitis. Undeterred, he signed up again on May 21, 1917, and this time was shipped off to France as a gunner with the 8th Army Brigade.

Brown served right up until he was demobilized in April 1919 and seemed to have made it through the war relatively unscathed, at least physically.*

JOHN FOWLER

John Fowler was a coal miner in Staffordshire, England, before immigrating to Vancouver in 1909. In February 1916, the thirty-six-year-old father of three signed up with the 121st Overseas Battalion.

Fowler, the Salvation Army's deputy band sergeant, had shown incredible bravery immediately after the collision on the *Empress* when he gave up his lifebelt to a young mother, then stopped to retrieve a rope to help Eliza Willmot get up to the deck and into a rescue boat. Willmot told everyone that Fowler had saved her life, and as a thank you, she gifted him a Bible. According to Fowler's obituary, during his time fighting at the front, Willmot's Bible stopped a bullet and saved his life. There are many stories of a pocket Bible in a soldier's breast pocket saving him from a bullet to the heart. If this one was true, Fowler's Bible appears to have been lost to history.

What we do know from Fowler's war records is that Private 763103 served two years and three days in Canada, England, and France. On Easter Monday, April 9, 1917, he was part of the first wave of Canadian soldiers to attack at Vimy Ridge. For the next three days the soldiers fought to capture the ridge under heavy machine-gun fire and amid huge casualties. On April 12, 1917, the last day of the battle, just before victory, Fowler received multiple gunshot wounds to the face, arm, hand, and leg. Two of his fingers were amputated, and he was shipped back to Canada in February 1918 as medically "unfit to continue."†

---

* Archie Brown married fellow Salvationist Beatrice Paddock of Newfoundland in 1925. They lived in North Burnaby, BC, and had two children. Brown became a sales rep for Nalley's Foods. He outlived his wife and died at the Shaughnessy Military Hospital in Vancouver, aged 83.

† After being demobilized in 1917, John Fowler worked as a CPR car inspector for the next twenty-five years. He died in Vancouver in 1966, aged 86.

John Fowler's grave at Mountain View Cemetery, Vancouver, 2024 | *Wayne Worden*

ROBERT CUNNINGHAM

In May 1914, Robert Cunningham, a twenty-six-year-old chemistry professor at Manitoba Agricultural College, was a first-class passenger on his way to Edinburgh for a working holiday. The Manitoba government had commissioned Cunningham to exhibit Canadian grains and produce at agricultural fairs and to solicit Scottish immigration to Manitoba.

While some soldiers talked about the pressure to enlist, others truly believed in the cause. On March 1, 1916, Cunningham enlisted as a lieutenant with the 196th University Battalion. The following month, he married Mildred McKee from Brandon, Manitoba. Cunningham shipped out with his unit to Bramshott, England, taking Mildred with him to live with his mother at the family home in Edinburgh.

While Cunningham was keen to join in the fighting at the Western Front, his knowledge of science and his skills in the classroom initially kept him in England. He was employed as an agricultural instructor at the soldier's college, which later became the Khaki University, offering soldiers classes in everything from history to engineering, French, and agriculture to prepare them for jobs after the war.

Early in the fighting, the Germans' use of poison gas quickly became a daily event and grew more deadly as the war progressed. The gas blinded, burned, and choked soldiers before they died a horrible death. The gas mask became the most important piece of equipment that a soldier owned, but the necessity of knowing when to put it on, when to remove it, and properly fitting it, was crucial. A divisional gas officer was appointed in 1916, and Cunningham's science background made him a great fit for the important anti-gas work.

A letter Cunningham wrote on December 9, 1917, to a colleague named Jackson was published in the agricultural department's newsletter, the *MANAGRA*, and retrieved for me by archivists at the University of Manitoba. Cunningham wrote that after the first poison gas attack at the Ypres Salient, every soldier headed to France had to

Robert Cunningham on the University of Manitoba Roll of Honour, 1914–18 | Courtesy of University of Manitoba Archives & Special Collections (Winnipeg, MB)

take a gas mask and be trained in its use. "The training of all ranks in auto gas work is checked at the base, so I had my hands full getting the men up to a high pitch of training. The rush has died down now, but I'm going ahead with the fitting so as to be ready when the next call comes."

Cunningham told Jackson that there was concern over the issue of conscription in the upcoming election. "There is quite a bit of excitement over here concerning the election issue, but there is no doubt which way the soldiers are voting. If the folks back home are true to the boys over here, there can be no doubt as to the issue. If Laurier gets in, rather than return to Canada, I'll transfer to the Imperials."*

Cunningham took pride in his military duties but was frustrated about being kept away from the front. "It seems as if the harder I try to get to France, the further I seem to be from getting there. I have this one consoling fact, that when free from educational work I'm going to France as a gas officer."

In August 1918, Cunningham got his wish. "The Battalion has been out on rest since I joined it, but things won't always be that way. The boys have seen some hard fighting," he wrote to Jackson. "The morale of the troops could not be better and is very much in contrast with that of the Hun at the present time. While the end of all this bloodshed is not in sight, we are perhaps nearer than we actually think."[156]

On September 22, 1918, five days after writing this letter, Cunningham, a bright, promising young man, was dead at thirty.†

Midway through 1916, voluntary recruitment began to decline. The government gradually eased its restrictions, lowering medical standards and the minimum height. The recruitment door was thrown

* Conscription was an issue bitterly fought over leading up to the Canadian federal election of December 1917. Robert Borden (for conscription) won, beating Wilfred Laurier (against).

† Robert Cunningham is buried at Triangle Cemetery, Inchy-en-Artois, in Pas-de-Calais, France, at grave reference D19.

open for Indigenous and Black Canadians and those of Chinese and Japanese descent. Government propaganda also changed from a message of enlisting for the greater good to one of public shaming.

JOHN WISE LANGLEY

All that stopped John Langley from enlisting earlier was the several months he spent recuperating in hospital after a kick to the head from a horse he'd been breaking in April 1916. By January 1917, he felt sufficiently recovered. He leased Willow Grange, the family's cattle ranch in Canford, BC, and took his wife, Bessie, and their three small children to the Glencoe Lodge in Vancouver, a boutique hotel owned by sugar baron Benjamin Tingley Rogers and run by the CPR-trained Miss Jean Mollison. Then he enlisted.

Langley's attestation paper describes a fresh-faced twenty-nine-year-old standing a little shy of six feet, with slightly flat feet, though it wasn't enough of a problem to cause his rejection, and a deep scar between his eyebrows. Another scar above his left eyebrow was a memento from the horse's kick, which had also given him a fractured skull and a broken nose.

Unlike many immigrants to Canada in the early 1900s, Langley was already a property owner in his native Ireland. His family owned several hundred acres in Tipperary, in the south of Ireland, but while Langley came from means, he'd had a sad childhood. His mother died from a blood clot in the lungs before his second birthday, and four years later, his father died from cirrhosis of the liver. Langley's aunt, Sarah, stepped in to raise him. At twenty-three, the "gentleman farmer," as he was described in the 1911 Census, met Bessie Lenthall of Oxfordshire, England. They were married at the little church at Bessels Leigh Manor, the estate that had been in the Lenthall family since William Lenthall, speaker of the House of Commons, bought it in the early 1600s.

John Langley married Bessie Lenthall in 1911 at the Lenthall family estate in Oxfordshire, England. The couple immigrated to BC in 1913. | *Langley family collection*

Langley was Private 200226 with the Canadian Expeditionary Force's 9th Infantry Battalion. In early 1918 he received his commission and transferred to the Royal Army Service Corps, British Army, as lieutenant. He served in France until September of that year, when he was gassed near Péronne and sent back to England. He returned to Vancouver in August 1919.

In 1919, a reporter called him "the cat with nine lives."[157] He'd survived a kick to the head from a horse, a motorcycle accident, the sinking of the *Empress*, and World War I, and all this by the age of thirty.

Langley opened the Corfield and Langley Motor Company with John Corfield on Seymour Street. The garage sold Fageol tractors and repaired and serviced cars. After their tenant Robert Grant was killed in a car crash in August 1922, the Langleys returned to the Nicola Valley and the ranch. Langley made improvements to the ranch, but not a lot of money, and in the early 1930s he did a land swap with J.T. Willgoose, retired chief of police, for a house and land in Merritt, BC.

Langley threw himself into politics, running in the electoral district of Yale for the newly formed Co-operative Commonwealth Federation (CCF) in 1933. If elected, the party promised to seek economic reform to help Canadians affected by the Great Depression.* The CCF won seven of the forty-seven available seats, but Langley wasn't one of them—he came in third, with 221 votes.

He took a job with Kamloops Stages as a driver on the Merritt-to-Spences Bridge run and co-managed the Spences Bridge Hotel. Still interested in politics, he ran in the next BC provincial election. In a letter to the editor, he wrote, "We believe work is for all and we will see to it that all work. We intend to abolish exploitation of labour in every shape and form. We believe in constitutional methods and are opposed to the forces of Communism."[158] This time he came second, with 442 votes. Later he split with the party over the CCF's anti-war stance. As he told a reporter for the local paper, while Canada's system was imperfect, it was better than fascism, and fascism must be destroyed.

Langley's grandson, Geoff, says that his grandfather never fully recovered from being gassed in the trenches during World War I; he suffered various health-related problems all of his life. He was hospitalized for nearly a year between 1940 and 1941, and he died the following year at the age of fifty-seven.

DR. JAMES GRANT

At the end of June 1914, Dr. Grant, the ship's surgeon on the *Empress of Ireland*, returned to a hero's welcome and reunion with his family in Victoria, BC. He set up practice as a general practitioner, partnered

* The CCF merged with the Canadian Labour Congress to form the NDP in 1961.

John Langley's grave at Mountain View Cemetery, Vancouver | Langley family collection

with two of his brothers in a logging company, and quickly became a highly regarded member of the community.

Grant's grandson, Doug Secord, tells me that Grant was one of the few physicians who would go out to D'Arcy Island, a "leper colony" where people were quarantined with Hansen's disease. Most of those left to suffer in isolation were the Chinese, while their white counterparts were sent to Eastern Canada for medical treatment. Undeterred by illness or race, Grant took the supply boat to D'Arcy Island every three months to give medical attention to those banished there.

Grant served as chief medical officer for the CPR on Vancouver Island, performed postmortems when required, taught classes for the Royal Life Saving Society, and became medical officer to the 5th Regiment Canadian Garrison Artillery in July 1915. After three years of militia service, Grant enlisted on August 6, 1918, as a captain with the Canadian Army Medical Corps.

Two months later, his beloved wife, twenty-eight-year-old Lizzie, was dead from the influenza pandemic of 1918–19.

Dr. Grant was demobilized in May 1919. He married Dorothy Harris in June 1922, and they had two children. He never discussed the *Empress* incident. Doug Secord says that his grandfather was bipolar and struggled with post-traumatic stress disorder all of his life. Grant retired in 1945 and died two years later from a duodenal ulcer. His death certificate notes that he was divorced and that manic depression contributed to his death.

By war's end, some 619,000 Canadians had enlisted in the Canadian Expeditionary Force for service overseas. This was an enormous contribution from a nation with a population of just under eight million in 1914. Approximately 7 percent of the total population of Canada was in uniform at some point during the war, and hundreds of thousands of others worked on the home front in support of the war.[159]

14. The Captains' War

PUBLICLY, CAPTAIN KENDALL WAS absolved of all responsibility for the actions that had caused the sinking of the *Empress*. But not everyone thought he was blameless, and the tragedy left a black stain on his near-perfect record. Kendall would no longer command the CPR's beautiful liners. Instead, he was promoted to a desk job: the CPR's temporary marine superintendent at Antwerp, Belgium.

CAPTAIN HENRY KENDALL

Kendall had been at his job for just over a week when Germany invaded Belgium. Thousands of British, Canadian, and American citizens were stranded in ports all over Europe. Their American cash and traveller's cheques were useless, and many were dead broke, scared, and hungry.

"Nothing could stop the onrush of enemy troops and it was only a question of time before they would be pouring into Antwerp. The day came when we must either remain and be German captives or get away to England," said Kendall in his memoir. "Most of the shipping had now departed and hundreds of refugees were daily besieging the British Consul's office."[160]

There were only two available CPR ships in port: the aging steamer *Montreal*, currently out of commission, and the *Montrose*, which was

Captain Henry Kendall of the Empress of Ireland, *circa 1914 | Société d'Histoire du Bas-Canada (Beloeil, QC), Guy D'Astous collection*

undergoing an overhaul. Within thirty-six hours, Kendall had assembled a scratch crew of engineers and stokers on shore leave and two officers from the *Nankin*. He hurriedly refitted the *Montrose*—the same ship he'd commanded in 1910 with Dr. Crippen aboard. Kendall arranged with the British Consul in Antwerp to tow the *Montreal* down the Scheldt River, then he assumed command of the *Montrose* and the more than four hundred refugees and headed across the English Channel as fast as he could safely manage.*

* In October 1914, the *Montrose* was sold to the British Admiralty, where she was filled with cement and used to block the entrance to the harbour at Dover, England. Two months later, she broke free of her moorings and drifted on to Goodwin Sands, where her story ended.

The RMS Calgarian *made her first voyage on May 8, 1914. Within months she would be refitted and repurposed into a Royal Navy armed merchant cruiser.* | *Société d'Histoire du Bas-Canada (Beloeil,* QC*), Guy D'Astous collection*

There was very little food. The crew and human cargo survived on the ship's biscuits, porridge, and corned beef until they were met by a British torpedo destroyer, escorted to the mouth of the Thames, and taken to Gravesend.

The Calgarian

As a reward for his bravery, Kendall was made lieutenant commander of the HMS *Calgarian*, second-in-command under Captain Thomas Webster Kemp. The *Calgarian* was a palatial Atlantic liner, and she'd had her maiden voyage from Liverpool to Quebec City on May 8, 1914, exactly three weeks before the *Empress of Ireland's* last departure.

After war broke out, the *Calgarian* was completely gutted of inflammable wood and fittings and given eight six-inch guns and a crew of over six hundred men. Now armed as a British merchant cruiser, the *Calgarian* began her naval career on September 15, 1914.

That October, a Welsh newspaper published a letter from an unnamed crew member describing what life was like aboard the *Calgarian*. He was careful not to divulge exactly where the ship had been or where it was going next, but was able to say that they'd visited the Grecian Archipelago, the Rock of Gibraltar, and Portugal.

"The ship is fast, ordinary running 22 knots but when we require 25 or 26 knots she can do it, so that if in nothing else, we are more than a match for most German ships in speed. As long as their submarines or mines don't interfere with us, we are prepared for anything," he wrote.

When not conducting their seaman's duties, days were taken up with heavy gun practice twice a day, daily rifle practice, and twenty-four-hour vigilance. "We sleep in our clothes with only our caps and boots off so as to be ready for anything at a moment's notice."

The SS Calgarian *in 1914, now an auxiliary cruiser at anchor | Library and Archives Canada (Ottawa, ON), The Mariners' Museum (Newport News, VA), Neg No. PB 11881*

According to the anonymous writer, Emmy the cat, who fled the *Empress of Ireland* on the eve of her departure from Quebec City, was now aboard the *Calgarian*.

"The stewards tell me that she was for nearly eight years on the *Empress* and the day the ship sailed the cat left and was brought back twice and finally she deserted just previous to sailing. I am going to keep my eye on her. As long as she sticks, we shall take it as a good omen."[161]

That November, Kendall was named the ship's commanding officer.

In the summer of 1915, Kendall was sailing the *Calgarian* up the St. Lawrence River to Montreal. His orders were to escort four submarines built in Quebec for the British Navy to Gibraltar. Over the next year the *Calgarian* made several trips across the Atlantic. She took Canadian troops to England and at times carried distinguished passengers such as Canadian prime minister Sir Robert Borden.

The Halifax Explosion

On December 6, 1917, Kendall was steaming toward Halifax when he received a message that there had been a huge explosion.

The French munitions ship *Mont-Blanc* had left New York and was entering Halifax, where she would pick up an escort to take her across the Atlantic. The *Mont-Blanc* was filled with between four and five thousand tons of explosives: benzol, picric acid, TNT, and gun cotton. The Norwegian ship *Imo* was departing Halifax for New York, where she would pick up food and clothing to take to Belgium. Both ships would pass each other in the Narrows, the harbour's tightest navigation section. It was a bright winter morning, and both steamers had a pilot aboard. After a series of whistles and miscommunications between the officers and pilots of the two ships and failed manoeuvres to avoid a collision, the *Imo* struck the starboard bow of the *Mont-Blanc*. After a few moments, the two ships parted, leaving a gash in the *Mont-Blanc*'s hull and generating sparks that ignited volatile grains of dry picric acid stored below its decks.

The crew fled the ship in lifeboats, and those on shore watched as the *Mont-Blanc* drifted to Pier 6. Teams of firefighters and sailors from other ships headed toward the ship, hoping to put out the fire. But it was too late. The *Mont-Blanc* exploded, sending out a shock wave in all directions, and burning metal fragments showered down over Halifax. The explosion caused a tsunami that washed over the Halifax and Dartmouth shores. Homes, offices, churches, factories, vessels, the railway station and the freight yards, and hundreds of people in the immediate area were obliterated. The blast shattered windows a hundred kilometres away in Truro, Nova Scotia, and was heard in Prince Edward Island.

The *Imo* was tossed onto the shore, killing everyone, including the pilot. The death count of the disaster was more than seventeen hundred. Another nine thousand were injured, and many more were left homeless.

When the *Calgarian* steamed into Halifax early the next morning, they found a city in chaos. Doctors and nurses sent by the Red Cross by train had not yet arrived, temporary hospitals that were hastily set up couldn't cope with the onslaught of injuries, and snowstorms impeded the search for survivors. Kendall and the crew of the *Calgarian* sprang into action and began to assist with the rescue and medical relief.

One of Kendall's first duties was to view the body of his friend, Captain James Murray. Murray was killed in his office at Pier 9 when the explosion ripped through the city.*

"It seemed surprising that with both pilots being old and respected Halifax citizens a collision in broad daylight should not have been

* Murray was incorrectly identified in several newspapers as the commanding officer of the *Empress of Ireland* when she sank in May 1914. At the time, he was the harbourmaster at Quebec City.

possible; yet both before and since that date ships have accidentally crashed into each other,"[162] wrote Kendall, perhaps ironically.

The crew of the *Calgarian* had a lucky escape, but her luck wouldn't hold.

Torpedoed

On March 1, 1918, the *Calgarian* and her crew of 610 were escorting a convoy of thirty ships off the coast of Northern Ireland toward the North Channel.*

"We had been met by the destroyers and it seemed likely that a valuable armed merchant cruiser of 17,515 tons steaming at that slow pace through such a confined passage would be inviting trouble," wrote Kendall. The *Calgarian* received permission to proceed independently and increased speed to 20 knots (37 kilometres per hour). "We were approaching Rathlin Island, the weather being fine and clear. I was walking up and down the highest lookout-bridge, while the ship kept up a confusing zigzag and a couple of destroyers protected us." Kendall told his lieutenant that he'd be pleased to shake hands with a German submarine officer who could "plant" them under those conditions.[163]

He spoke too soon.

The first torpedo struck the *Calgarian* from close range, about 500 metres (1,640 feet) out. It hit between her two funnels, killing twenty-nine men on watch. The ship's watertight doors were closed, and she stayed afloat. Eleven trawlers, three sloops, and seven destroyers rushed forward to surround the *Calgarian*, one making a smokescreen for additional protection.

There were less than a dozen men on deck with Kendall. Some had been blown overboard by the explosion, others had dived into the sea. A trawler came around the *Calgarian*'s stern carrying dozens of men

* In response to German U-boat attacks, convoys were established to protect cargo ships by consolidating merchant vessels into large groups escorted by a British warship riding shotgun.

who had been plucked from the water. Kendall found a rope and was able to slide down it to the trawler and safety.

Tommy Agney, a merchant seaman from Liverpool who had joined the Royal Navy when war broke out, was the leading fireman on the *Calgarian*. He and fourteen of his colleagues managed to get off the ship to safety. When they saw that she was still afloat, the men volunteered to go back to the ship and try to put out the fire and bring the ship into port.

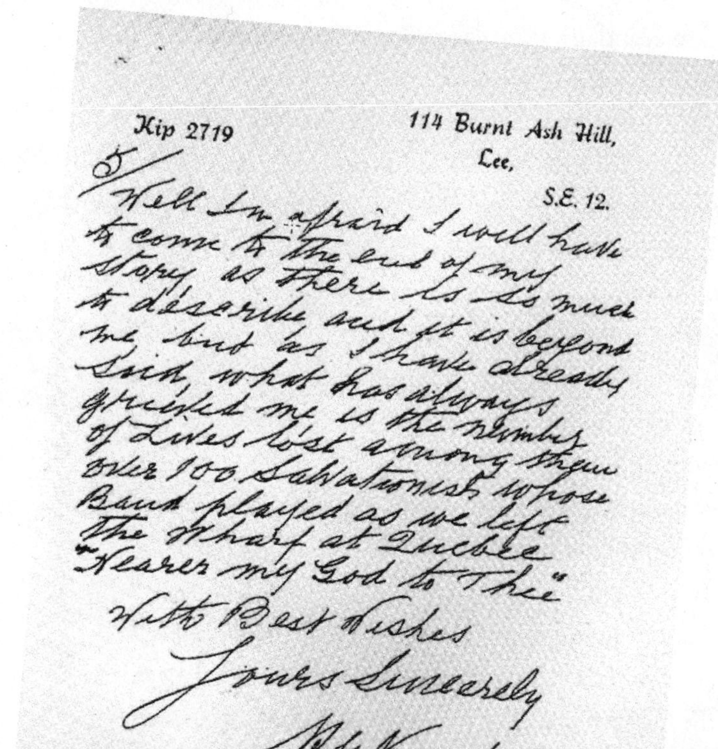
Kip 2719
114 Burnt Ash Hill,
Lee,
S.E. 12.
5/
Well I'm afraid I will have
to come to the end of my
story as there is so much
to describe and it is beyond
me, but as I have already
said, what has always
grieved me is the number
of Lives lost among them
over 100 Salvationists whose
Band played as we left
the Wharf at Quebec
"Nearer my God to Thee"
With Best Wishes
Yours Sincerely
HG Kendall
Should be
God be with you till
we meet again

Letter from Captain Kendall to Wally Court of the Salvation Army in England, August 14, 1963 | Used by permission of the Salvation Army Canada and Bermuda Archives (Toronto, ON)

Forty-six minutes later, the German sub dived below the vessels and fired two more torpedoes into the *Calgarian*, killing Agney and all the crew who were trapped in the engine room. The *Calgarian* sank below the waters. Altogether, four torpedoes hit the *Calgarian*. Forty-nine officers and crew members died.

The remaining crew held a memorial service at a little church on the waterfront. Later that night, they crossed to England to report for duty.

Retirement

The rest of Captain Kendall's war was relatively uneventful. The following June, he was appointed commodore of convoys. America had joined the war, and troops were pouring over the Atlantic. Kendall was in charge of the New York convoy. "The fullest freedom and power were given to each Commodore, and the pay was excellent."[164] All in all, Kendall brought 196 ships across the Atlantic during that time.

Within a few days of the Armistice of 11 November 1918, Kendall was released from the Admiralty. He returned to the CPR and was put back in a desk job as marine superintendent at Southampton, England. Six years later, he moved to London and retired after thirty years of service with the CPR.

Kendall's 256-page memoir sums up his experience as captain of the *Empress of Ireland* in just one paragraph:

> The year 1914 for me personally promised to be more than ordinary, for I had been transferred to the Liverpool–Montreal route and given command of the finest ship in the CPR fleet—the *Empress of Ireland*. It was no small honour to be Master of such a magnificent vessel, but one day the *Storstad* collided with us in the River St. Lawrence and that was the end of the *Empress*. Even today this sad incident is too painfully engraved on my memory for me to enlarge on the matter. It will suffice if I state as a result of the inquiry, the Court found the whole blame rested on the *Storstad*.[165]

Fifty years after the sinking, Kendall still blamed the *Storstad* for the accident, never taking any personal responsibility for his own failure to have the watertight doors closed when fog first set in, an action that could have potentially saved so many lives. In May 1964 he told a reporter, "The *Empress* was the finest ship afloat and a finer crew never trod a ship's deck ... As for the *Storstad*, she was carelessly handled. Despite that dense fog, her speed was never reduced. So, there you had a captain asleep with an officer at the bridge, and that moving mass of tonnage steaming toward me on that black river."[166]

When Kendall died in November 1965 at a London nursing home, he was ninety-one. His obituary in the *Times of London* focused on his remarkable maritime career but not once mentioned his time as captain of the *Empress of Ireland*.

Captain Thomas Andersen of the Storstad, *circa 1914* | *Société d'Histoire du Bas-Canada (Beloeil,* QC*), Guy D'Astous collection*

CAPTAIN THOMAS ANDERSEN

Unfortunately, Captain Thomas Andersen did not write a memoir, and there is far less information available about his time during the war. We know that he was absolved by the Norwegian Inquiry of any responsibility for the accident with the *Empress of Ireland*, and he continued as captain of the *Storstad*, plying the St. Lawrence between Sydney and Montreal. After war broke out, the *Storstad* operated as a relief ship, carrying supplies for people in German-occupied Belgium.

While Norway remained neutral during the war, German subs sank more than four hundred Norwegian merchant marine ships

Loading flour onto a Belgian relief ship in Montreal, 1917 | *McCord Stewart Museum (Montreal,* QC*),* VIEW-*17112*

between 1914 and 1917, killing more than fifteen hundred Norwegian sailors. On March 8, 1917, the *Storstad* was off the coast of Ireland, taking a cargo of food consigned to the Commission for Relief in Belgium. Although she was flying the Norwegian flag and was clearly marked with "Belgian Relief" in large letters on either side, the *Storstad* was attacked by a German U-boat in broad daylight.

"The German submarine when it sighted us, began to fire shells. We called out that we were a Belgian relief ship, but when we thought that the danger had passed and that they would not sink us, they fired a torpedo," said John Roy Christian, an American aboard the *Storstad*. "We took to the lifeboats and the Germans began to fire shells all round the place and some of them fell near the boats though we were a good distance from the vessel. They appeared to be firing about for fun. I do not know any other reason."

Christian said that twelve of the crew and passengers of the *Storstad* were stranded in a lifeboat, surrounded by heavy seas, for thirty-six hours. "We had to be constantly bailing out and everybody was exhausted through being out on the seas in such terrible weather. The fourth engineer was very ill in the boat and died, although we tried everything to revive him. During the night we could not light our torches because we had not a single dry match amongst us."[167]

Captain Andersen told the reporter that there was absolutely no doubt that the Germans knew that they were firing on a Norwegian relief ship. "When we were in the open boats, I asked the German commander would he give us a tow and told him that it was a bad business. He made no reply but made away from us at full speed. They then commenced to fire shells and some of them fell dangerously near us. We had a most trying ordeal during the time that we were in the boat."[168] By the time they were rescued, said Andersen, the crew were dying from exposure to the cold.

Alfred Toftenes, circa 1913 | *Jan Hauge Nilsen, Toftenes family collection*

CHIEF OFFICER ALFRED TOFTENES

While Alfred Toftenes, Captain Andersen's second-in-command, was blamed by the English Inquiry for the sinking of the *Empress*, he was absolved by the Norwegian government and returned to work. On June 24, 1914, Alfred's wife, Ingrid, sent a postcard to her in-laws.

> Dear Mother-in-Law:
> This evening Alfred and I will return to Montreal once again. The newspapers are horrible, especially with Alfred. He was on the bridge after all and is thus the most important witness. The newspapers said that he was nervous, but he wasn't. The *Storstad* will be sold, and we hope for a little decency, even if it seems virtue is absent here.[169]

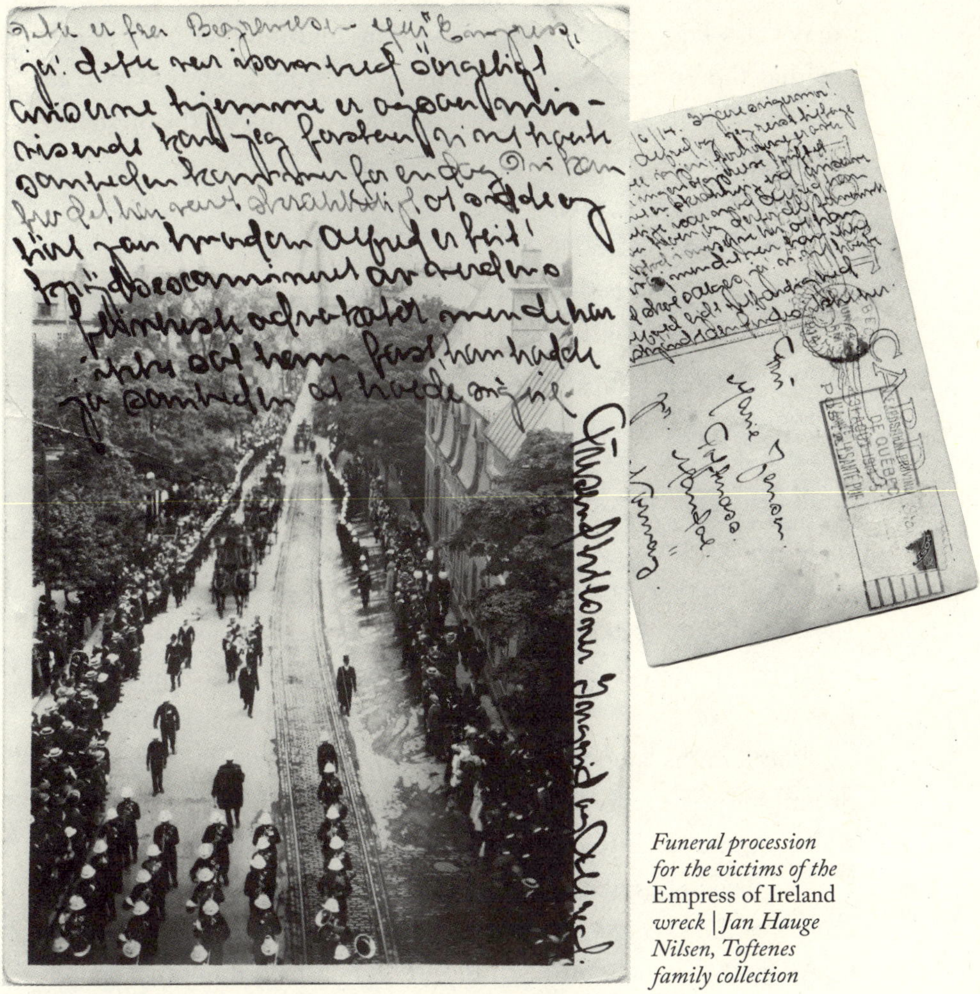

Funeral procession for the victims of the Empress of Ireland *wreck | Jan Hauge Nilsen, Toftenes family collection*

Along the side of the photo, Ingrid wrote:

This is the funeral after the *Empress*. Yes! It's so sad. The newspapers at home are also wrong, I can tell you. We must hope that the truth comes out one day. As you can imagine it was truly terrible to sit and hear how Alfred was cross-examined by the best lawyers in the world, but they couldn't really bring him down. The truth, after all, is on his side.

We also know from a postcard sent by Ingrid to her mother-in-law that the Tofteneses were still living in Sydney, Nova Scotia, at the end of August, and Alfred had returned to work on the *Storstad*.

> Sunday August 30, 1914.
> Dear Mother-in-Law!
> I'm in Sydney in our old place. The *Storstad* is in Montreal. Alfred talked about writing. Hopefully he will take the initiative. Otherwise, we are all well. It's expensive to live here, but it must be worse back home.

Shortly after Ingrid wrote that postcard, Alfred was promoted to captain.

On January 27, 1918, Alfred Toftenes was in command of the *Carolus* off the south of Dodman Point on the UK's South Cornish coast. The ship was torpedoed and sunk by a U-boat. Fortunately, no lives were lost.

Four months later, Toftenes's luck ran out. His death is somewhat of a mystery. The story in the family is that his ship was torpedoed by a U-boat, and he drifted in a lifeboat for weeks before being rescued, then he died in hospital. But at the time of his death, Toftenes was the captain of the SS *Sildra*, which was still afloat in 1919. Toftenes died in an American hospital on April 19, 1918. He is buried in Greenwood Cemetery, Brooklyn.

Toftenes's wife and mother placed the following notice in a Norwegian newspaper on May 1, 1918.

> My dearly beloved husband, and my dear only son Captain Alfred J. Toftenes, Commander of SS Sildra died in New York on April 18 from Pleurisy. He was 36.
> Ingrid Toftenes (Ramsaas) and Marie Jensen Toftenes (Herolden)[170]

15. Shell Shock

MORE THAN 172,000 CANADIANS who fought in World War I returned with debilitating injuries. Those who were disabled because of lost arms or legs received some help and sympathy, but psychological casualties often went undiagnosed or were just misunderstood.

The term *shell shock*, now more easily understood as a form of post-traumatic stress disorder that affects soldiers, was first used in 1915. Those who suffered from it described being easily surprised or scared and having symptoms that ranged from confusion, tiredness, and trouble concentrating to flashbacks, nightmares, and depression. Psychiatry was still in its infancy, and the belief was that shell shock resulted from physical damage to the brain from exploding artillery shells in the trenches.

A German dugout in WWI | *City of Vancouver Archives (BC), Gr War P23*

For the most part, though, those with shell shock were considered to be hysterical or cowardly, and there was little treatment available for the more than nine thousand returning soldiers suffering from mental trauma. Most veterans suffered in silence.

ONE VETERAN'S STORY

The last time Gertrude Palmer saw Gordon Davidson was when she served him breakfast in the dining room at 8:30 on the morning of May 30, 1922. After that, he went back up to his room. "I called him when his brother phoned. I also called him at luncheon and rang the bell, and I judged by his cap being gone, that he was out."[171]

Palmer, a nurse whose family owned the boarding house where Gordon lived, went upstairs around 2:00 p.m. The first thing she noticed was blood running in two streams from under his door. She ran downstairs and phoned James, Gordon's brother. James arrived ten minutes later to find Gordon's door unlocked.

Gordon was leaning back in a wicker chair just inside the door. There was a large hole in the top of his head, and blood was pouring down his face and right shoulder, along the chair, and onto the floor. James could see Gordon's service weapon lying on his lap, between his hands. He ran downstairs and phoned Dr. William Burnett. Gertrude Palmer hadn't heard a thing.

"He had evidently been dead a few hours—I should say three or four hours," Burnett testified at the Coroner's Inquest the next day. "The blood on the clothing was beginning to dry up, and one place on the floor, a small amount was quite dry and the rest of it was liquid."[172]

Everything else in Gordon Davidson's room was neat and tidy. He was fully dressed except for his hat, which sat on top of the chest of drawers. His bags were packed, ready for his train trip to Ontario that evening, and the holster for his gun sat on top of his open steamer trunk. There was no note. Burnett believed that Davidson had made

Gordon Davidson at the family farm in Union, circa 1919 | Courtesy of Margaret Patmore

the impulsive decision to take his gun out of its case, sit down, and shoot himself.

Constable Edgar Campbell arrived shortly after Burnett. He noted several shells in the magazine and one empty shell in the chamber that had been fired. He searched for a suicide note but could find only a few letters from Davidson's parents, a silver watch, a bank book with eight hundred dollars, and just under sixty dollars in cash.

Gordon Davidson rented a room in a large three-storey house on West 12th Avenue not far from the University of British Columbia, where he taught history. He suffered from severe anxiety, and he felt his teaching wasn't up to the standard that he expected from himself. The 979 days that he'd served in the military were evident from the gunshot wounds to his right leg and left thigh and the scars etched into his face where shrapnel had entered his lip, smashed through his teeth, and exited underneath his right ear.

UNION, ONTARIO

When Gordon Davidson demobilized in 1919 and returned to Canada, he went to his parents' farm in Union, Ontario, and stayed there for two years. He lived off a small pension for his teeth, and his parents were told to pretend that nothing was wrong. That all Davidson needed was rest.

I was curious about Union, a deeply religious farming community that had produced two sons with PhDs, another with a theology degree, and a fourth with a master's in science. Gordon's niece, True Davidson, was the first female publishing sales rep in Canada, became the mayor of East York in 1972, and, after retiring, wrote a column for the *Toronto Sun* and provided commentaries for CBC Radio.

In September 2023, I went on a road trip. Union is a two-and-a-half-hour drive from Toronto. When the Davidsons settled there

Gordon Davidson's parents and a few of his siblings and nieces are buried at the cemetery in Union | Eve Lazarus

Canadian soldiers on parade at the Western Front, circa 1916 | City of Vancouver Archives (BC), Mil P281.50

in the late 1870s, it was a thriving community with retail stores, factories, a pub, and a school. The only remnants of the town left now are a shuttered general store, a few houses, the Union United Church—formerly the Union Wesleyan Methodist Church, which the Davidsons attended—and the cemetery. Most of the family are buried there, including Gordon's parents, his brothers, John and James, and his niece, True. Gordon Davidson is buried in the World War I soldiers' plot at Mountain View Cemetery in Vancouver.

HE SEEMED LOST

"There was no indication of anything wrong mentally, except that he was very quiet, like so many of the boys are," said his brother, James, a physics professor at UBC. He told the Inquest that Gordon Davidson had returned to Vancouver the previous August to lecture in history.

"He said a number of times that life did not seem real; his work did not seem real anymore, but a great many of our students said that, and I paid no attention, except before Christmas. He was afraid of a nervous breakdown. I did not advise him to quit, but I advised him not to kill himself and not to hurt himself if the work was too much. He decided to carry on but worried a great deal."[173]

Gordon dropped by his brother's house on Marine Drive the Thursday before his death. "In the middle of the conversation he said, 'Jim, is it one or two men you have got following me?' That was the first erratic thing that I had seen of any kind," said James. He took him to see their family doctor, who blamed Gordon's university work as the source of his problems and advised him to immediately go home to the family farm in Union and rest.

Gordon Davidson's grave at Mountain View Cemetery in Vancouver, 2024 | Wayne Worden

"He seemed lost. If you spoke to him, he would wait for a while and say, 'I cannot understand,' and then he seemed all right again," said James. "There was every indication that he was proceeding to get ready to go home and was all ready, and simply saw this revolver and saw a way out of his troubles and worries. Had he got away, the doctor still thinks that he would have been all right."[174]

Gertrude Palmer wasn't so sure. Gordon had told her that he liked his university work and didn't want to leave. "He seemed rather distressed about it, and he said physically he thought he was quite all right. But evidently the work was too hard for him in his nervous condition."[175]

One juror seemed to understand that Gordon Davidson's anxiety and paranoia was a by-product of the horrors of war rather than stress from work. He said, "I think it is about time the government did something for these men. I am speaking for myself. I have not done anything this year, and can't do anything, and perhaps he was in the same predicament."[176]

DEATH NOT DUE TO SERVICE

The six-member jury determined that Gordon Davidson's death "on May 30, 1922, in his room at 1055 West Twelfth Avenue, Vancouver, was the result of a revolver shot wound inflicted by his own hands while temporarily mentally deranged." Or, as the *Vancouver Daily World* reported the next day, "Gordon Davidson is believed to have become suddenly insane as he was packing the last bag to go east for his health."

Handwritten across Davidson's military records in black felt pen is "death not due to service."

Davidson's childhood friend, the Reverend G.O. Fallis, officiated at his funeral service. He told mourners that Davidson's death was a direct result of the war. "The effects of the war on the nervous systems

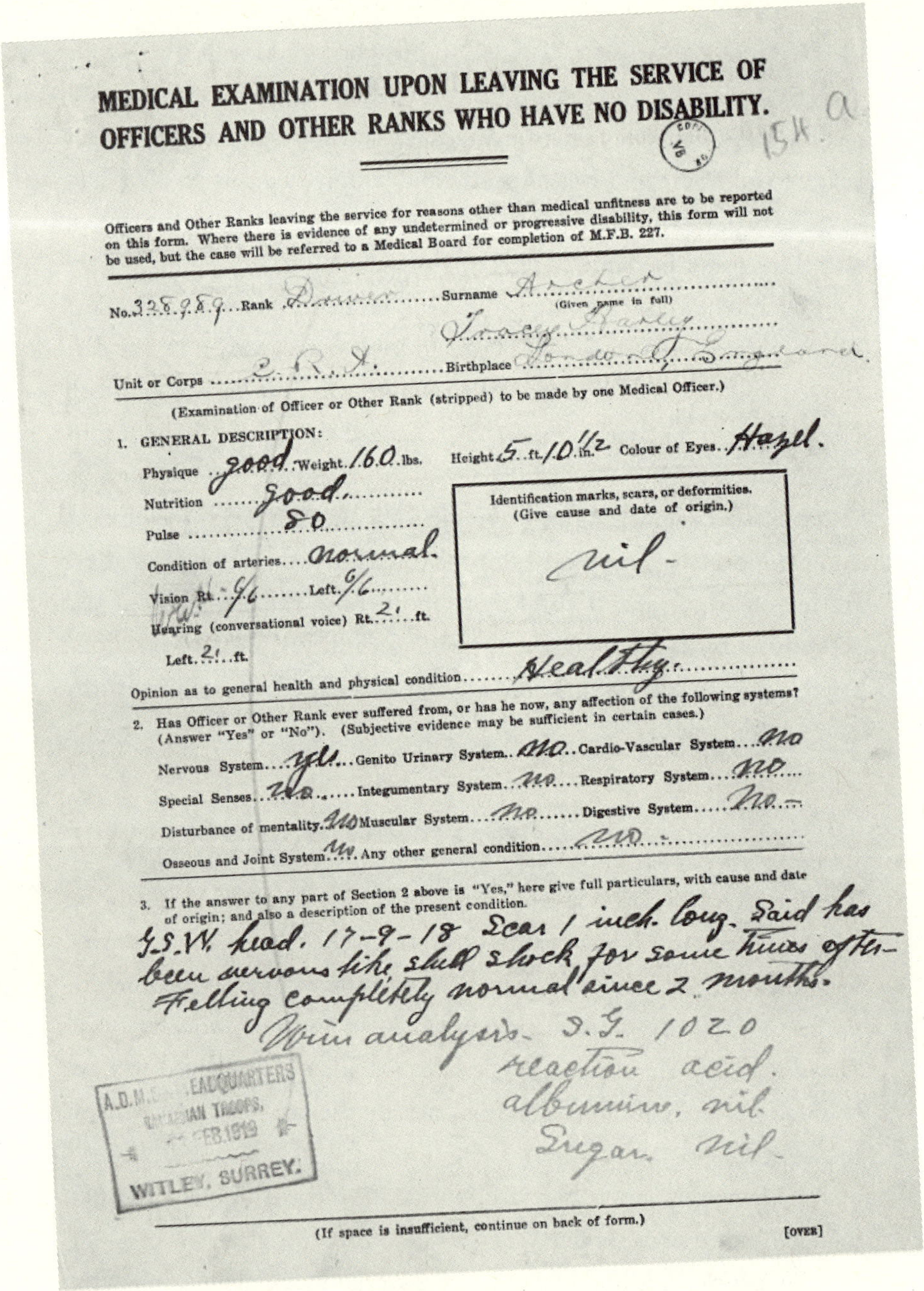

MEDICAL EXAMINATION UPON LEAVING THE SERVICE OF OFFICERS AND OTHER RANKS WHO HAVE NO DISABILITY.

154 a

Officers and Other Ranks leaving the service for reasons other than medical unfitness are to be reported on this form. Where there is evidence of any undetermined or progressive disability, this form will not be used, but the case will be referred to a Medical Board for completion of M.F.B. 227.

No. 328989 Rank Driver Surname Archer
(Given name in full) Tracey Harley
Unit or Corps C.R.T. Birthplace London, England

(Examination of Officer or Other Rank (stripped) to be made by one Medical Officer.)

1. GENERAL DESCRIPTION:

Physique good Weight 160 lbs. Height 5 ft. 10½ in. Colour of Eyes Hazel.

Nutrition good

Pulse 80

Condition of arteries normal.

Vision Rt. 6/6 Left 6/6

Hearing (conversational voice) Rt. 21 ft. Left 21 ft.

Identification marks, scars, or deformities. (Give cause and date of origin.)
nil –

Opinion as to general health and physical condition Healthy.

2. Has Officer or Other Rank ever suffered from, or has he now, any affection of the following systems? (Answer "Yes" or "No"). (Subjective evidence may be sufficient in certain cases.)

Nervous System yes Genito Urinary System no Cardio-Vascular System no

Special Senses no Integumentary System no Respiratory System no

Disturbance of mentality no Muscular System no Digestive System no –

Osseous and Joint System no Any other general condition no –

3. If the answer to any part of Section 2 above is "Yes," here give full particulars, with cause and date of origin; and also a description of the present condition.

G.S.W. head. 17-9-18 Scar 1 inch long. Said has been nervous like shell shock for some times after. Feeling completely normal since 2 months.
Urine analysis. S.G. 1020
reaction acid.
albumine, nil.
Sugar, nil.

A.D.M.S. HEADQUARTERS CANADIAN TROOPS, FEB 1919 WITLEY, SURREY.

(If space is insufficient, continue on back of form.)

[OVER]

Attestation papers of Tracey Harley Archer | 328989 © Government of Canada. Reproduced with permission of Library and Archives Canada (2024). Library and Archives Canada / Canadian Expeditionary Force (CEF) / Acc. 1992–93/166, Box 210–30

of thousands of men must go on for many years," he said. "Many of you are critical of nervous and unsteady returned soldiers. My friends, had you to go through the shot and shell, the mud and blood of the Great War, you might be in a worse state."[177]

We now know that Davidson was suffering from post-traumatic stress disorder, but at the time, the psychological effects of the Great War were not well understood. Attitudes seem to range from understanding that it was a mental illness caused by the impact of war to viewing soldiers with PTSD as cowards who just needed to snap out of it.

Jonathan Scotland is a historian who studied soldier suicide in World War I for his dissertation at Western University in 2014. He says that initially, at least, people were understanding of mental health issues in returned soldiers, but they became less accepting as more veterans came back from the war and couldn't assimilate back into society. Scotland's research found that the suicide rate in returned men ranged from two to four times as high as civilians of the same age group. In Davidson's case, he told me, there were multiple reasons that might explain his suicide. "Is it the *Empress* going down? Is it a shrapnel wound to the head? Is it the loss of his job or just difficulty with life? Who knows."

Tracey Archer was close in age to Davidson. He survived the sinking of the *Empress* but lost his wife and baby boy. He also enlisted in the war, spent a considerable stretch overseas, and took a shot to the head. Unlike Davidson's military records, which contain no mention of mental illness, Archer's personnel file states that he experienced nervousness and shell shock. But, by the time he was discharged in 1919, he was considered mentally and physically healthy. Archer remarried, had two children, and lived to the age of eighty-six.

"And that's the difficulty of working with veteran stories," says Scotland. "They are as different as the individual. The way they came to terms with the war, if they ever did, was unique."

16. Arthur Delamont's Musical Legacy

WHILE MANY OF THE *Empress*'s survivors went on to make their mark through their heroism during the war, their work, or their families, Arthur Delamont's musical legacy continues through the hundreds of boys he taught over five decades, their successes, and the importance placed on musical education in schools.

Arthur was born into a musical family. His father, John, worked as a leather tanner and volunteered with the local fire brigade in Hereford, England, but his passion was music, and he played bass horn in the Salvation Army band. When in 1909 the Army put a call out for bandsmen willing to immigrate to Western Canada, the Delamonts chose Moose Jaw, Saskatchewan, which at that time had a population of around twelve thousand.

It wasn't the Delamonts' first time in Canada. They had immigrated in 1883 to Oxford, Ontario, where Elizabeth (Lizzie), their oldest child, was born, but soon afterward, they moved back to Hereford. By 1909 they had eight children, and all five Delamont boys learned to play a musical instrument at a young age. Five years later, John and his two sons, Leonard and Arthur, were chosen to play in the staff band at the National Congress in England. John's wife, Seraphine, and his daughter, Lizzie, decided to come along, and the family booked third-class passage on the *Empress of Ireland*.

Arthur Delamont playing in vaudeville at the Pantages Theatre in Vancouver, 1922 | Courtesy of Warfleet Press, Delamont Library, Metro Guides

After the sinking, Lizzie, ill and still deeply traumatized, returned to Moose Jaw.* John, Seraphine, and Arthur had a change of heart and continued to London on the *Empress*'s sister ship, the *Empress of Britain*.†

THE DELAMONTS MOVE TO VANCOUVER

After returning to Moose Jaw in July 1914, twenty-two-year-old Arthur Delamont spent most of his time playing in the local theatre's orchestra pit and racing motorbikes. He fell in love and married Lillie Krantz in 1916, and two years later they had a son, Gordon. Arthur

* Lizzie continued with the Salvation Army and was promoted to captain in 1916. She married Arron Hultquist and lived in Saskatchewan until her death in 1972, aged 87.

† John played in the Moose Jaw Salvation Army band until 1922, when he and his wife moved to Toronto. Seraphine died on May 29, 1935, the twenty-first anniversary of the sinking of the *Empress*. John died exactly two weeks later. Both were aged 72 and are buried in Toronto's Mount Pleasant Cemetery opposite the Salvation Army's *Empress* memorial.

The house that Arthur Delamont built for his family is still standing on West 7th Avenue in Kitsilano, Vancouver, in 2024 | Eve Lazarus

moved his young family to Vancouver, which had a thriving theatre district and an active vaudeville scene. His daughter, Vera, was born in 1923, and by this time Arthur was running the Delamont Grocery store in Kitsilano and playing at the Strand and the Pantages Theatres at night. In 1925, he bought three lots in Kitsilano, built three houses, rented out two of them, and moved his family into a five-bedroom home that flanked the playground of General Gordon Elementary in Kitsilano.

The grocery business only lasted a couple of years, and by 1927 vaudeville was nearing the end of its life. Gordon was learning the trumpet, and Arthur was looking for something new. He talked to the school principal about starting a boys' band, then immediately began preparing the boys to play at a welcome-home parade for Olympic champion runner Percy Williams in June 1928.

The Kitsilano Boys' Band parading down Burrard Street in Vancouver, circa 1946 | *City of Vancouver Archives (BC)*, AM303-S2 CVA 294-063

BOYS' BAND WINS CANADIAN CHAMPIONSHIP

Three years later, the boys' band won the Canadian Championship at the Toronto Exhibition. The legendary Dal Richards joined in 1933. The band was now open to boys from any school and was renamed the Kitsilano Boys' Band, after the area of Vancouver where Arthur Delamont lived. Richards was taking music lessons for clarinet and saxophone after losing his eye in a slingshot mishap, and his mother took him to meet Delamont. "He was a tough bird, I'll tell you. He'd drill us and drill us until the kids playing the horns thought they couldn't play another note. Then he'd ask us, please, if we'd go through it all one more time, just to get it right," Richards told *Vancouver Sun* columnist Denny Boyd. "He wanted perfect posture, rigid concentration on the sheet music, and no jacking about. He'd tell his kids: 'If your nose runs while you're playing, don't stop to wipe it, let it run and keep playing.'"[178] To his boys, he was a formidable mentor—crusty, impatient, and dedicated.

In August 1933, forty-three boys, including Dal Richards, travelled to the Chicago World's Fair in a private railcar that was taken off the main track and shunted to the side so the boys could stop and play concerts in Moose Jaw, Calgary, and Banff. Delamont's boys won World's Champion Junior Band at the Fair.

A postcard sold by the Kitsilano Boys' Band, 1953 | City of Vancouver Archives (BC), AM1052 P-423

Delamont funded his trips partly by charging the boys twenty-five cents for music lessons, charging venues a performance fee when he could, and selling postcards of photos of the boys standing in front of Vancouver City Hall or the Vancouver law courts. The boys sold the postcards at intermission for ten cents each.

In 1936, Delamont and his boys chalked up another win at the Crystal Palace National Festival in London, England. "Whirling the baton as 'drum major' was Vera Delamont, the pretty young daughter of Arthur Delamont, the only girl member of the band."[179] The reporter was being generous—Delamont did not allow girls in his band. While his daughter, Vera, played percussion, her role was more that of cheerleader or mascot.

WORLD WAR II

In the summer of 1939, Delamont took fifty boys on a tour of England, planning to return at the end of September. Instead, war broke out, and Delamont immediately made arrangements to return to Canada. He was told that some could travel immediately on the *Athenia* but the rest would have to wait for a later ship. He chose to have the band wait and travel together on the *Empress of Britain*.*

Delamont sent a telegram to the boys' parents, telling them that he was bringing the boys home early, but it was an anxious week for families; the day after the boys left England on the *Empress of Britain*, 125 people died when the *Athenia* was torpedoed by a German U-boat.

After learning the fate of the *Athenia*, the *Empress of Britain* went dark, and the captain started evasive movements. Carson Manzer,

---

* This was the second *Empress of Britain*, built in the late 1920s. The original *Empress of Britain*, sister ship to the *Empress of Ireland*, was renamed the *Montroyal* in 1924. By the late 1920s, she was sold as scrap in Stavanger to a Norwegian recycling company, but before she was completely demolished, the first-class smoking room was sold to the Sola Strand Hotel, who turned it into a dining room. In 1937, the bell from the *Empress/Montroyal* was given to the Hausken Cemetery in Rennesøy, about 20 km (12.5 miles) from Stavanger, where it remains to this day.

one of Delamont's boys, wrote a letter to the *Province* when the ship reached Canadian soil.

> We were genuinely scared. Nobody except the captain knew our exact position. The ship's wireless could receive messages but couldn't send them. We received news that the *Athenia* had been sunk, and that didn't help our spirits any. We started to zigzag. Every eight minutes we made a complete turn to avoid torpedoes. The boat was overcrowded with 500 extra on board. They had set up beds in tennis courts and in the nursery.[180]

Vancouver billionaire Jimmy Pattison joined Delamont's band during the years of World War II. Pattison told the *Vancouver Sun*'s Denny Boyd, "He was so tough. I still remember very clearly when the trumpet player in the next chair to me was having problems at a rehearsal in a classroom. Mr. Delamont got one of those quart bottles of ink that were used to fill the inkwells. While we were still playing, he walked over and very carefully poured the entire bottle down the bell on the kid's horn. He certainly made his point."[181]

AFTER THE WAR

Vancouver architect Bing Thom joined Delamont's band in the early 1950s, shortly after his family arrived from Hong Kong. Thom was twelve and barely spoke English when his mother took him and his two older brothers to meet Delamont. Thom told author Christopher Best (who joined the band in the 1960s) that Delamont stuck a clarinet in Thom's mouth and said, "Blow!" Delamont's discipline was so effective that even as an adult, Thom still woke up in a cold sweat a couple of times a year, terrified that he'd forgotten his instrument or that his socks didn't match. Thom said that Delamont was a scary guy, with his shock of white hair and piercing blue eyes. "We were all living in fear. Sometimes he would single you out and tell you to play in front of everybody else. If you played badly or squeaked, he would give you this look or hit you on the head with his baton or a rolled-up newspaper."[182] Thom said the three biggest influences in his life were Arthur Delamont, Arthur Erickson, and the Maharishi Mahesh Yogi.

Delamont held the first reunion concert in 1963, on the band's thirty-fifth anniversary. The reunion coincided with Delamont's seventy-first birthday, and among the four hundred "boys" who came to play that night at the Queen Elizabeth Theatre were a Benedictine monk from Mission, BC, who played bass drum and a chemist with Shell who flew in from Texas.[183]

Christopher Best has written six books on Delamont's boys' band. He told me that he'd gone on three European trips with "Mr. D" to play in music festivals and later interviewed 160 former band members. "From a social point of view, what he did is very important," said

Arthur Delamont rehearsing with his alumni band in a church at 67th and Hudson, Vancouver, 1976 | John Denniston

Best. "The example he set travelling with his boys across Canada by train in the 1930s, '40s, and '50s made everyone want to have a youth band like his. His band became the example of what can be accomplished, and it got instrumental music onto the curriculum of public schools across Canada."

While Delamont remained connected to the Salvation Army, his first love was Freemasonry. So, it was fitting that he died at the age of ninety on September 11, 1982, at the Meridian Lodge after making a presentation to a fellow Mason. Mr. D was given a musical farewell at the Kitsilano United Church, his baton and coronet resting on his coffin.[184]

"I would say the almost-death scenario of surviving the *Empress* disaster drove him to succeed and not let anything get in his way, and that was exactly what he was like," said Best. "Headstrong, single-minded of purpose, he wouldn't listen to anyone else, and the music always came first. After the disaster, what does he do? He assembled a band made up of neighbourhood boys who had never played a note before and turned them into a world-class organization by marching them through the provincial, national, and world band competitions and winning them all. His boys grew up to fill the seats of orchestras, bands, and concert halls all across Canada. They were the who's who of the Canadian music industry."

Arthur Delamont was named Vancouver's Good Citizen of the Year in 1946 and became a Member of the Order of Canada in 1979. Delamont Park at 7th Avenue and Arbutus Street in Kitsilano was named after him in 1980. Delamont was posthumously inducted into the BC Entertainment Hall of Fame in 1994. He is buried at the Masonic Cemetery in Burnaby, BC.

17. Women and Children

SHARON BRITZ OF LADNER, BC, sent me an email in June 2024. She'd heard that I was writing a book about the *Empress of Ireland* and wanted to tell me about her personal connection to one of the passengers.

Margret Heavey, a twenty-six-year-old Irish lass, immigrated to Canada in 1911. She was the cook at Camp 103 just outside Duncan, on Vancouver Island—the only woman working on the Canadian National Railway grade between Alberni and Cowichan Lake. There she met her husband, Hugh Potts, and they were married in Vancouver two years later. Hugh, or Hughie, as he was known in the family, was Sharon's grandfather's brother from Cheshire, England.

Margret Heavey Potts was pregnant with their first child and returning to her family in Ireland via the *Empress* to have her baby. As Sharon pointed out, it was common practice for women to return to their country of birth to have their children.

"Margret's pregnancy was the prime reason for her being on the ship," said Sharon. "My grandfather and my mum said that Hughie was never the same after losing her and his unborn child. He was still very distraught two years later and enlisted in the Canadian Overseas Expeditionary Force in 1916."

Margret Potts certainly wasn't the only pregnant woman on the *Empress* travelling back to her family and country of birth to have her baby. There were women in all three classes who were either travelling alone or with small children. This wasn't surprising, as at the turn of the century, infant mortality was at a crisis high in Canada, with Montreal having the highest death rate in North America: one in four children there died before the age of one.[185]

WOMEN AND CHILDREN FIRST

When it came to abandoning ship, the idea of "women and children first" became engrained in our culture after the *Titanic*. In that tragedy, Captain Edward Smith employed what was known as the Birkenhead drill, an unofficial code of conduct that was adopted after a British troopship called the *Birkenhead* sank off the coast of South Africa in 1852. Because there were few lifeboats available, two dozen women and children were given priority, and all of them were saved. Captain Smith had reportedly threatened to shoot any man who took a seat in a lifeboat away from a woman or a child. Because of Smith, who went down with the *Titanic*, more than 70 percent of the women and half of the children survived compared to only one in five men.

Women and children first is not a maritime law, and it wasn't applied on the *Empress*. This was typical, say Mikael Elinder and Oscar Erixson in a 2012 study of eighteen shipwrecks, including the *Titanic*, the *Lusitania*, and the *Empress of Ireland*.[186] The authors point out that when this unwritten law was not applied, a ship's crew had the highest survival rate, followed by the captain and then the male passengers, and lastly, women and then children. This was particularly evident before World War I, when men learned to swim more often than women, wore much less restrictive clothing, and had the physical strength to move quickly through congested and listing stairs and corridors. The *Empress* crew had the survival advantage because they were familiar with the layout of the ship and had emergency training, and about half were on shift at the time of the collision.

Margaret Greenaway, circa 1950 | Courtesy of Denise Reynolds

MARGARET GREENAWAY

Margaret Dalzell Greenaway, the twenty-nine-year-old Salvation Army bride, was one of only fifteen women from second class to survive the sinking. Denise Reynolds was only eight when her grandmother died but remembers her grandparents' visits and spending time at their house in Toronto. Margaret's father was a lighthouse keeper at Swallowtail Lighthouse on Grand Manan, a remote island in the Bay of Fundy, off the coast of New Brunswick. To get to the school on the main part of the island, Margaret and her eleven siblings had to cross a rope bridge that was strung up between high cliffs and dangled over unpredictable waters. Margaret, at just five foot two, was small but feisty. "My sisters and I think her harsh upbringing must have helped her to cope during the collision and afterward," Denise says.

Margaret joined the Salvation Army in 1903 and had a ten-year career as an officer, serving in Nova Scotia, New Brunswick, Quebec, and finally in Toronto, where she met and married Tom Greenaway. Tom spent most of his working life in the human resources department of Bell Canada. He never returned to his native England, but Margaret made the trip in 1950 as a convention delegate for the Women's Christian Temperance Union, where she served as provincial president.

What Denise remembers most about her grandmother was that she had long dark hair that she wore pinned up on her head, that she smelled of lavender, and that she was always smiling. "She was always dressed in a skirt and blouse or dress. In the colder weather, she would wear a real fox collar, and the fox head had caramel-coloured beady eyes," says Denise. "After she passed away, the collar found its way into my playclothes box."

Denise was always aware of her family's connection to the *Empress of Ireland* tragedy, but it wasn't until after her father's death that she found Margaret's letter, with details of the final minutes aboard the ship and their rescue, and realized its significance to the story of the *Empress*.

Margaret and Tom Greenaway died in 1954 within a few months of each other. They are buried in Toronto's Mount Pleasant Cemetery.

Out of the 139 children under the age of thirteen aboard the *Empress*, only three survived: in first class, ten-year-old Helen O'Hara, and in second class, eight-year-old Florrie Barbour and seven-year-old Grace Hanagan. All of the 103 children travelling in third class died.*

And, although Helen, Florrie, and Grace survived, all three suffered terrible losses. Helen lost her father, Florrie lost her mother and her younger sister, and Grace, an only child, was orphaned.

---

* For a full list of the children aboard the *Empress of Ireland*, see Appendix 1.

HELEN O'HARA

Helen O'Hara had been travelling to England with her parents and their maid, Alice Brown. Hours after her rescue, Helen told a reporter that she had been separated from her father in the water, but she could swim. She found a piece of wood to hang on to until she was taken into a rescue boat. She was reunited with her mother, May, in Rimouski.

For years after the sinking, Helen's name was linked to public service announcements in newspapers about the importance of learning to swim. Health problems dogged her throughout her short life, and after the tragedy, Helen and her older sister, fourteen-year-old Kathleen, who had stayed behind in Toronto, spent the Canadian winters with May in Long Beach, California.

In April 1920, the O'Haras were staying at Ferry Apartments and making plans to head home to Toronto when sixteen-year-old Helen died. Her death certificate notes cause of death as "myocarditis acute, following menorrhagia, extensive," with renal tuberculosis as a contributing factor. In layman's language, this means her heart was damaged, possibly by a viral infection, and she had heavy and prolonged menstrual bleeding and tuberculosis of the kidney.

GRACE HANAGAN

Grace had been travelling on the *Empress* with her father, Ted Hanagan, the Salvation Army bandmaster, and her mother, Edith. They would be attending the Congress and planned to holiday in England afterward. Instead, Grace returned to Toronto to live with her grandparents and later, her uncle John and his wife, Annie.

Grace married Maurice Martyn, a customs and excise officer, in 1929, and they had a son, Gordon, who became a doctor in St. Catharines, Ontario.

Grace Martyn (Hanagan), 78, talking to the media on the seventy-first anniversary of the Empress of Ireland *sinking | Canadian Press*

Over the years, Grace stayed in touch with other survivors from the *Empress* until, one by one, they died, leaving only Ronald Ferguson, the English marconi operator.

In May 1987, Grace told a reporter that the memories of the tragedy never got easier. For years afterward, she had nightmares, and just hearing water running into the bathtub would send her into a panic attack, remembering being sucked down into the icy-cold St. Lawrence River in the middle of the night. Maurice managed to talk her into taking a cruise from Alaska to Vancouver in 1981—it was the first time she had been on a boat in sixty-seven years. She felt trapped in their windowless cabin, so they moved to an outside cabin with a window. But still, she found it hard to sleep.

Maurice died in February 1993. Alone for the first time at the memorial service in May of that year, Grace told a reporter that she'd had a happy life.[187*]

* Grace died in 1995, aged 88, two weeks before the annual May memorial service to honour her parents and all the others who died on the *Empress of Ireland*.

TOP: *Ernie Green looks on as Grace Martyn (Hanagan) places a wreath on the memorial for the thirty-sixth anniversary of the wreck at Mount Pleasant Cemetery in Toronto in 1950. Green and Martyn were the only members of their families to survive.* BOTTOM: *Grace Martyn attends the May memorial service in Toronto in 1985 | Used by permission of the Salvation Army Canada and Bermuda Archives (Toronto,* ON*), photos 73540 & 82927*

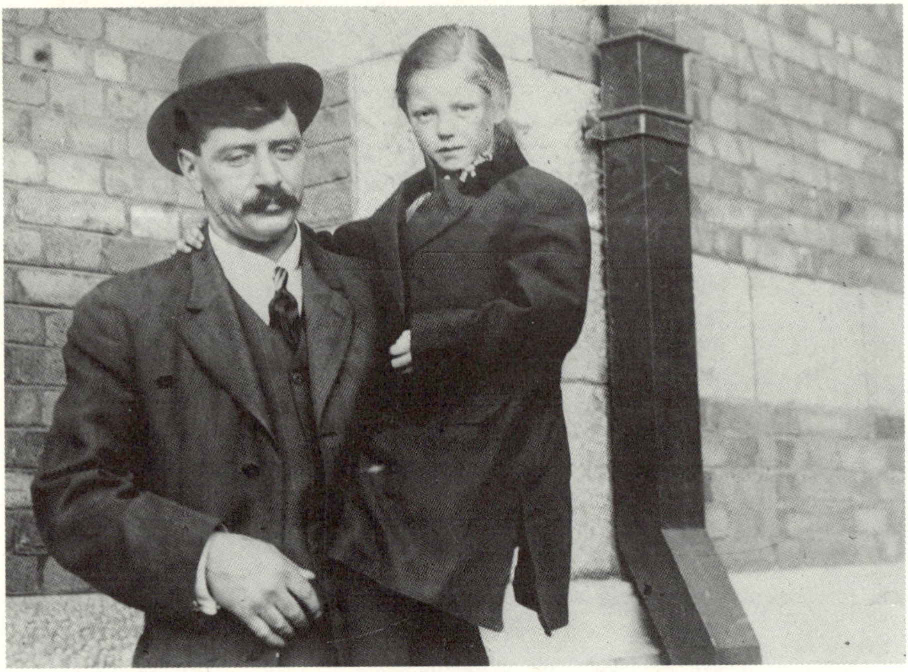

Robert Crellin with Florrie Barbour outside the Château Frontenac, June 1914 | *Library of Congress (Washington, DC), LC-B2-3079-7*

FLORRIE BARBOUR

For a brief time after the sinking, Florrie Barbour became the darling of the media. Her picture appeared in newspapers all over the world, and offers to adopt her poured in.

Robert Crellin, the thirty-five-year-old miner from Silverton, BC, who saved her, had been engaged to Florrie's mother and wanted guardianship of her, but the McQuillans, a wealthy Quebec family, had taken her in and were keen to adopt. Crellin believed that they would give her a better life than he could provide, and so he left for England on the *Alsatian*. As far as he was aware, Florrie stayed in Canada. What Crellin did not know was that after he left, a custody dispute broke out between Florrie's two sets of grandparents. On July 14, 1914, Florrie was sent to live with her paternal grandparents in Cumberland, England, not far from where Crellin was staying in Whitehaven.

It's not known whether Crellin saw Florrie while he was on leave from the war or if he even knew that she lived in England, but Florrie's 1964 memoir indicates that he did. She wrote that, after the war, Crellin married and returned to Canada. "No one will ever know how much I wanted to go back with him, to where I had so many happy memories, but again it was not meant to be."[188]

Florrie lived with her grandmother until her grandmother's death, then went to live with her uncle and his wife until she was twenty-four. She married Leonard Harker at the start of the Great Depression. In August 1964, half a century after the sinking of the *Empress of Ireland*, Florrie was finally able to make her first trip back to Canada. She arrived in Quebec just weeks after divers rediscovered the wreck.

Florrie reconnected with her school friends in British Columbia. She visited her father's and Crellin's graves at the cemetery in New Denver, the mine where her father had worked, and her first home at Three Forks, now a ghost town. Each of the three different houses the family had lived in at Silverton were still standing. "The last one we left when coming to England was still there with people living in it," wrote Florrie. "My heart ached such a lot when I looked at them and I wondered what they would have been like for me if we had never set sail on the *Empress of Ireland* ... I have often wondered what happened to my sister and my mother. Maybe they had a swift death. I hope so. They found my mother's body, and she was buried in Quebec, but my sister and Billy [Barry] were never found."

Crellin's family—his two sons and his sister—still lived in New Denver. Florrie met Crellin's son, Ellison, who showed her the watch his father had had in his pocket the night of the shipwreck.* "I don't

* Robert Crellin's watch was passed down to his son, Ellison, and now belongs to his grandson, who lives in British Columbia.

know who were the most excited—we had lots to talk about. I thought Ellison looked very much like Uncle Bob," Florrie wrote.[189]

Soon after her three-week stay in Canada, Florrie wrote a memoir, which she dedicated to Robert Crellin and hoped to have published. She planned to use the money from its sales to return to Silverton to live. The memoir exists as twenty-four handwritten pages in an elementary school exercise book.

Florrie did not get her wish. Her book wasn't published, and she never returned to Canada.[190]

18. Homesteading and Immigration

IT'S THE MORNING OF May 28, 2024, exactly 110 years to the day that the *Empress of Ireland* left for her final voyage down the St. Lawrence River. I'll be flying to Quebec City tomorrow, but first I'm stopping over in Edmonton and making the two-hour drive to Stettler, Alberta.

A few weeks ago, Karen Wahlund, the manager of the Stettler Town and Country Museum, sent me information about Theo Bartschi, one of the town's pioneers and one of only two Albertans to survive the sinking. In the early 1990s, the museum received an old trunk that had belonged to Bartschi, but it hadn't been processed and was still in storage. I was on my way to help with that and, with any luck, tell a whole new story.

Whenever lost history is found or resurfaces, there's always a hope that we'll find personal letters, even a diary. But, while the contents of Bartschi's trunk were intriguing, most of the documents concerned his land holdings, his dealings with the CPR, and tourism information from the 1920s that he kept for some reason. I was excited to find some photos of Bartschi and his older brother, Chris, a pastry chef at Carl Stettler's National Hotel who was lost on the *Empress*. Most interesting were several interviews with Bartschi published in the *Stettler Independent*, which gave me insight into his personality and his life.

During my visit to Stettler, Wahlund connected me with Stefan Kiener from Burgdorf, Switzerland, a fourth-generation descendant

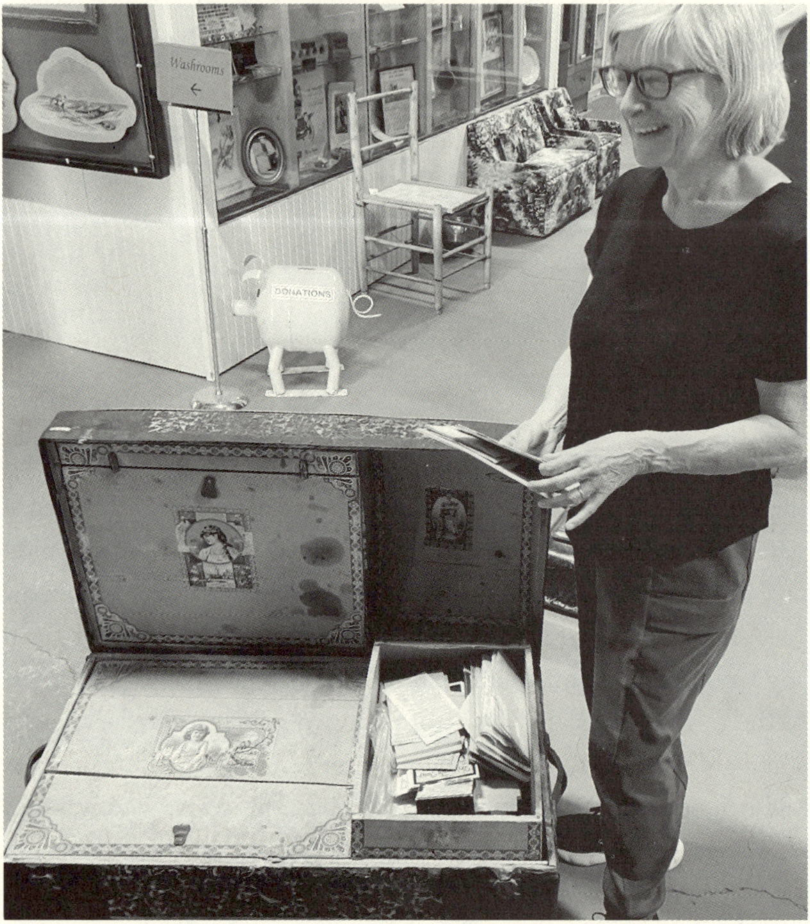

Eve Lazarus at the Stettler Town and Country Museum in 2024, opening the chest of documents and photos that belonged to Theo Bartschi | Mike Dunn

of Theo Bartschi. Kiener's great-uncle, Hans Ermel, visited Bartschi on his first trip to Canada in 1974. Ermel was born in 1941 and still lives in Langnau im Emmental in Switzerland.

Ermel had more photos and articles about Bartschi, as well as a typed transcript from a tape-recorded 1974 interview where Bartschi chatted to fellow Swiss immigrant Alfred Stecher. Bartschi told him about his life before Canada, the sinking of the *Empress*, his return to Stettler, and his first visit back to Switzerland in 1919.

Theo Bartschi playing the accordion | Stettler Town and Country Museum (AB)

THEO BARTSCHI

In 1902, twenty-one-year-old Theo Bartschi was reading his local newspaper when an ad caught his attention. Carl Stettler, a man he knew from their village outside Berne, Switzerland, was a land agent for the CPR, and he was looking for people interested in forming a Swiss colony in Alberta on land formerly occupied by the Blackfoot and the Cree.* Stettler had named the colony Blumenau.† Bartschi was intrigued by Stettler's slogan—"Every Swiss must have his own nesting place"—and his descriptions of the fertile prairie lands available cheaply to immigrants to Canada.

The following spring, Theo and Chris Bartschi and two other men from their village were on their way to Canada.

Theo Bartschi worked on a survey gang and spent the summer of 1903 scouting for a property. The homestead land had been taken

* Stettler is situated on Treaty 7 territory, the traditional lands of First Nations people and also home of the Métis Nation Region 3.

† *Blumenau* is a German word meaning "flowery field."

up, and he and Chris each bought 160 acres in Botha from the CPR. They built log shacks and lived off rabbits in the summer and prairie chickens in the winter. The winter of 1903 was the coldest on record. Feed was scarce, and many cattle died of starvation.

Stettler was incorporated in 1906; Carl Stettler became its namesake and the town's first postmaster. In 1908, fire destroyed more than twenty businesses, but within a year, Stettler was rebuilt to twice its original size.

In 1962, Theo Bartschi was interviewed by Bill Wuest, the son of one of the original pioneers from Switzerland. Wuest asked Bartschi, now eighty-one years old, why these people, including his own parents, had left their homes in Switzerland for Canada, a country they knew little about. Carl Stettler was the son of a tanner, another pioneer worked in a watch factory, and a couple were tradesmen. None had any real knowledge of farming.

Bartschi told Wuest that Switzerland could support only so many people. "The oldest son usually inherited his father's business or land, a second or third son might become a tradesman, a craftsman, even a doctor or lawyer. But inevitably some younger boy would leave his hometown out of sheer boredom or because of some not so innocent misdemeanour."[191] Carl Stettler, he said, had been in love with a local girl, the daughter of the wealthiest man in town. But because he was the son of a tanner, he was not allowed to marry her, and his heart was broken when a more socially suitable match was made.[192]

In 1914 the Bartschi brothers decided to return to Switzerland on the *Empress of Ireland* to marry and bring their brides back to Stettler. But instead, Theo Bartschi lost almost everything in the wreck, and Chris lost his life. "Chris and I carried all our cash in waistbelts and mine was torn away with other parts of my clothing. All I could recover was the $300 we had in American Express cheques," Bartschi said. Chris's body was never recovered.

Before Bartschi could plan another trip to Switzerland, war broke out. He stayed in Stettler. Financially, he was in dire straits, and a few of his friends reached out to Richard Bennett, then MP for Calgary, explaining his circumstances. Bennett met with Thomas Shaughnessy, president of the CPR, who said he would do what he could. Bartschi still owed about eight hundred dollars on his land. According to an article in the *Stettler Independent*, Shaughnessy forgave the loan and gave Bartschi clear title.*[193]

Bartschi leased out his farm in 1916 and went searching for a different kind of adventure. He worked as a gardener at the Chateau Lake Louise and was put in charge of flower displays. He became a mountain guide for a time and later worked in an underground electrical plant. From there he took up carpentry and went from job to job in various cities in Washington state and as far down the coast as San Diego.

When he was able to return to Switzerland in 1919, Bartschi found that the woman he'd planned to marry had instead married a police officer and lived in Zurich. He returned briefly to Stettler, where the *Red Deer Advocate* wrongly reported that he had survived the sinking of the *Lusitania*. Then Bartschi returned to Lake Louise because, he said, it was the area most like his homeland. He ran a CPR boat in the summers and served customers in the Chateau.

Soon restless again, Bartschi spent a few years in Alaska before settling in Edmonton in 1925. He moved into a small apartment on the upper floor of the Arcade Building and started up an accordion repair and tuning shop.

In 1936, he and J. Alvin Tupper, a chartered accountant, bought a small bakery together. With Tupper as general manager and Bartschi as president, Sunland Biscuits quickly expanded into graham wafers, ginger snaps, and sandwiches, with distribution extending from

* Over $21,000 CAD in 2024.

Manitoba to British Columbia. In 1939, the company won a large contract to supply Canadian soldiers with hardtack, and the following year, they started an ice cream cone manufacturing company. Bartschi sold his interest in the business to his partner in 1945.

In April 1964, Bartschi took a train to Montreal to celebrate his eighty-third birthday. The following day, he boarded a Lufthansa plane to Zurich, where he told reporters that he intended to meet up with fellow survivor Walter Erzinger. The two men had made a pact that if both were still alive in fifty years, they would meet again in 1964.

Over the years, the Stettler town council discussed financing a memorial for Carl Stettler. In 1972, and as the last of the original settlers, Theo Bartschi, now under the care of the Canadian Institute for the Blind in Edmonton, offered to donate five thousand dollars. The memorial reads, "In memory of Carl Stettler and all his Swiss compatriots who settled the colony Blumenau April 1903 and the town of Stettler May 1905. Donor Theo Bartschi, Pioneer Settler."

Theo Bartschi died in 1976, aged 95. He is buried at Lake View Cemetery in Stettler.

Lakeview Cemetery in Stettler, 2024 | *Eve Lazarus*

COLONIZATION

Nothing on the Stettler memorial mentions the region's first inhabitants—the Indigenous peoples who occupied the Prairies and whose lives were intrinsically linked to the migration of the bison that clothed and fed them. Settlers wiped out the bison and brought disease. Those who survived were further victimized by legislation that used a policy of starvation to force Indigenous leaders to sign treaties that put their people on reserves. By 1883, the majority of Indigenous peoples were living on reserve land, under the control of the Department of Indian Affairs. Canada's Prairies had been cleared for European settlement.

HOMESTEADING IN SASKATCHEWAN

By the early 1890s, land agents were aggressively advertising all over Europe in hopes of attracting people adventurous enough or desperate enough to immigrate to Western Canada. The hook was free land—for a ten-dollar registration fee, they could own 160 acres of the Prairies. What the land agents glossed over was the difficulty of finding oxen and machinery to clear the land and materials to build houses and barns, the harsh winters, and the fact that crops didn't always materialize right away.

Land ownership in a new country looked very attractive to Peter Rask. Thirty years old in 1893, he was a trained stonemason and saw few prospects in his home in Jämtland, Sweden. While his father did own a large tract of land—almost sixteen thousand acres—it would all eventually be passed down to his eldest son—Peter's brother, Andrew.

Another draw for Peter Rask was that, in the 1880s, Scandinavians had established New Stockholm, Saskatchewan, the largest Swedish settlement in Canada at the time. These early settlers were known to help newcomers by giving them a place to stay and work while they

Poster enticing immigrants to Canada, 1890 | Library and Archives Canada (Ottawa, ON), C095320k

waited for their own land. Along with his sweetheart, Brita Hanson, Brita's brother and sister, and their families, Peter bought a ticket to Canada.

Peter and Brita married in November 1893, and their first daughter, Martha, was born the following year in New Stockholm. That spring, the family was living on their own land in a three-room log

Peter and Brita Rask | Courtesy of Rask family collection

cabin about 12 kilometres (7.4 miles) from Broadview, a town on the CPR mainline. Annie was born on the homestead in 1896.

"It was such a lovely home. Mother had a way, and Dad was a skilled person who could do almost anything," wrote Annie. The floors were covered with rugs made from a loom that Peter had built. Later, he added a kitchen at the back. "There were always lively discussions about current affairs, politics, religion, all sorts of topics every day, and it kept us a close-knit unit."[194]

The Rask family lived on the farm for almost a decade, but when it was time for Martha and Annie to start at Clifton, the little stone school in Percival that their father helped build, Peter and Brita

Students with their teacher, Miss Hedden, in front of Clifton School, 1908 (back row: Hilda Hawkes, Mabel Hawkes, Annie Rask, Clara Cope, Nancy Vickberg, Lillian Cope; front row: Esterh Vickberg, Pauline Norman, Hugo Rask, Martha Pearson, Emma Pearson, Ted Cope, Lewis Hawkes, Dick Vickberg, Bil Hawkes) | Provincial Archives of Saskatchewan (Regina, SK), R-A20963

thought the long trek along rough trails would be too much for the girls. They bought land that abutted the school grounds, and Peter became chair of the school board.

Peter developed severe asthma, which forced the family to give up farming and move into Broadview. He built stone houses and barns in and around the town. In winter, he cut ice from the lake south of the town and sold it to customers who used the melted ice to wash their clothes. In the summer months, he worked on the road gangs as a grader or hauled cinder from the CPR dump to spread on the roads around Broadview.

Peter's brother, Andrew, inherited his father's estate as expected, but when Andrew died in 1913, he left a third of the estate to his wife and the balance to Peter's seven children, who by then were aged between six and twenty. Peter made plans to leave for Sweden on the *Empress of Ireland* the following May—the first time he would have been back to Sweden since immigrating to Canada twenty-one years before.

After surviving the sinking of the *Empress of Ireland*, Peter returned to Broadview. World War I caused all travel plans to be put on hold, and he never did make it back to Sweden.

TOP: *train station in Broadview, Saskatchewan;* BOTTOM: *Main Street in Broadview, Saskatchewan | Courtesy of Glen Lundeen, prairie-towns.com*

The Rask family (back row: Alfred, Martha, Isabella, Annie; front row: Francis, Betty, Hugo) | Courtesy of Rask family collection

The following summer, Peter moved the family to the Northwood district, where he served on the school board and the municipal council and helped set up the Northwood Rural Telephone Company in 1919. His son Francis later wrote that one of the district's first Christmas concerts was held in their small house in 1916. "The day before, Dad went out to the bush and cut a small, well branched poplar tree. He made a stand for it and it was decorated with tinsel and wax candles. The house was packed full," said Francis. "Everything except the piano had been moved out for that one night."[195]

Peter Rask died from cancer in October 1923. "It was the first break in the family circle," said Annie. "Dad was only sixty and to us seemed so young, so vital, so interested in everything."[196] The funeral service was conducted by Reverend Dr. Hugh McKay, the same man who had officiated at Peter's wedding in 1893.

More than three million people immigrated to Canada between 1896 and 1914. Almost half of those immigrants settled in the cities, one in five worked in mines or for the railway, and the rest bought homesteads in Western Canada.[197]

From 1906 to 1914, the *Empress* carried more than 117,000 passengers between England and Canada. When dozens of news stories were printed in 2014 about the hundredth anniversary of the sinking, several articles noted that a million Canadians—roughly one in thirty-five of us—can trace their roots back to an ancestor who came to Canada on the *Empress*. As a relatively recent immigrant—I arrived in Vancouver from Melbourne, Australia, in the mid-1980s—in today's multicultural country, I find this number staggering. It's also difficult to fact check. Newspaper stories referenced the "federal government" as the source, and these numbers are repeated on the Canada's Historic Places website. I asked Steven Schwinghamer, historian at the Canadian Museum of Immigration in Halifax, about this, and he said that while the statistic is believable, it's impossible to verify. "Tracing the genealogies of more than 100,000 passengers is tricky," he wrote me in an email. "Similarly, a straight prediction based on normal family growth or averaging is difficult, as after the *Empress* sank came periods of very high levels of deportation and return by immigrants, and the impacts of deaths and mobilities around the world wars would frustrate many population models."

HOMESTEADING AFTER WWI

Tom Smart and his wife, Bessie, immigrated to Canada from Luton, Bedfordshire, in 1905 on the *Lady Champlain*. His immigration papers list him as a bricklayer headed to Winnipeg to take up farming. Their first child, Florence, was born in Teulon, Manitoba, in 1908. Gertrude was born in Prince Albert, Saskatchewan, in 1910, and Jessie was born in Shellbrook, Saskatchewan, in 1912. Soon after, the family returned to England. Their fourth daughter, Alice, was born in 1914.

Earlier that same year, Tom (thirty-six) and his older brother, Syd (forty-one), had come back to Canada to search for a place to settle. Tom was heading back to his family in England the following month when the *Empress* sank.

Tom and his family stayed in England during the war, while Syd enlisted, serving in England and France. Upon his discharge in 1918, Syd applied for a homesteading land grant under the Soldier Settlement Act. Joined by Tom and his family, he took up farming in Grimshaw, in Alberta's Peace River Country. The family including Syd homesteaded in a 12 × 16 foot (3.7 × 4.9 metre) log cabin with a sod roof; the girls slept in a tent until Tom was able to build an addition. In January 1919, George was born in the cabin.

Two years later, Gertrude (Gert) Smart joined her brothers in Canada. She made quite an impression in her huge English hat when she was collected by Jim Kennedy's taxi—a horse-drawn sleigh—from the Grimshaw train station. Gert bought more land, and the family expanded their holdings and their houses. Things were going quite well until 1929, when the Great Depression landed with full force.

Times were tough on the land. Tom sold their cattle. He moved the family into Immigration Hall and took janitor work at the hospital to keep the family going. He planted crops in the spring and eventually moved everyone back to the farm in 1931.

Because there was no Anglican church in the area, Reverend Potter would occasionally drive his horse and buggy to the Smarts' home and hold services there. Tom decided the town should have its own church; he donated four acres of land and helped to build the church and establish the Briarcliffe Cemetery. Back in England, Tom's brother, Harry, made a cross out of a wooden beam from a church that was being demolished and shipped it to Alberta. The last reverend of the church was hired in 1972.

Tom and Bessie Smart donated the land for Briarcliffe Cemetery and helped build the Anglican Church in 1931. Still standing in 2020, the stone structure in the foreground is a grave marker for the Smart family. | *Glen Bowe*

Gordon Zaichowsky has lived in the area for sixty years, the last twelve as caretaker for Briarcliffe Cemetery. He knew Tom's grandson, George—in fact, he gave a eulogy at George's funeral in 1999. He was the school bus driver when George's son, Tom (named for his grandfather), was in school. Tom, an RCMP officer, died in 2023.

According to the cemetery's burial records, Zaichowsky said, the first was Thomas F. Brown in September 1931. "A couple of farmers were measuring out the parcel of land for the church and this Tom Brown was going by with a team of horses." Brown told the farmers that if anything happened to him, he wanted to be buried in the northwest corner. "Well, lo and behold, three days later he was killed when something scared his horses, and his body is buried in that northwest corner."

Tom Smart's youngest daughter, twenty-three-year-old Alice, died in 1936 and is buried in the family plot of the cemetery. Tom's wife, Bessie, died in 1941. Tom left the farm to George and moved into Grimshaw, about 7 kilometres (4.5 miles) away. He couldn't quite face retirement, though, and became the caretaker of the curling rink, did some bricklaying and carpentry work, and turned his garden into a local showpiece, winning the 1951 competition for most beautiful home and grounds in Grimshaw. He died later that year at the age of seventy-five.

The watch that Tom Smart was wearing on May 29, 1914, which stopped at the exact moment he hit the water, has stayed in the Smart family.

19. Rediscovering the Empress

IN 1964—ON THE FIFTIETH anniversary of the sinking of the *Empress*, newspapers around the world ran stories about the tragedy.

One of those stories caught the attention of five divers from Gatineau and Montreal. Civil servants Andre Menard and Jean-Paul Fournier, salesman Fernand Bergeron, and factory workers and brothers Claude and Robert Villeneuve had never before heard of the *Empress*.

Their first challenge was to find her.

Since the CPR had renounced all rights to the wreck, divers could keep anything they managed to bring up to the surface as long as they declared their finds to the local Receiver of Wrecks. Rimouski resident and businessman Aubert Brillant, who owned Quebec Telephone, offered the divers the use of his yacht, *La Canadienne*, for their expedition. In return he would receive half of all the artifacts they brought up or half of their value when they were sold. Donald Tremblay from the Institut Maritime du Québec had the ship's original position from the 1914 Inquiry. They attached a cable to an anchor and dragged it around in circles until it hooked onto part of the wreck.

The *Empress* was officially rediscovered on July 17, 1964.

Those early dives were especially tough. Up until the early 1970s, only commercial divers and the military had access to drysuits, and wetsuits weren't made for cold water. A diver could quickly become

The 20 ton propeller salvaged from the Empress of Ireland *in 1968 | Site Historique Maritime de la Pointe-au-Père (Rimouski, QC), donated by Donald Tremblay*

hypothermic, even in the middle of summer, and the colder the water, the greater the risk. This meant that the divers could only stay down for short periods of time. Even so, the divers salvaged a 30 kilogram (66 pound) wooden pulley from the main deck on the first dive, and on subsequent dives they brought up the ship's telegraph and compass. Later they would bring up the brass bell from the navigation bridge with the ship's name on it and a plaque inscribed with "First Class Passengers Only."

Brillant financed a second expedition the following year to recover the 10 ton anchor from the ship's forward deck.

By 1968, the race to strip the *Empress* was well underway. This time Tremblay and a new group of divers were after one of the ship's bronze propellers. The propeller weighed 20 tons and measured over

Marconi operator Ronald Ferguson returned to the wreck site in 1980 | Canadian Press

6 metres (20 feet) in diameter. The salvage operation dynamited a hole in the stern and then towed the propeller to the dock at Rimouski. Along the way, the propeller struck bottom and lost one of its four blades on the river floor. With nowhere to display it, the rest of the propeller sold to a scrap dealer for $5,300.*

In 1971, Tremblay and three other divers were surprised to find that the ship's wheel from the wheelhouse was still intact. The team had to saw through the wheel shaft in order to raise it.

In 1980, the *Empress* received renewed attention when French ocean explorer and filmmaker Jacques Cousteau and his son, Jean-Michel, explored the St. Lawrence River on the *Calypso*. The expedition became a co-production between Cousteau and the

* Close to $47,000 CAD in 2024.

National Film Board of Canada. Several hundred people crowded together at the dock in Rimouski, waiting for the ship to return each evening. "Police had to be called to keep the crowds away so the twenty-seven-man crew (twenty-three French and four Americans) could get some sleep."[198] Accompanying the crew were Quebec diver Philippe Beaudry and Ronald Ferguson, eighty-four-year-old *Empress* survivor. Ferguson was the young marconi operator who calmly sent out the SOS moments before the power died on the night of the sinking.*

PHILIPPE BEAUDRY AND MIKE SOEGTROP

Philippe Beaudry made his first dive to the wreck in 1970. He became so obsessed with the *Empress* that he left his accountancy practice, moved to Rimouski, and opened a diving shop so that he could spend more time following his passion. He made more than six hundred dives to the *Empress* and, at one time, owned the largest private collection of artifacts brought up from the ship. His collection included everything from the ship's bell to dinner plates and champagne bottles, and he sold most of it to the Canadian Museum of History in 2012. Beaudry told a reporter that he had spent about half a million dollars on his collection. "It was an obsession. I was addicted to that work," he said. "The *Empress* is part of the story of Confederation."[199]

Mike Soegtrop made his first dive when he was just thirteen years old. By the early 1980s he was a diving instructor, a photographer, and the associate editor of Toronto-based *Diver Magazine*. He teamed up with Beaudry and made over twenty dives to the *Empress* while taking photos and gathering information for feature stories that would

* Ferguson was decorated for serving in the Royal Flying Corps during World War I. He joined the British Wireless Marine Service in 1927 and later became managing director of Marconi International Marine Communication Co. He received the Order of the Nile for managing Egypt's state broadcasting system during World War II. Ferguson retired in 1961 to Chelmsford, Essex, and died in 1985, aged 91.

A porthole from the Empress of Ireland, *2024* | *Eve Lazarus*

eventually run in both *Diver Magazine* and *Equinox* in 1984. "It's very gritty, very tough diving," Soegtrop told me. "And it's cold, not that pretty, and it's even more hazardous now."

Beaudry met with Salvationist survivor Bert Greenaway, who helped him to locate the storage compartment where the band instruments were kept on the ship. Greenaway had overseen their loading at the dock in Quebec City.* Soegtrop visited Grace (Hanagan) Martyn at her home in Kitchener, Ontario. Martyn was the youngest person to survive the *Empress*, and she was the last of the survivors when she died in 1995. Soegtrop told her that he and Beaudry would search

* Bert Greenaway married and had four children. He died in 1979, aged 89.

The 25 brass letters that spelled "EMPRESS OF IRELAND LIVERPOOL" salvaged from the wreck are now on display at the Site Historique Maritime de la Pointe-au-Père, 2024 | Eve Lazarus

for her father's baton on their upcoming dive. Unfortunately, of all the band instruments that went down with the ship, only a cornet was recovered.*

Soegtrop's prized possession taken from those days before the *Empress* was designated a heritage site was an 18 kilogram (40 pound) brass porthole. "It turns out that the number on the porthole is 171, the same as my address," he said. "You can imagine those poor people trying to squeeze through—only the thin ones could make it. It must have been very difficult." On one dive, Soegtrop said, what he thought were pottery shards turned out to be parts of human skulls. They were on display for a short time until Soegtrop lobbied to have them reinterred.

Soegtrop still dives with his wife and his children, but no longer to the *Empress*. He prefers warmer waters.

---

* The cornet was donated to the Salvation Army Heritage Centre in Toronto.

The 1990s produced the twenty-five brass letters spelling "EMPRESS OF IRELAND LIVERPOOL." Quebec divers Dany St-Cyr and Pierre Lepage, who died near the wreck a few years later, recovered the letters over a hundred dives. Twelve of the letters were still attached to the hull, while thirteen had fallen onto the riverbed floor. Each letter weighed up to 7 kilograms (15 pounds).

GUY D'ASTOUS

Guy D'Astous first dived to the wreck in 1989 and has been obsessed with the *Empress of Ireland* ever since. He shows me the tile he found on that first dive. "The tile from the kitchen is the very first artifact that I brought back from the wreck. I started with this and told myself that it would be nice to have a plate or a porthole."

D'Astous made a total of thirty-five dives to the *Empress* over the next decade, amassing a collection that includes cups and plates, champagne bottles, spoons, a model of the *Empress*, a passenger's top hat, a shoe, a gold walking stick, portholes, paintings, and thousands of documents, including photos, brochures, books, postcards, and letters.

He says that his most treasured possession from those dives is the memory. "The artifacts are very interesting, but it's not as touching as seeing the *Empress* with your own eyes for the first time. You hear about it, you see pictures, you hear the stories, but when you touch it with your hands and you see it with your own eyes, it's an amazing feeling."

His favourite artifact is the ship's phone, which he bought from Philippe Beaudry in the early 2000s. "Having an artifact that comes from the bridge is quite rare," he tells me. "The last order that Captain Kendall gave to the engine room was through that phone."

Amazingly, the phone still works.

CLOCKWISE FROM TOP LEFT: *Guy D'Astous holding a salvaged pot in front of some of his* Empress of Ireland *collection at his home in Montreal, 2024 | Dominique Guertin, Société d'Histoire du Bas-Canada (Beloeil, QC); artifacts brought up by diver Mark Reynolds, circa 1980 | Société d'Histoire du Bas-Canada (Beloeil, QC), Guy D'Astous collection; the telephone used on the bridge of the* Empress | *Guy D'Astous*

HISTORICAL DESIGNATION PUTS A STOP TO PILLAGING

Over the decades, the elements have weakened the structure of the ship, but it was two large commercial operations during the 1990s that led to the protection of the wreck. In 1993, commercial salvagers ripped out more than five thousand planks of teak decking to resell to yacht owners. Much of the metal underdecking came away with the teak decking, accelerating the corrosion process.

Then in 1998, a salvage operator invested tens of thousands of dollars in a plan to blast open the cargo hold and collect close to a million dollars' worth of nickel ingots. Experts warned that this would most likely destroy what remained of the wreck and scatter hundreds of skeletons into the St. Lawrence River. The prospect of desecrating the underwater cemetery was so upsetting to the families of the dead that the Salvation Army lobbied for legislation that would protect the remains of the victims.

In 1999, the *Empress of Ireland* was designated a site of historical and archaeological importance by the Government of Quebec. This put an end to for-profit and souvenir-hunting divers, the underwater equivalent of animal-trophy hunters.*

MODERN-DAY EXPLORERS

It's chilly on the St. Lawrence River, and Matt Mandziuk is already wearing his drysuit for the forty-five-minute boat trip out from Rimouski Harbour. Once at the wreck site, he inspects each piece of equipment and reviews the route that he plans to follow. The drysuit covers every part of his body, and that's important because the water temperature is cold; even in summer it varies from two to seven degrees Celsius. Two steel tanks and additional bottles of air, lighting, and lead weights to counteract the neoprene suit's buoyancy add up an extra 70 to 90 kilos (150 to 200 pounds) that Mandziuk needs to carry into the water.

At the beginning of the spring diving season, a marker is attached to the *Empress of Ireland* wreck by a rope at midship. Divers prefer to tackle the wreck at low tide, which can save them up to 4 metres (12 feet) in depth and valuable decompression time on the way back

---

* Thanks to the designation, removing objects from the wreck or the wreck site without an archaeological permit is strictly prohibited, and offenders can be prosecuted through the Cultural Property Act.

Matt Mandziuk after a dive to the Empress *wreck in 2014 | Matt Mandziuk*

up. Once in the water, it takes Mandziuk only a few minutes to follow the rope down to the wreck, stopping once at about the 9 metre (30 foot) mark to tie twin tanks to the line to use for decompression on the way back up to the surface.

When he reaches the *Empress*, Mandziuk will typically run a line from the wreck so that he can find his way out if visibility is bad. It's the equivalent of leaving breadcrumbs to find your way out of the forest, he says. "I had to pull a couple of guys out of there one year because they didn't run a line, and they got lost."

Mandziuk made his first dive to the *Empress of Ireland* in 2000, when he was twenty-one years old. He's the owner of Dan's Dive Shop in St. Catharines, Ontario, the business his father founded in 1974. He grew up hearing stories of the great wrecks—the *Titanic*, the *Lusitania*, and the *Empress of Ireland*. Because the *Empress* was the only one of the three ships in Canadian waters and accessible to scuba divers, when Mandziuk took over the business in the 1990s, he started reading about the ship, collecting deck plans, and talking to other divers who had made the descent. "Even though it's shallow, it's a very challenging dive. It's only 30 to 45 metres (100 to 150 feet) down, but you've got ripping fast currents, you've got low visibility, and you've got really cold water," he tells me. "As the tides change or the currents change, the personality of the wreck changes substantially as well. It can get darker and a little more ominous."

The wreck itself is 173.7 metres (570 feet) long by 19.8 metres (65 feet) wide and lies on her starboard side. Visibility can vary between 3 to 15 metres (10 to 50 feet), and the currents are strong and unpredictable.

Six divers have died over the years. The first was Edward Cossaboom in June 1914, a hard hat diver from New York hired by the CPR to bring up bodies from the wreck. It was his third dive of the day. He lost his footing and was swept off the bow and onto the river bottom by the current. In 1981, Hector Moissan, a twenty-nine-year-old welder and commercial diver, died of an air embolism. His body was recovered from the forward deck. Two divers from Quebec, Lisa Parent, forty-one, and Xavier Roblain, twenty-five, died in 1996. Parent drowned, while Roblain died from a burst lung during a visit to the dive site. Although Pierre Lepage, forty-six, was an experienced diver to the *Empress*, he died from decompression sickness at 45 metres (150 feet) in 2001. In August 2002, thirty-three-year-old Serge Cournoyer became disoriented while exploring the wreck and ran out of air. His body was recovered from inside the wreck later that day.

Fortunately, there have been no deaths since 2002. Equipment and lighting are brighter, neoprene suits are heated, and closed-circuit breathing apparatuses allow for longer dives and less decompression time. But the *Empress* is still the Mount Everest of Canadian diving. "It's definitely a tough dive, and it needs a lot of equipment," says Mandziuk.

Mike Babiski and Dany St-Cyr demonstrating 1914 hard hat diving gear in Rimouski, 2024 | Olivier Barthell

Mandziuk has made more than fifty dives to the *Empress*, sometimes taking out other divers for the first time. He calls these "tourist dives." Depending on the group, he may start at the top railing, which is a little forward of the gangway doors, and then go through to the grand stairway up the first-class deck. From there he can lead his group through the kitchen, the galley, the dining hall, and the bathrooms.

"We've usually got ambient light all the way down to about 20 metres (70 feet). From 20 to 25 metres (70 to 80 feet), it basically goes from day to night. It's like somebody turned off the light switch on you, and you have to let your eyes adjust."

Typically, Mandziuk books a charter boat for a week and makes around twelve dives. He limits each dive so the time spent on the bottom is no more than forty minutes. The longer he stays down there, the longer he will need to decompress on the way up. That can turn a forty-minute exploration of the wreck into seventy-five minutes in frigid water. Failure to do this could result in a lethal bout of the bends. Even with all the precautions he takes, Mandziuk has had a mild case of the bends a couple of times. "You can actually feel your body fizzing in a specific area. It's like somebody's pushing a nail into you."

Mandziuk explains the effects in terms that I can understand. Every 10 metres (33 feet) you descend is the equivalent to drinking one martini. "As you go down, the nitrogen increases so that at about 30 metres (100 feet) most divers are feeling the effect of three martinis," he tells me. After that, motor skills diminish, and you're at risk of blacking out. Some divers, he says, have switched to helium, a lighter, non-narcotic gas. But that's also risky for inexperienced divers. If a diver ascends too fast, the nitrogen and helium dissolved in the blood can cause injury and even death.

Over time, divers' breathing apparatuses have also impacted the wreck's integrity. "We are advised not to go in the wreck as much as

A buoy at the wreck site in 2019 indicates that it is a federally protected National Historic Site, for expert divers only | Eve Lazarus

we used to," Mandziuk says. "The bubbles have quite a bit of force to them. If I was above a diver exhaling bubbles, it could push me up 2 to 3 metres (5 to 10 feet), if not more. The bubbles from the diver can dislodge matter from the ceiling, and you get rust, so some of us have switched to breathers where there are less bubbles or no bubbles."

Over the years, salvagers have chiselled out the tiles in the kitchens and bathrooms and pillaged the faucets. They've also made off with portholes, bathroom sinks, showerheads, and unopened champagne bottles. "Kitchen stoves have been taken away. Anything that's not nailed down is gone," Mandziuk says. "The outside shell of the wreck is all still there, but the decks are sliding a little bit now. The fantail and everything on the stern still looks beautiful."

While much has been hauled out of the *Empress* and sold, given to museums, or taken as souvenirs, Mandziuk says there is still a lot down there, especially in the deepest part of the wreck. "Going through the cargo holds, I could still see dress shoes. I've seen remnants of bones, but not in a long time. I don't know if somebody brought them out or if they just leeched into the silt. It is a grave site."

At one time, the wreck would see around a hundred divers a year between June and September. Now it sees half that number, and divers need to book up to two years in advance. "Quebec has some great diving, but the *Empress* is definitely the crown jewel," Mandziuk says.

LOST MATERIALS RESURFACE

Sébastien Hudon is an art historian based in Quebec City who scouts auctions around the world searching for archival film and photographs related to his province. Hudon learned of the existence of a 1914 newsreel that featured some of the *Empress* survivors when he read a story in the *Kutne Reader*, a blog by former *Nelson Star* editor Greg Nesteroff in 2019. Nesteroff wrote about the lost footage and how unlikely it was ever to be found.

Nesteroff was thrilled when Hudon and Louis Pelletier, a film historian from Montreal, reached out to him the following year. Hudon had seen a description of an old film that mentioned the ship in an auction in London, England. He took a chance and bought the two-minute film. It took several months to prepare the delicate old film for digitization, but they succeeded, and it is now online. "When we finally saw what was on the film, it was amazing. We were very excited," Hudon tells me. "It was quite a long wait, but it was worth it."

The newsreel was shown around the world and turned shy Robert Crellin from Silverton, BC, into a hero and little Florrie Barbour, the girl he saved, into a celebrity. In the last ten seconds of the film,

Sébastien Hudon and Louis Pelletier holding the 1914 newsreel they bought unseen at an auction in London in 2020 | Courtesy of Sébastien Hudon

Crellin, a handsome man wearing a suit and hat and sporting a moustache, holds the newly orphaned eight-year-old in front of the Château Frontenac.

Hudon dug deeper into Florrie Barbour's life. He discovered that Crellin had been in love with Florrie's mother, Sebena, and that they planned to marry when they reached their hometown in the Cumbria region of England. "I came to be very emotionally involved in Florrie's story, and it still breaks my heart to know that she wasn't aware that Crellin was about to marry her mother. After rereading the whole story of her adoption and her diary, it seems likely that it was a secret kept from her," Hudon says.

In the fall of 2021, Hudon was searching eBay, an online auction site, when he noticed two photographs showing sailors carrying heavy equipment along a wharf. The writing on the back identified the site as the Gaspé Lighthouse in 1908. He sent the link to his friend, maritime historian David Saint-Pierre, who immediately recognized the Pointe-au-Père lighthouse and noticed that the sailors wore British Navy uniforms. "As soon as I saw the two photos, I knew that they showed the men carrying salvage equipment on the dock at Pointe-au-Père in June 1914," Saint-Pierre told me. "Only a few images of these operations have survived. These two photos were already exceptional."

Saint-Pierre bought the photos and noted that they had paper from an album still attached to them. He contacted the seller and found that she was dismantling a photo album found at a flea market. The album contained 525 photos taken between 1908 and 1917. "She had just started to take it apart to sell all the photos separately. My heart started racing. What was in this album had the potential to be a major discovery for the maritime history of Canada," said Saint-Pierre.

In September 2023, divers took a photo of a 2.4 metre (8 foot) tablelike structure that they had seen on the river floor near the *Empress*. They sent the photo to Saint-Pierre, who immediately identified it as the ship's compass platform. Saint-Pierre knew that divers had dropped it while attempting to remove it from the wreck in 1994. In fact, he has one of the eight brass fixtures that once secured the compass platform to the deck. The compass platform played a large role in the ship's navigation and its eventual demise, says Saint-Pierre. "[Captain Kendall] actually mentions (in his testimony at the Inquiry in 1914) that he was standing on that compass platform when he corrected the direction of the *Empress*. And that's where he first personally spotted the *Storstad*."

HEIRLOOMS

The story of the *Empress of Ireland* is far from over. I have no doubt that more artifacts currently held in private collections all over the world will eventually surface. Ephemera—everything from postcards to ticket stubs and posters to articles in long-defunct newspapers to menus to sheet music—is still out there in people's attics, waiting to be sold at future garage sales, in flea markets, and on eBay. Personal items such as Florrie Barbour's little ring and Martin Gill's pocket watch have been given to museums or passed down to grandchildren and great-grandchildren, along with their stories. Events such as the 100th anniversary in 2014 and the 110th, held at the Site Historique Maritime de la Pointe-au-Père, brought descendants of the passengers and the crew from the *Empress* and the *Storstad* to Rimouski. These descendants brought with them treasured letters, photos, and family stories that have been passed down through the generations. Many of these heirlooms have already been donated to museums and archives in towns and cities across Canada. These items expand our knowledge of the *Empress* and raise awareness of the shipwreck, while the passed-down stories of immigration and war, heroism and sacrifice, human endurance, and modern-day shipwreck hunters add to our understanding of Canada.

EPILOGUE
Honouring the Dead

IT'S SUNDAY, JUNE 2, 2024, and I'm in Rimouski for the 110th anniversary of the sinking of the *Empress of Ireland*. It's been almost five years since I first visited this small French Canadian city, took a Zodiac out to the wreck site, and decided to write this book.

This week's activities revolve around the Site Historique Maritime de la Pointe-au-Père, or in English, the *Empress of Ireland* Museum. I'm standing in the shadow of the 1909 lighthouse with a couple of dozen others, including seventeen members of the Salvation Army dressed in full uniform. They have come from different parts of Canada to conduct a memorial service later this morning.

Our group includes Ron and Donna Millar, the Salvation Army archivists who helped me on my visit to Toronto last September. There is Mike Babiski, a commercial diver from Niagara, Ontario, whose ancestor, Wasili Babiski, died in the sinking in 1914. I meet Marilyn Hurd, whose great uncle, Lieutenant Alfred Keith, was one of only twenty-eight Salvation Army members to survive.

We gather around David Saint-Pierre, former Rimouski resident, author, and marine historian, as he prepares to take us on a bus tour of the town.

Both Saint-Pierre and the Salvation Army are intrinsically tied to the *Empress of Ireland* and want more people to know about this Canadian tragedy. "This story doesn't belong to anyone in particular,"

LEFT: *David Saint-Pierre standing in front of the Site Historique Maritime de la Pointe-au-Père at the start of his tour of Rimouski, 2024* | *Eve Lazarus;* BELOW: *a postcard of Avenue de la Cathedrale in Rimouski, circa 1940* | *Public domain*

Saint-Pierre told me the first time we talked. "I don't think we should be protective. History is collective."

Saint-Pierre points out that while the ship is often referred to as the "forgotten *Empress*," the people of Rimouski have never forgotten, and neither have the Salvation Army. Salvationists call the tragedy "Black Friday." The entire upper echelon of their Canadian organization was wiped out in the sinking. It took the organization fifty-five years to rebuild the staff band.

Major Ron Millar is the director of archives for the Salvation Army in Toronto, and it's his and Donna's first trip to Rimouski. "For every single individual who journeyed on that fateful trip, lives were changed and families were altered in dramatic ways for all times," he tells me. "The *Empress* tragedy is the single most important event that shaped the history of the Salvation Army in Canada, and because of that, the connection with Rimouski, the museum here, and the people in this place will be forever bonded. And in the midst of the tragedy that caused it, that is something to celebrate and be thankful for."

QUEBEC CITY

I arrived in Quebec City on May 29, 2024, and posted a photo on Facebook of the St. Lawrence River taken from the balcony of the Hôtel Terrasse Dufferin. Saint-Pierre saw my photo and pinpointed the exact location where the *Empress* was moored 110 years before and from where it departed for its final voyage.

"Go to the Château Frontenac and take a minute to walk across the street toward the Basilica," he messaged me. "Two buildings there are important to the *Empress* story. The grey stone building is the old courthouse where the Inquiry was held. Just a few metres farther down, across the little square, you will see the back of the English cathedral where the main funeral was held just a few days after the sinking. This is the funeral where Captain Kendall was present, along

View of the St. Lawrence River from the Hôtel Terrasse Dufferin, 2024 | Eve Lazarus

with other surviving officers and Dr. Grant, who wrote to his wife that the CPR had new uniforms made for them for the occasion—a uniform he vowed he would never wear again."

For me, living in Vancouver, a city of steel and glass with little in the way of heritage, Quebec City is a powerful reminder that buildings can convey not only architectural history but also a sense of place and story.

Saint-Pierre suggested that I visit Rue de la Barricade in the area of Basse-Ville and look for a large squarish brick building, which once housed the Seaman's Institute. This was where a few crew members were signed on to the *Empress* the day before she sailed. These last-minute hires included three firemen: Edward Fitchett, Bernard Tumilty, and Henri Fournier, the only French Canadian on the crew and the only one of the three to survive. "Fitchett was a famous boxing champion," said Saint-Pierre. "Tumilty wrote to his brother complaining that the *Empress of Ireland* was a bad ship, and he couldn't wait to leave her—'All Scotland Road, you know.'"*

---

* Scotland Road was a working-class area near the Liverpool docks.

RIMOUSKI

Outside the museum at Pointe-au-Père, Saint-Pierre finishes his introduction, and we board the bus that will take us to Rimouski, about 9 kilometres (5.6 miles) away.

The first street on the way into town is Rue Marconi, named after the wireless station established there in 1906. John McWilliams, manager of the Great Northwestern Telegraph, lived there in 1914, and it was here the young telegraph operator tapped out an SOS in morse code (three short taps, three long taps, and then three short taps) on his doorbell in the middle of the night to convey that there was an emergency. His house is long gone. Presently it's a closed distillery.

Our first stop is the wharf at Rimouski where the 465 survivors and 212 bodies were brought by the *Lady Evelyn* and the *Eureka* early in the morning of May 29.

News of the disaster quickly spread through the town. Residents waited at the wharf with clothes and blankets and anything they could grab from their homes and their stores. They brought horses and buggies and carts to transport the freezing and traumatized survivors into town, just over a kilometre away. Many lined the street, shocked by the enormity of the tragedy and the massive loss of life.

The sick and injured were cared for by the Sisters of Mercy in a building next to the Catholic church. More than a hundred survivors were taken there, while others filled every available hotel and the homes of residents. "The people of Rimouski did what they could, but the town could not handle such a large situation," says Saint-Pierre.

Today, Rimouski is a city of around fifty thousand, but in 1914 it was a French Canadian lumber town with a little over three thousand residents.

Our bus stops right on the spot where a coal shed once stood. Immediately following the sinking, the shed was converted into a temporary morgue until the bodies could be transported to Quebec

City. Across the street, a grey building has replaced the school where the Inquest was held on the same day as the disaster.

We head into town along Rue St. Germain and pull up opposite the Catholic church in what was once the heart of Rimouski. It's the only building in the old part of town that wasn't destroyed by fire in 1950. Saint-Pierre points to the former location of the general store, which threw open its doors early that morning in 1914, generously clothing the survivors.

"There was no insurance at that time. If they gave out everything in their store, then that was the end of their business," says Saint-Pierre, adding that few store owners received any compensation from the CPR.

Marilyn Hurd and Mike Babiski pay their respects at the 110th anniversary memorial service while the Salvation Army staff band play in the background, June 2, 2024 | Eve Lazarus

We continue up the hill, past the old post office and the train station, to Rimouski's Catholic cemetery, and stop at the second monument for those who died in the sinking. Non-Catholics were buried in a plot of land purchased by the CPR at Pointe-au-Père. We go there now, taking the old road that hugs the curve of the river. Many of the stone houses and cottages are well over a hundred years old. In 1914 they would have had a view of the rescue boats at the wreck site.

The final resting place for the twenty-seven names inscribed on the stone and for sixty-eight unidentified bodies sits on the side of a hill looking out onto the St. Lawrence River. This is our last stop and the location of today's memorial service.

The names on the stone include second officer Roger Williams, who turned thirty the night he died, and twenty-five-year-old third officer Charles Moore, who was on the bridge at the time of the collision. There is Thomas Gerard, the bartender in the first-class smoking room who worked the maiden voyage and was on every sailing up until the last. And William "Billy" Thomas, a former pro soccer player. When his career began to fade, he became an assistant steward and team captain for the *Empress of Ireland*'s soccer team. There is also first-class stateroom steward Harold Jones, the thirty-four-year-old father of four who died when, instead of trying to save himself, he heroically went back down into the ship to help passengers get up on deck.

Marilyn Hurd and Mike Babiski stand at the memorial and pay their respects, while members of the Salvation Army band gather with their trumpets, trombones, cornets, and horns. The ceremony is a powerful tribute to the passengers and crew of the *Empress of Ireland*.

Every schoolchild knows the story of the *Titanic*, the luxury ocean liner that hit an iceberg and sank in 1912. So, why has the *Empress of Ireland* tragedy, which claimed even more passenger lives a little over two years later, failed to embed itself in our collective national consciousness?

Likely it's because, while the *Titanic* was filled with big names from the New York social register, the *Empress of Ireland* was a comfortable workhorse filled with ordinary Canadians. Most of those who drowned were in the third-class hold, and a large number of them were immigrants and labourers. It wasn't the maiden voyage, people didn't want to think that these ships were vulnerable, and in most people's minds, the *Empress* liners were synonymous with safety, reliability, and comfort. After colliding with a Norwegian collier, the *Empress* sank in just fourteen minutes, not nearly enough time to make a motion picture about it. It was also a matter of timing. Two months after the *Empress* sank in the St. Lawrence River, Archduke Ferdinand of Austria was assassinated, bringing about World War I and more fatalities and horror than anyone could imagine. Mostly, though, it was a Canadian story, and as Canadians, we like to bury the lede.

APPENDIX 1

Passenger List

The passenger information is compiled from several online sources, including National Museums Liverpool (www.liverpoolmuseums.org.uk), Peter Engberg-Klarström's website,* Ancestry.ca, and Family Search.org.

Empress of Ireland followers will notice that my numbers differ slightly from those found online. We may never know the names of everyone who travelled that night, or their places of permanent or intended residence. Hundreds of Europeans were aboard the *Empress*, and their names were frequently misspelled or anglicized by the CPR. I've identified different spellings wherever I could find them, but often just initials were used, and it's impossible to determine if those individuals were male or female. Even determining who was Canadian is subjective at best. If a person lived in a Canadian city for more than two years, I've considered them Canadian, but many immigrants were returning to their original homes, either by choice or through deportation.

Where I am unable to verify the person's last place of residence, I have listed the location where passage was booked, as well as their final destination (if known), using vague pre–World War I borders. After World War I, the geography of Europe changed dramatically and then changed again following World War II.

Children's names are in italics. I have defined children as those under the age of thirteen. Any child under the age of two is listed as an "infant," and if their age is unknown, they are listed as a "child."

---

* Peter's Empress of Ireland Page, https://empressofireland.wordpress.com/.

As imperfect as the list is, my hope is that it will give future researchers a place to start or at least an easy way to identify where I may have gone wrong.

Boldface indicates that the passenger was rescued.

FIRST CLASS

Out of the eighty-seven passengers travelling in first class, thirty-six survived and fifty-one were lost.

Name	Residence
Abbott, Frank Ernest	Toronto, ON
Abercrombie, John Robertson	London (England)
Adie, Marion Sharp	London (England)
Adie, Percy James	London (England)
Anderson, Albert Bruce	England
Averdieck, Percy Clifford	England
Barlow, Dr. Alfred Ernest	Montreal, QC
Barlow, Frances	Montreal, QC
Bloomfield, Lt. Col. Robert William	Auckland (New Zealand)
Bloomfield, Isabella Louisa Clarke	Auckland (New Zealand)
Bloomfield, Hilda Isabel Read	Auckland (New Zealand)
Blyth, Jennie P.	Toronto, ON
Bowes-Lyon, Charles Lindsay Claude	London (England)
Brandon, Vernon Gething	Manchester (England)
Burrows, Alfred John	Nottingham (England)
Burt, Clayton Ray	Toronto, ON
Cash, John Harwood	Nottingham (England)
Cash, Mary Kate White	Nottingham (England)
Cay, Catherine Beatrice	Golden, BC
Cayley, John Joseph	Hamilton, ON
Clark, Charles Robert	London (England)
Cox-Edwards, Joseph Francis	England
Crathern, Waneta	Montreal, QC
Cullen, Maude Young	Toronto, ON
Cullen, Albert (2)	Toronto, ON
Cullen, Isobel (6)	Toronto, ON
Cunningham, Robert Alexander	Winnipeg, MB
Darling, Merton Daniel Addison	London (England)
Dickson, Peter	Ottawa, ON
Duncan, James Fergus	London (England)
Dunlevy, Mrs. Grace Fiske	Denver, CO
Fenton, Walter	Manchester (England)
Gallagher, Cedric Aubrey Wools	Winnipeg, MB
Gallagher, Charlotte Harman Wools	Winnipeg, MB
Gaunt, Doris Winifred	Birmingham (England)
Godson, Frederick Philip	England
Goldthorpe, Charles	England
Gosselin, Louis Aldei	Montreal, QC
Graham, Elizabeth Humphreys	Hong Kong
Graham, Walter Douglas	Hong Kong
Haggerston, Mabel Hilda	England
Hailey, Elizabeth Rhodes	Vancouver, BC
Hart-Bennett, Ella Mary Tuck	Nassau (Bahamas)
Henderson, George William Simpson	Montreal, QC
Herxheimer, Walter Salomon	England
Hirst, Arthur	Birmingham (England)
Holloway, Charlotte Elizabeth Oliver	Quebec City, QC
Howes, Frank William	England
Hyamson, Lionel Alexander	London (England)
Irving, Laurence Sydney Brodribb	England
Irving, Mabel Lucy Hackney	England
Johnston, David	Fredericton, NB
Kent, John Lionel	Montreal, QC
Kohl, Grace Margaret Fairbanks	Montreal, QC
Lee, Ailse Holland	Toronto, ON
Lindsay, Dr. Murdoch Alexander	Halifax, NS
Lyman, Florence Holwell Kirkby	Montreal, QC

Lyman, Henry Herbert — Montreal, QC
Maginnis, Alexander Gordon — London (England)
Malloch, Charles — Howser, BC
Marks, Gabriel Jacob — Melbourne (Australia)
Marks, Marion Alexander — Melbourne (Australia)
Miller, Catherine — Montreal, QC
Mullins, Albert — England
Mullins, Eileen (10) — England
Mullins, Kate Emily Piercy — England
O'Hara, Henry Robert — Toronto, ON
O'Hara, May Laura Cutting — Toronto, ON
O'Hara, Josephine Helen **(11)** — Toronto, ON
Palmer, Wallace Leonard — London (England)
Palmer, Ethel Courtney Short — London (England)
Paton, Ethel Sabina Grundy — Sherbrooke, QC
Price, Fanny Emma Plumley Wynne — Auckland (New Zealand)
Rutherford, Frederick James — Montreal, QC
Seton-Karr, Sir Henry — London (England)
Seybold, Edward — Ottawa, ON
Seybold, Mrs. Susanna Bricker — Ottawa, ON
Smart, George Bogue — Ottawa, ON
Stork, Mary Louisa Reeve — Toronto, ON
Taylor, John Thomas — England
Taylor, Dorothy Maud — England
Taylor, Helen Marjorie — England
Townshend, Tiria Vere Ferrer — New Zealand
Tylee, Charles David — Montreal, QC
Tylee, Mrs. Martha — Montreal, QC
Wakeford, Alfred Joseph — Cardiff (Wales)
Wallett, Rev. Joseph Webster — England

SECOND CLASS

Out of the 255 passengers travelling in second class, 48 survived and 207 were lost.

Aldridge, Ernest, William — Toronto, ON
Archer, Alfred (infant) — Regina, SK
Archer, Mary Ruth Congdon — Regina, SK
Archer, Tracey Harley — Regina, SK
Assafrey, Alma Fedora Maude — Scotland
Atkin, Martha Jane — Prince Albert, SK
Attwell, George Ernest Stephen — Toronto, ON
Attwell, Hattie Eva Frink — Toronto, ON
Axten, Dorothea Kelly — Vancouver, BC
Axten, Leonard (3) — Vancouver, BC
Bach, Edith Chistina — Rochester, MN
Bach, Reinholdt — Rochester, MN
Balcolme, Alice (6) — Vancouver, BC
Bales, Ada Alice — Toronto, ON
Barbour, Evelyn Beatrice (3) — Silverton, BC
Barbour, Florence Jessie **(8)** — Silverton, BC
Barbour, Sebena Hicks — Silverton, BC
Barrie, William Simpson — Silverton, BC
Bawden, Elizabeth — Indiana
Bawden, Florence Annie — Indiana
Baxter, Anna May — Toronto, ON
Beale, Edward — London, ON
Beauchamp, Ruth Foster — Michigan
Beckstead, Adj. Jane — Winnipeg, MB
Berry, Ethel De La Tour — North Vancouver, BC
Bigland, Lt. Joseph Stanley — Halifax, NS
Birkett, Rev. Henry James — Carstairs, AB
Bishop, Thomas George Tetley — Vancouver, BC
Black, John Wilson — Ottawa, ON
Black, Rosina Letch — Ottawa, ON
Blackhurst, Ada Ratcliffe — Paris, ON
Bonthrone, Alex — Scotland
Bonynge, Ens. George — Toronto, ON
Boynton-Lee, Frances Elisabeth — St. Thomas, ON
Brooks, Frank Percy — Toronto, ON
Brown, Alice — Toronto, ON
Brown, Overend — Kenora, ON
Buhler, Costa — Germany
Bulpitt, Reginald George — England
Burgess, Susan Robertson — Hamilton, ON
Butler, Rose — Toronto, ON
Byrne, Edward — Australia
Byrne, Eliza Ann Bickford — Australia
Byrne, Selina Gertrude — Australia
Caughey, Albert Edward — Ottawa, ON
Caughey, Helen Hughes — Ottawa, ON
Chignell, Eliza Leys — Victoria, BC
Clark, Lavinia Simpson — Toronto, ON

Clark, Nellie (9) — Toronto, ON
Cole, Annie — Princeton, BC
Cook, Annie Emma Jane Rampling — Vancouver, BC
Court, Emily Florence — Victoria, BC
Creighton, Bertha Jane Dixon — Toronto, ON
Creighton, Maj. David Law — Toronto, ON
Crellin, Robert William — Silverton, BC
Dale, Mary Parker — York, ON
Dale, Rita Betty Cleveley (infant) — York, ON
Dandy, James Ferguson — Pierson, MB
Dargue, Annie Isabella Barrass — Kenora, ON
Davidson, Gordon Charles — Vancouver, BC
Davies, Thomas William Henry — Toronto, ON
Davies, Eliza Ethel Gough — Toronto, ON
Davison, Daisy May Barling — Vancouver, BC
Davison, Dorothy Ada (infant) — Vancouver, BC
Death, Arthur Henry — Regina, SK
De Bow, Adj. Everett Stanley — Toronto, ON
De Bow, Mary Ann McKim — Toronto, ON
Dodd, Capt. John Edward — Toronto, ON
Dodd, Violet Victoria Howson — Toronto, ON
Dunn, Jane Elizabeth Elliott — England
Eastes, Frances Hannah — Toronto, ON
Edwards, Adj. George — Ottawa, ON
Elmslie, Jane Christine — Moose Jaw, SK
Erzinger, Walter — Winnipeg, MB
Evans, Ernest Joshua — Toronto, ON
Evans, Emma Willett — Toronto, ON
Evans, C. (infant) — Toronto, ON
Farr, Bessie (3) — Moose Jaw, SK
Farr, Dorothy (5) — Moose Jaw, SK
Farr, Kathleen Helen (8) — Moose Jaw, SK
Farr, Nancy Annie Meggit (7) — Moose Jaw, SK
Felstead, George Philip — York, ON
Findlay, Maj. Hugh — Winnipeg, MB
Findlay, Isabella Ivison — Winnipeg, MB
Findlay, Johnson McWilliam — Liverpool (England)
Fisher, Margaret Lightfoot — New York
Fisher, Wilfred — New York
Foard, Herbert — England
Foord, Alfred Ernest — Toronto, ON
Foord, Alice Margaret (4) — Toronto, ON
Foord, Alice Ward — Toronto, ON
Freeman, Henry — Wisconsin
Freeman, Mary Massoth — Wisconsin
Goddard, John Arthur — Toronto, ON
Grafton, Susanna Woodbridge — Vancouver
Gray, Edwin Philip — Toronto, ON
Gray, Madeline Shirt — Indiana
Gray, Mary Winifred (6) — Indiana
Green, Adj. Harry John — Toronto, ON
Green, Nellie Adams — Toronto, ON
Green, Ernest Harry — Toronto, ON
Green, Jessie — Toronto, ON
Greenaway, Herbert Booth — Toronto, ON
Greenaway, Margaret Ellen Dalzell — Toronto, ON
Greenaway, Thomas Hartley — Toronto, ON
Griffin, Grace Withnell — Burnaby, BC
Griffin, Winifred Pauline (2) — Burnaby, BC
Grigg, James — Chilliwack, BC
Grigg, Pricilla White Matthews — Chilliwack, BC
Groom, Capt. Charles Henry — Toronto, ON
Hakker, Harriet — Winnipeg, MB
Hakker, Judith (infant) — Winnipeg, MB
Halliday, Christopher — Pierson, MB
Hanagan, Adj. Edward James — Toronto, ON
Hanagan, Edith Grace — Toronto, ON
Hanagan, Miss Grace Edith (8) — Toronto, ON
Hart, William — Moose Jaw, SK
Hart, Emma Roach — Moose Jaw, SK
Hart, Edith (4) — Moose Jaw, SK
Hart, William (infant) — Moose Jaw, SK
Hayes, St. Capt. Emma — Toronto, ON
Heath, Hugh Lester — Chicago, IL
Heath, John Russell (4) — Chicago, IL
Hepburn, Barbara Meredith (3) — Vancouver, BC
Hepburn, Mary Katherine Meredith — Vancouver, BC
Hepburn, Owen Meredith (infant) — Vancouver, BC
Hoggan, Rosinda Blakey — Nanaimo, BC
Holcombe, Florence Louisa Newton — Calgary, AB
Hope, Chrissie Burgess (4) — Hamilton, Ontario
Horwood, William — Toronto, ON
Howarth, William — Calgary, AB
Howarth, Rebecca Ellen Brien — Calgary, AB
Howarth, Melvin (4) — Calgary, AB
Hudson, William — Montreal, QC
Humphreys, William John — Toronto, ON
Hunt, Miss Eleanor Grace — Ireland
Hunt, Dr. Rennsaleer Wilkins — Hamilton, ON
Hunter, Brigadier John — Gorakapur (India)
Hunter, Grace — Gorakapur (India)

Hunter, Jessie Catherine Ogilvy Tulloch — Gorakapur (India)
Hunter, John Stewart (11) — Gorakapur (India)
Johnson, James — Toronto, ON
Johnston, George — Santa Barbara, CA
Jones, Edward Thomas — Toronto, ON
Jones, Ens. Emily — Calgary, AB
Kavalesky, Ivan — Russia
Keith, Lt. Alfred Thomas — Toronto, ON
Knudson, Captain Anna Elizabeth — Toronto, ON
Kruse, Herman — Rochester, MN
Kruse, Freda Josephine — Rochester, MN
Langley, John Wise — Merritt, BC
Langley, Mary Anne — Vancouver, BC
Law, Ernest — Calgary, AB
Law, Jack (4) — Calgary, AB
Law, Margaret Haythornthwaite — Calgary, AB
Lennon, James Joseph — Winnipeg, MB
Longley, Gertrude Eva Day — Brantford, ON
Longley, Leonard Hurlock — Brantford, ON
Longley, Miriam Violet (infant) — Brantford, ON
McAlpine, Mr. A. — Montreal, QC
McAmmond, Capt. David Foster — Winnipeg, MB
McGrath, Captain Matthew James — Winnipeg, MB
McIntyre, Kenneth Arnon — New York
McLean, John McQueen — Agassiz, BC
Maidment, Harriett Peckham — Toronto, ON
Maidment, Col. Sydney Charles — Toronto, ON
Malone, Robert — Toronto, ON
Mardall, Ens. Oliver Pinnock — Vancouver, BC
Matier, Alexander — Indiana
Meacher, George William — Toronto, ON
Measures, William Howard — Toronto, ON
Moir, Euphemia Sanders Prior — Toronto, ON
Morgan, Lilian Else — Toronto, ON
Morgan, James Oswald — Winnipeg, MB
Morgan, William Leslie — Winnipeg, MB
Morris, St. Capt. Arthur — Toronto, ON
Morris, Daisy — Toronto, ON
Morris, Major Frank — London, ON
Mounsey, Fannie Sewell — Chicago, IL
Myers, Capt. James Patterson — Toronto, ON
Neeve, Ernest Edward — Toronto, ON
Newton, Jane Roberts — England
Noneley, Annie — Hamilton, ON
Nuttall, Christina McColl — Winnipeg, MB
Nuttall, Ralph George (infant) — Winnipeg, MB
Nuttall, Tom (infant) — Winnipeg, MB
Oslender, Joseph — New Jersey
Pantling, Sarah Ann Hurst — Toronto, ON
Patrick, Julian — Unknown
Pattenden, Ens. Bertram John — Toronto, ON
Patterson, John Rea — Calgary, AB
Patterson, Robert Stuart — Calgary, AB
Patterson, Sarah — Calgary, AB
Perkins, Richard Henry — Toronto, ON
Perry, William Henry — Petersborough, ON
Peturson, Hannes — Winnipeg, MB
Peturson, Tilly Anna Sigurdson — Winnipeg, MB
Potter, Brig. William Scott — Toronto, ON
Potter, Willard (9) — Toronto, ON
Potts, Margret Heavey — Vancouver, BC
Price, Adj. Anna — Hamilton, ON
Priestley, Alice — England
Priestley, Martha — England
Prior, Edith Mary Ann Auger — Winnipeg, MB
Pugmire, Ens. Ernest Ivison — Toronto, ON
Rees, Annie — Toronto, ON
Rees, David — Toronto, ON
Rees, Capt. Harding Willford — Toronto, ON
Rees, Ruth Hephzibah Babington — Toronto, ON
Rees, Capt. Ruth Maybury — Toronto, ON
Richards, George Clement — Indiana
Richards, Sarah Ann Ward — Indiana
Richardson, Mary Ann (Griffin) — Australia
Richardson, William John — Australia
Riley, John — Hamilton, ON
Sampson, Samuel James — Guelph, ON
Schongut, Josephine Pepi Kleinberg — Montreal, QC
Scott, John M. — Mortlach, SK
Searle, Eva Ruth — Seattle, WA
Shattock, William Noah — Nesbitt, MB
Simco, Maj. Annette Wallis — Vancouver, BC
Simmonds, Mary Mahoney — London (England)
Simmonds, Reginald Frank — London (England)
Smith, Mrs. Lewis — Calgary, AB
South, Elsie Marian Roberts — England
South, Harold Neville — England
Spooner, Capt. Rufus Thompson — Toronto, ON
Spoor, Margaret Calpin — Edmonton, AB
Spoor, Robert — Edmonton, AB
Stage, Isabel — Toronto, ON

Name	Residence
Stainer, Edith Elizabeth	Medicine Hat, AB
Stillman, Arthur Edward	Calgary, AB
Stitt, Clara Bell Cofield	Toronto, ON
Stitt, Adj. Fitzwilliam	Toronto, ON
Swindlehurst, Sarah Agnes Ann	England
Taplin, Elizabeth Turner	Kamloops, BC
Turpin, Maj. Richard	Toronto, ON
Veitch, Mary Elizabeth	Victoria, BC
Vincent, John	England
Vincent, Clara Searsib	England
Wakefield, William Henry	Vancouver, BC
Walker, Brig. Henry William	Toronto, ON
Weinrauch, Bernard	Montreal, QC
Whatmore, Capt. Giovanni Guido	Toronto, ON
Whyte, Jennie Amy (infant)	New Westminster, BC
Whyte, Mary Jane Knox	New Westminster, BC
Whitelaw, Isabella Joplin Henderson	New Westminster, BC
Willmot, Eliza	Ontario
Wilson, Capt. George H.	Toronto, ON
Wolter, Agnes Isabella Liston	England
Wood, Mary	Regina, SK
Woods, Fanny Simmons	Toronto, ON
Yates, Harry	Hamilton, ON
Yates, Mary Ann Taylor	Hamilton, ON
Zebulak, Josef	Austria

THIRD CLASS

Out of the 714 passengers travelling in third class, 136 survived and 578 were lost.

Name	Residence
Adamiak, Kasper	Michigan–Austria
Adamiec, Franciszek	Michigan–Russia
Adamovich, Jovo	Michigan–Austria
Adamowicz, Joseph	Wisconsin–Russia
Afanassief, Mary Francis	Winnipeg
Ainsworth, Edith Smith	Cleveland, OH
Ainsworth, Maude (12)	Cleveland, OH
Ainsworth, Eric (7)	Cleveland, OH
Ainsworth, Jack (11)	Cleveland, OH
Alborg, Johan	Illinois–Russia
Alexejew, Leonty	Russia
Alexoff, Demeter	Serbia
Allgrove, Florence Alice Dawes	Windsor, ON
Allgrove, Evelyn (infant)	Windsor, ON
Allgrove, Vera Ellen (6)	Windsor, ON
Anderson, Amanda Albin	Minnesota–Norway
Anderson, Eric Albert	Sweden
Anderson, Joseph	Sweden
Anderson, Albert Bruce	England
Anderson, Olof	Sweden
Andrews, Herbert John	England
Antonuk, Nikolai	Russia
Appleton, Charles	England
Atkinson, John	Scotland
Babezuk, Basil	Regina, SK
Babezuk, Mrs.	Regina, SK
Babezuk, Mary (infant)	Regina, SK
Babiski, Wasili (Vasil)	Michigan–Germany
Baie, Sima	Michigan–Hungary
Bangen, Mary	Calgary, AB
Barsk (Parsk), Maria	Chicago, IL–Sweden
Bartschi, Christian	Stettler, AB
Bartschi, Theofil	Stettler, AB
Basta, Andrew	Michigan–Russia
Bednarz, Jan	Michigan–Russia
Befara, Nazzarino	Minnesota–Italy
Bekoeff, Tartari	Vancouver, BC
Bell, Dan	Michigan–Hungary
Bellucci, Luciano	Minnesota–Italy
Bellucci, Sante	Minnesota–Italy
Belser, Katherine	Ireland
Benari, Pete	Montreal, QC–Germany
Berari, Ilie	Michigan–Hungary
Bercsan, Sandor	Michigan–Hungary
Bergman, Reino (infant)	Michigan–Finland
Bergman, Senja	Michigan–Finland
Bernabei, Antonio	Minnesota–Italy
Berry, Daniel	Illinois–England
Bevan, William George	Swansea (Wales)
Biondi, Nazzareno	Minnesota–Italy
Birch, Ellen Gertrude Turner	Toronto, ON
Birch, Elsie (infant)	Toronto, ON
Birch, John Reuben Henry (7)	Toronto, ON

Bjordal, Peder Luritz — Bellingham, WA
Blackham, Arthur James — Toronto, ON
Blakeburn, Ethel May — Halifax, NS
Blomqvist, Marcus August Sylvester — Saskatchewan–Sweden
Blomqvist, Elisabet Katanna Eriksson — Saskatchewan–Sweden
Blomqvist, Erik Walfrid (9) — Saskatchewan–Sweden
Blomqvist, Olov Sigfri (12) — Saskatchewan–Sweden
Boardman, Charles — Hamilton, ON
Boardman, Catherine Ellen Pugh — Hamilton, ON
Bokic, Mile — Michigan–Hungary
Bolanian Zacharie — Michigan–Hungary
Bolton, George Bruce (3) — Toronto, ON
Bolton, George Henry — Toronto, ON
Bolton, Lillian Maud Smith — Toronto, ON
Bolton, Sadie (infant) — Toronto, ON
Bonne, Jacobus — Illinois–Brussels
Borsik, Fred — Fernie, BC
Braet, Victor Polydore — Antwerp (Belgium)
Braga, Carolina Tamorini — Minnesota–Italy
Braga, Egildo — Minnesota–Italy
Braga, Rino (infant) — Minnesota–Italy
Braithwaite, John (2) — Assiniboia, SK
Braithwaite, Martha Dora Ellis — Assiniboia, SK
Braithwaite, William Ellis (3) — Assiniboia, SK
Brischuk, Dimian — Michigan–Russia
Bristow, Charles Henry — Burnaby, BC
Bristow, Charles Junior — Burnaby, BC
Bristow, Selina Clayton — Burnaby, BC
Britten, Joseph — St. Thomas, ON
Bronchin, Jules — Brussels (Belgium)
Bronken, Mrs. Petronille Nilsine — Edmonton, AB
Bronken, Ella (11) — Edmonton, AB
Brooks, Henrietta Westwood — Toronto, ON
Brooks, Dorothy Caroline Mary (8) — Toronto, ON
Brooks, Harry — Vancouver, BC
Brown, Archie — Moose Jaw, SK
Bryan, Caroline Agnes — England
Brzozowski, Jan — Michigan–Russia
Bucciaretti, Giovanni — Minnesota–Italy
Buchacs, Leonty — Montreal, QC–Hungary
Buck, Mary — Lloydminister, AB
Burrows, Charlotte Ann Heyes — Nottingham (England)
Burrows, Elizabeth (6) — Nottingham (England)
Burrows, William (11) — Nottingham (England)
Burrows, William Thomas — Toronto, ON
Butacs, Demeter — Michigan–Hungary
Carlson, Andrew — Minnesota–Norway
Carter, Harold Hewitt — England
Chmilewsky, A. — Montreal, QC–Hungary
Chomicz Moisej — Michigan–Russia
Churcia (Cacich), Pava — Indiana–Hungary
Clark, Ellen Wainwright — Vancouver, BC
Clark, Stephen — Unknown
Clark, Thomas — Vancouver, BC
Clausen, David — Sweden
Clements, Robert H. — Port Hope, ON
Cooper, Percy Daniel — St. John, NB
Costa, Dalahea — Michigan–Hungary
Costea (Coste/Costca), George — Michigan–Hungary
Cotterill, Liza Oakley Hamilton — England
Cox, Henrica Maria — Dauphin, MB
Crawford, May Baines — England
Cresswell, Fanny Giles — Lethbridge, AB
Cresswell, Joseph — Lethbridge, AB
Czelisok, Valenti — Hamilton, ON–Russia
Dab, Eliza — Minnesota–Germany
Davies, Eliza — Edmonton, AB
Deliman, Constantin — Hungary
Delamont, Arthur William — Moose Jaw, SK
Delamont, Elizabeth — Moose Jaw, SK
Delamont, John — Moose Jaw, SK
Delamont, Leonard Samuel — Moose Jaw, SK
Delamont, Seraphine Cooper — Moose Jaw, SK
Dellamorte, Francesco — Minnesota–Italy
Demarsis, Luigi — Montreal, QC–Italy
Deveson, Frederick George — Quebec
Deveson, Phoebe Jane Giles — Quebec
Diski, Philip — Unknown
Dixon, Polly — Toronto, ON
Dowker, George Reader — Nelson, BC
Dowker, Mary Ann Peen — Nelson, BC
Dransfield, George — Saskatoon, SK
Dreha, John — Michigan–Russia
Dudka, Roman — Chicago, IL–Russia
Duffy, Mary Ann Speak — Vancouver, BC
Dulevich, Stefan — Michigan–Russia
Duma, Alexander — Michigan–Hungary
Durrant, Frances Harrington King — England
Durrant, James — England
Dutton, Kathleen — Hamilton, ON
Dzurik, Iwan — Hungary
Edwards, Christopher John — Broadview, SK
Ekqvist, Arvid — Finland
Elliott, Ellen Florence Donald — Quebec
Elliott, Ernest — Quebec

Elliott, Frederick Ernest (infant) — Quebec
Elliott, George Bruce (4) — Quebec
Engel, Jules — France
Engstrom John — Sweden
Eriksen Anthon (Anton) — Illinois–Norway
Ericksson, Erik Johan — Rossland, BC
Eriksson, Nils — Sweden
Evans, Alfrida Johnson — Nelson, BC
Evensen, Arthur — Chicago, IL
Evich, Dementi — Michigan–Russia
Evinson, Eli — Winnipeg, MB
Evinson, Fanny Levi — Winnipeg, MB
Evinson, Julius (infant) — Winnipeg, MB
Fabbri (Falni), Davide — Minnesota–Italy
Fant, Mikael — Minnesota–Finland
Farkas, Georg — Cincinnati, OH–Hungary
Faulkner, Ellen Meredith — England
Faulkner, James — England
Fell, Edith E. — Toronto, ON
Felstead, Edith Gladys (10) — Toronto, ON
Felstead, George William — Toronto, ON
Felstead, Louise Amelia Last — Toronto, ON
Ferguson, A.C. — England
Fishwick, Edmund — Windsor, ON
Flack, Edith Frances Harrald — Muskoka, ON
Flack, Percy George — Muskoka, ON
Fliflet, Josephine Holm — Wisconsin–Norway
Forstrom, Anna Amanda — Minnesota–Finland
Forstrom, Johann Wilhelm — Minnesota–Finland
Forstrom, Tauno (infant) — Minnesota–Finland
Forstrom, Waldo William (3) — Minnesota–Finland
Fowler, John — Vancouver, BC
Fransen, Oscar — Fernie, BC
Fraser, Frank — Montreal, QC
Fregoriczuk, Wasil — Ontario–Hungary
Furniss, Samuel George — Liverpool (England)
Fuss, Vavroshenetz — Russia
Gaguloff, Naluk — Vancouver, BC–Russia
Garbuzew, Ewdokim — Michigan–Germany
Gard, Johannes — Chicago, IL–Norway
Garnett, Mary Heward — Calgary, AB
Garnett, William — Calgary, AB
Gasieff, Stephan — Vancouver, BC
Gassenhuber, Frank, — Milwaukee, WI–Germany
Gattrell, Adela Rachel Jasper — Johannesburg (South Africa)
Gattrell, Ernest Maurice — Johannesburg (South Africa)
Giles, William — Lethbridge, AB
Gill, Martin — Nelson, BC
Glover, Frank — Unknown
Goddefroy, Leon — Belgium
Goff, Agnes — Toronto, ON
Gogoff, Tasko — Bulgaria
Goralski, Felix — Michigan–Russia
Goss, Beatrice Minnie Bath — Quebec
Goss, John Jr. (7) — Quebec
Goss, John Manning — Quebec
Goss, Joseph (5) — Quebec
Goss, Violet May (11) — Quebec
Grasa, Antonie — Michigan–Hungary
Grdisa, Miko — Minnesota–Hungary
Green, Florence Roberts — Islington, ON
Greenfield, Ruth Amy Johnston — Winnipeg, MB
Gregovich, John — Michigan–Hungary
Griffin, Violetta Jane Boaz — Brantford, ON
Grinevich, Alexander — Michigan–Russia
Gupka, Riprijan — Golden, BC
Guppy, Eleanor — England
Gustafson, John — Minnesota–Sweden
Guszczo, Adam — Russia
Haertjens (Aerjtens, Emiel) Emil — llinois–Belgium
Hakala, Maria — Michigan–Finland
Halasch, Wasil — Michigan–Germany
Hall, Henry — England
Hamalainen, Vilho — Michigan–Finland
Hammer, Emma — Lethbridge, AB
Hannunen, Aino — Michigan–Finland
Hannunen, Edviin, — Michigan–Finland
Harkonen, Reinhold — Minnesota–Finland
Harrison, Hugh — Belfast (Ireland)
Harvey, Carrie — Windsor, ON
Hatischky (Hatiosky), Tanasky — Montreal, QC–Hungary
Haverinen, Kreeta Sonia — Finland
Hedgecoe, Richard George — Montreal, QC
Heikkila Annti Ola — Michigan–Finland
Heikkila, Hilja Maria Eskola — Michigan–Finland
Heikkila, Vieno [Viena] (infant) — Michigan–Finland
Heller, Abram — Toronto, ON
Hill, Mary Emma Clegg — England
Hoad, Kathleen Emily — Quebec
Hoad, Kathleen Mavourneen Lane (infant) — Quebec
Hobbs, Louisa — Brantford, ON
Hobbs, Mary Ann Evans — Brantford, ON
Hokley, Edward — Fernie, BC
Holl, Edith — Toronto, ON

Holmberg, Edvard — Finland
Holmi, Mrs Liisa Johansdotter — Minnisota–Finland
Hopper, Frank — England
Hopper, William — England
Horowitz (Horwitz), Mollie — Chicago, IL–Belgium
Howanicz, Albert — Alberta–Germany
Howarth, Beatrice Morgan — Calgary, AB–England
Howarth, Emmie Majory (4) — Calgary, AB–England
Howarth, Leonard (5) — Calgary, AB–England
Howell, Alice Waters — Brantford, ON
Howell, Lillian Alice Maytom (10) — Brantford, ON
Hunt, Beatrice Elizabeth — Windsor, ON
Ilie, Boris — Chicago, IL–Bulgaria
Ilieff, Pavell — Ontario–Hungary
Ingleton, Violet May — Hamilton, ON
Ispas, Alexander — Michigan–Hungary
Ivane, M. — Ontario–Hungary
Ivane, W. — Ontario–Hungary
Jack, David (2) — Toronto, ON
Jack, Sarah Swift Coutts — Toronto, ON
Jaksic, Mile — Missouri–Hungary
Jaksic, Vaso — Missouri–Hungary
Jay, Clifford James (4) — Toronto, ON
Jay, Emily Foley — Toronto, ON
Jay, Emily Annie (6) — Toronto, ON
Jay, Florence Lillian — Toronto, ON
Jay, Frederick William Arthur (11) — Toronto, ON
Jay, Stella Dorothy (8) — Toronto, ON
Jeffrey, Mary Ann — Calgary, AB
Jeffries, Mary Elizabeth Unwin — England
Jeffs, Kate Holiday — Brantford, ON
Jeffs, Ernest Wilfred — Brantford, ON
Jelisavac, Simo — Michigan–Hungary
Jensen, Annie — Winnipeg, MB
Johnson, Alida — Chicago, IL–Sweden
Johnson, Andrew — Racine, WI
Johnson, Edward — Toronto, ON
Johnson, Mrs. — Toronto, ON
Johnson, Jens — Minnesota–Denmark
Johnson, Johanna — Minnesota–Denmark
Johnson, Matilda — Minnesota–Denmark
Johnson, Ulf — Minnesota–Norway
Johnson, W — Ontario–England
Jokinen, Frank — Minnesota
Jones, Sara Ellen — Montreal
Joukainen, Simo — Michigan–Finland
Jovitz, Jacob — Ohio–Hungary
Jovitz, Jola Gyula — Ohio–Hungary
Juniper, Annie Elizabeth — England
Juniper, Arthur (3) — England
Jussila, Kalle — Minnesota–Finland
Kadieff, Hangeri — Vancouver, BC–Russia
Kallio, Hilma — Unknown
Kaminski, Joszef — Michigan–Hungary
Kangas, Einar — Minnesota–Finland
Kangas, John — Minnesota–Finland
Karanes, Michael — Michigan–Russia
Kasparowicz, Joseph — Wisconsin–Russia
Keeley, Thomas, — Toronto, ON
Kerney, James — Edmonton, AB
Kerr, Catherine Russell (2) — London, ON
Kerr, George Russell (8) — London, ON
Kerr, Maggie Russell (11) — London, ON
Kerr, Mary Currie Russell — London, ON
Kerr, Peter — London, ON
Kerr, Sarah Russell — London, ON
Kerr, William Russell (4) — London, ON
Kesaniemi, Matt — Sudbury, ON
Kestila, Ivar — Finland
Kiczak, Wojciech — Ohio–Hungary
Kilsby, Charles — Toronto, ON
Kinos, Eino — Ontario–Finland
Kirtley, Elizabeth Frank — England
Kirwin, Amelia Gertrude Sellers — Quebec
Kirwin, James (infant) — Quebec
Kitson, Ada Mary Long — Winnipeg, MB
Kitson, Herbert — Winnipeg, MB
Kitson, Monica (infant) — Winnipeg, MB
Kivisto, Helen Laura (2) — Finland
Kivisto, Hilma Sofia Rajamaki — Finland
Kivisto, Toivo (5) — Finland
Klemens, Josef — Cincinnati, OH–Germany
Kleva, Wasili — Michigan–Russia
Klimchuk, Istafi — Ontario–Hungary
Klukacz, Adam — Michigan–Russia
Knisz, Andrej — Chicago, IL–Russia
Koivisto, Tuomas Fabian Jaakonpoika — Finland
Koivisto, Arvi (2) — Finland
Koivisto, Martti (infant) — Finland
Koivisto, Susanna Paulina — Finland
Kolometz, Mitrofim — Michigan–Russia
Korga, Jan — Michigan–Russia
Koskinen, Amanda Lager — Finland
Koskinen, Helmi (9) — Finland
Koskinen, Jaakko (child) — Finland
Koskinen, Milja (2) — Finland
Kostoff, Delcho — Unknown
Kowalski, Jan — Michigan–Russia

Koynyto (Kapusta, Saweli), Saveli — Michigan–Russia
Kozlowsky, Stanislow — Unknown
Kozoriz, Kuzma — Michigan–Russia
Kravetz, Larion — Ontario–Hungary
Krawczenko, Anton — Detroit, MI–Russia
Kroenig, Alfred — Invermere, BC
Kroenig, Edith — Invermere, BC
Kruchinsky, Andrej — Ontario–Hungary
Krutin, Jan — Montreal, QC–Hungary
Kryczuniak, Ivan — Montreal, QC–Hungary
Kubeless Frantz — Russia
Kuchiev (Kuchoj, Mike), Murkazan — Vancouver, BC–Russia
Kujala, Jaakoppi — Finland
Kupreczenko, John — Michigan–Germany
Kutzi, Grigor — Russia
Kuukar, Vihtori — Michigan–Russia
Kwarchek, Feodore — Michigan–Russia
Lahti, Hermanni — Minnesota–Finland
Lajesic, Jovan — Michigan–Hungary
Lammi, Matti — Michigan–Finland
Lampinen, Liini Lydia — Michigan–Finland
Langenicz, Peter — Michigan–Belgium
Larsen, Anton (5) — Minnesota–Denmark
Larsen, Patrina Laura Norberg — Minnesota–Denmark
Larsson, Nils — Omaha, NE–Sweden
Laskey, Frederick George — London, ON
Lawler, Ellen Garthwaite — Brantford, ON
Lawler, Herbert — Brantford, ON
Lawler, Philip — Brantford, ON
Laws, Robert — Brantford, ON
Lebedowicz, Ivan — Michigan–Russia
Lee, Ethel Mary Durham — Weyburn, SK
Leeks, Willie (infant) — England
Lehton (Lehto), Matti — Michigan–Finland
Leikas, Anselmi — Montreal, QC–Fiinland
Lejczuk, Marcin — Michigan–Russia
Levchik, Olef — Michigan–Russia
Levetz, Archiv — Michigan–Russia
Lewandowski, Becker — Ontario–Hungary
Liezner, Hrye — Ontario–Hungary
Lilek, T. — Montreal, QC–Hungary
Lindquist, Jonas — Shellbrook, SK
Lindquist, Marta Persdotter — Shellbrook, SK
Livanoff, Peter — Michigan–Russia
Loncar, Josip — Minnesota–Hungary
Lone, Anna — Norway
Lone, Alick (child) — Norway
Lone, Clara (2) — Norway
Lone, Hans — Norway
Lone, Rena (child) — Norway
Los, Harry — Michigan–Russia
Lubnjewsky, Adam — Wisconsin–Russia
Lubnjewsky, Jacob — Wisconsin–Russia
Luchovich, Luka — Michigan–Russia
Lukijanec, Maty — Michigan–Hungary
Lung, Ilia — Michigan–Hungary
Lupini, Nazzareno — Minnesota–Italy
Luren, Magnus — Minnesota–Norway
Luren, Sarah Lofthus — Minnesota–Norway
Luzensky, Ignotty — Montreal–Germany
Madsen, Signe Ostgaard — Minnesota–Denmark
Magyar, Toma — Michigan–Hungary
Makela, Juha — Unknown
Maki, Amanda — Oregon
Maki, Matti — Unknown
Maki, Orvokki (infant) — Oregon
Makinen, Oscar — Montreal, QC–Finland
Malachuk, Foma — Michigan–Russia
Malobasa, Dane — Michigan–Hungary
Mandryk, Harry — Winnipeg, MB–Hungary
Mandryk, Sydor, — Winnipeg, MB–Hungary
Marazewicz, Terenty — Detroit, MI–Germany
Marian, Juon — Michigan–Hungary
Marin, Jovan — Michigan–Hungary
Marini, Guiseppe — Minnesota–Italy
Marinkov, Gymo — Michigan–Hungary
Markkula, Aino (child) — Michigan
Markkula, Arvo — Michigan
Markkula, Eero (10) — Michigan
Markkula, Sofia — Michigan
Markkula, Tonio (2) — Michigan
Martin, Emma Smith Payne — England
Maric (Masic), Steve — Michigan–Hungary
Mason, Mrs. — England
Mason, Howard (infant) — England
Matiyos, N. — Montreal, QC–Hungary
Mattson, Ida — Sudbury, ON
Mattson, Sulo (infant) — Sudbury, ON
Maule, Mrs. Frances — England
Mawby, Elsie Mary Stubbings — Toronto, ON
Mawby, Kathleen Mary (2) — Toronto, ON
Mawhinney, George Waring — Ireland
May, Mark — Ottawa, ON
McGachen (infant) — London, ON
McGachen, Alice Mary Marjorie (12) — London, ON
McGachen, Gladys Maud — London, ON
McGachen, Maude Mary Nicholson — London, ON
McVeigh, James Henry — Michigan–England

Mezin, Dimitri — Michigan–Hungary
Mihekovic, Tomo — Missouri–Hungary
Mikulicza, George — Michigan–Hungary
Minardi, Luigi — Minnesota–Italy
Mincy, Petru — Michigan–Hungary
Mitchell, Sydney — Los Angeles, CA
Mitoff, Alexi — Quebec–Hungary
Mitoff, Gairo — Quebec–Hungary
Moorehouse, Frederick — Ontario–England
Morelli, Paolo — Minnesota–Italy
Morosuk, Moisei — Michigan–Russia
Morton, Jane (infant) — Fernie, BC
Morton, Kathleen (infant) — Fernie, BC
Morton, Lowther — Fernie, BC
Morton, Ruth Jane Spruston — Fernie, BC
Mose, Harold — Montreal, QC–Germany
Moskelli, K. — Montreal, QC–Hungary
Motki, Mike — Michigan, QC–Germany
Mott (Chew/Chou), Amelia — Oxford, ON
Mullen, Robert — Wisconsin
Muzichuk, Dimitri (Nikita) — **Michigan–Russia**
Murcsan, T. — Michigan–Hungary
Naulls, Louisa Rose Bills Holten — Toronto, ON
Naulls, William George — Toronto, ON
Nelson (Nilsson), Gustaf — Michigan–Sweden
Nevalainen, Otto — Montreal, QC–Finland
Nikula, John — Michigan–Hungary
Nikulaie, Ilie — Michigan–Hungary
Nilsson, Sigfrid — Sweden
Ninutear, Pavel — Michigan–Hungary
Nirny, Ilia — Michigan–Germany
Nissila, Frank — Montreal–Finland
Nissila, Sanni — Montreal–Finland
Nivala, John — Minnesota–Finland
Nivala, Lizzie — Minnesota–Finland
Nivala, Roy — Minnesota–Finland
Nixon, Emma (2) — Calgary, AB
Nixon, Ethel Mary Jeffrey — Calgary, AB
Nixon, Leslie (infant) — Calgary, AB
Nobiski (Noviski), Piotr — Michigan–Russia
Novikov, Speredon — Michigan–Russia
Numminen, Mauno — Finland
Oakley, George — England
Olecki, Onufrej — Montreal, QC–Germany
Olsen (Olscon), Gustav — Sweden
Pac, Vavyence — Michigan–Hungary
Paccozzachi, Guiseppi — Minnesota–Italy
Pajin, Nika — Michigan–Hungary
Parker, Thirza — England
Parkinson, Letitia — Toronto, ON
Parrish, Florence (child) — Toronto, ON
Parrish, Florence Ellen Baker — Toronto, ON
Parrish, Harry (7) — Toronto, ON
Paszkowicz, Iwan — Michigan–Germany
Paterson, Alex — Merritt, BC
Pawlowsky, Peter — Michigan–Hungary
Perkins, Louise Maria — Toronto, ON
Permiakov, Ivan — Michigan–Germany
Peryer, Jemima Richardson — Petersborough, ON
Pettersson (Petterson), George — Michigan–Finland
Petrovich, Simon — Michigan–Hungary
Petrus (Petruk), Metro — Saskatchewan–Russia
Phillips, Ethel — Saskatoon, SK
Phillips, Hubert (11) — Saskatoon, SK
Phillips, Rachel Pass — Saskatoon, SK
Piermatti, Lorenzo — Minnesota–Italy
Pierpaoli, Domenico — Minnesota–Italy
Piirainen, Erik — Michigan, Finland
Polic (Poliae), Izidor — Michigan–Hungary
Polic (Poliae), Stepan — Michigan–Hungary
Polkluf, John, — Ontario–Hungary
Pomichonski, Ignacy — Michigan–Germany
Pompei, Cesare — Minnesota–Italy
Pop, Gorygy — Michigan–Hungary
Pop, Veralin — Michigan–Hungary
Porii, Hilma — Finland
Powdeleski, Mr. — Ontario–Hungary
Powdeleski, Mrs. — Ontario–Hungary
Praksi, Frank — Minnesota–Finland
Pratt, MaryLouisa Holder — Toronto, ON
Pratt, Frances (2) — Toronto, ON
Presciutto, Ubaldo — Minnesota–Italy
Prince, Gilbert (5) — Hamilton, ON
Prince, Mary Alice Wilson — Hamilton, ON
Prince, William Lee — Hamilton, ON
Pukas, Iwan — Michigan–Hungary
Pykari, Jacob — Michigan–Finland
Pykari, Kalle — Michigan–Finland
Raasakka, Antti — Minnesota–Finland
Radburn, Mary Nicolls Wilson — England
Ragoschin (Rogozin), Alexei (child) — Chicago, IL–Russia
Ragoschin (Rogozin), Anastasia — Chicago, IL–Russia
Ragoschin (Rogozin), Vladimir — Chicago, IL–Russia
Rantala, Kalle — Minnesota–Finland
Rask, Per Johnson — Broadview, SK
Raven, Lorenzo Ross — Toronto, ON
Rebaljchenko, Feodor — Michigan–Russia
Reeves, Dora (4) — Windsor, ON

Reeves, Rose Elizabeth Wright — Windsor, ON
Reid, Charles — Brantford, ON
Rigby, Sarah Ann Bourne — St. John, NF
Robson, George Lisle — England
Robinsky, Adrian — Montreal, QC–Hungary
Roman, Petra — Michigan–Hungary
Romaniuk, Jacob — Michigan–Russia
Romanyszin, Pawlo — Hungary
Romanyszin, Ignatz — Hungary
Ross, Thomas — Michigan–Liverpool
Ruud (Reid), Laura — Norway
Ruddy, John — Ontario–Hungary
Russell, Sarah — London, ON
Russell, William — London, ON
Ryczko, Charyton — Michigan–Germany
Saarinen, David — Michigan–Finland
Saarinen, Hilm — Michigan–Finland
Saarinen, Niilo (2) — Michigan–Finland
Sagrafena, Aurelia — Minnesota–Italy
Salo, John — Michigan–Finland
Samuelson, Christian — Ontario–Norway
Samuelsson, Carl — Nebraska–Sweden
Sanden, Teresia, — Quebec–Sweden
Schakalida, Wassili — Michigan–Russia
Schwarz, Johann — Illinois–Russia
Scott, Mrs. Margaret — Edmonton, AB
Scott, Thomas — Edmonton, AB
Scott, Thomas (2) — Edmonton, AB
Sejmon, Dyonizy — Michigan–Germany
Seschinski, Josef — Detroit, MI–Russia
Shedlock, Steve — Illinois–Hungary
Shropas (Sroba), Joseph — Fernie, BC–Germany
Shurniak, Martin — Fernie, BC–Germany
Sidorowicz, Jakim — Michigan–Hungary
Sikorski, Lucjan — Chicago, IL–Russia
Simczesin, Jan — Hungary
Simper, Alfred — Montreal, QC
Simper, Mary — Montreal, QC
Sipka, Nikola — Michigan–Hungary
Sivula (Sihvola), Matti — Montreal, QC–Finland
Skocin, John — Hungary
Slyepovic, S. — Ontario–Hungary
Smart, Arthur Thomas — Grimshaw, AB
Smedberg, Charles (10) — Thunder Bay, ON
Smedberg, Rafael — Thunder Bay, ON
Smedley, Rose, — Toronto, ON
Smith, Edith Alice — Calgary, AB
Smith, Frederick — Toronto, ON
Smith, Isabella, — Toronto, ON
Smith, Maud — Toronto, ON
Sokar, S. — Montreal–Hungary
Sopan, Janos — Ohio–Hungary
Spooner, Margaret Hill — Vancouver, BC
Spooner, Mary Smith — Vancouver, BC
Spooner, Ralph — Vancouver, BC
Spurgeon, Kathleen Annie Britton — Hamilton, ON
Spurgeon, Kathleen Beatrice (6) — Hamilton, ON
Staley, Daniel — Vancouver, BC
Starowoitow, Alfanasi — Michigan–Germany
Statkus, Antoni (Stalkuss) — Montreal, QC–Russia
Steele, Elizabeth Flood — Brantford, ON
Steele, James (infant) — Brantford, ON
Steele, Lily Ada (child) — Brantford, ON
Steele, Norah Mary (6) — Brantford, ON
Stevenson, Alexander — Toronto, ON
Stevenson, Fanny Hardy — Toronto, ON
Stevenson, Margaret — Edmonton, AB
Stone, Emma — Montreal, QC
Strecha, Grigori — Michigan–Russia
Sundberg, Nil Jansson — Winnipeg, MB–Sweden
Suni, Matti — Montreal, QC–Finland
Sunich, Peter — Michigan–Hungary
Suvelean, George — Michigan–Hungary
Svniesuk, A. — Unknown
Swan, Charles Olsson — Wisconsin
Swanson, Amandus — Sweden
Swanson, Martin — Sweden
Swider, Stanislaw — Michigan–Russia
Sydonik, Petro — Montreal, QC–Hungary
Szabo, John — Michigan–Hungary
Szambargo, W. — Montreal, QC–Hungary
Szilagy Nikolae — Michigan–Hungary
Taavettila, Allan Mattias (7) — Thunder Bay, ON
Taavettila, Antti — Thunder Bay, ON
Taavettila, Hilma Kehto — Thunder Bay, ON
Tales, Matthew — Waterloo, ON
Tallbacker (Talbakka), Alexander — Michigan–Finland
Tankis, Demetre — Michigan–Hungary
Tarry, Albert Raymond (7) — Brantford, ON
Tarry, Annie Mobbs — Brantford, ON
Tarry, Hilda (9) — Brantford, ON
Taverner, Clara — Montreal, QC
Taverner, Eva (6) — Montreal, QC
Taverner, Henry (child) — Montreal, QC
Taverner, James Robert — Montreal, QC
Taylor, Florence (12) — Hamilton, ON
Taylor, James Thomas — Hamilton, ON
Thirkettle, Dudley — England
Tholix, Nestor — Michigan–Finland

Tholix, Sofia Jern — Michigan–Finland
Thompson, Mrs. Francis — Victoria, BC
Tiitus, Jaakoppi — Michigan–Finland
Tipuricze, Johan — Michigan–Belgium
Todorovich, Mladru — Michigan–Hungary
Tolander, Emma Louise — Iowa–Sweden
Tome, Luigi — Minnesota–Italy
Torikoff, Grigori — Illinois–Russia
Treherne, Allan Edwin — England
Trif, Kosta — Michigan–Germany
Tuffley, Laura — Kamloops, BC
Turcic (Turkich), Imbro — Minnesota–Hungary
Turnbull, Albert Reginald (11) — England
Turnbull, Caroline Ellen Norman — England
Turner, Joseph Henry — England
Tworkowski, Dominik — Illinois–Russia
Udin, (Yudin) Aaron (Harry) — Toronto, ON–Russia
Ugolini, Giovanni — Minnesota–Italy
Vagni (Vagre), Adele (child) — Minnesota–Italy
Vagni (Vagre), Ameriga (child) — Minnesota–Italy
Vagni (Vagre), Angelo — Minnesota–Italy
Vagni (Vagre), Anna — Minnesota–Italy
Vagni (Vagre), Luigi (child) — Minnesota–Italy
Vaisanen, Taavetti — Michigan–Finland
Valhott, Krancho — Ontario–Hungary
Valhott, Mico — Ontario–Hungary
Valimaki, Tuomas — Michigan–Finland
Van de moere, Victor — Illinois–Belgium
Vancaster (Van castre), Victor — Belgium
Vanner, Thomas Ewart — Calgary, AB
Varney, Louisa, Moran — England
Varney, Violet Gladys — England
Verniers, Camille Joseph Maria — Saguenay, QC
Verniers, Edmée-Marie Munaut — Saguenay, QC
Verniers, Edouard (7) — Saguenay, QC
Verniers, Francois Xavier (infant) — Saguenay, QC
Verniers, Jean Marie (9) — Saguenay, QC
Verniers, Louis Georges (9) — Saguenay, QC
Verniers, Renee Joseph (5) — Saguenay, QC
Verniers, Marie-Marguerite (4) — Saguenay, QC
Vequist (Vinquist), Carl Johnan — Omaha, NE
Viitala, Kalle — Michigan–Finland
Walker, Mrs. J. — Unknown
Walker, James — England
Walkky Hilda — Finland
Warne, Mrs. Jane Holloway — England
Warwick, Charles Ralph — England
Waszko, Pawlo — Winnipeg, MB–Russia
Watson, Eliza Edith Kemp — Toronto, ON
Weir, Violet Maud — Kerrisdale, BC
White, Alma May — England
White, Jessie — Guelph, ON
White, Mary Ann Mitchell — Guelph, ON
White, Selina Sara Tyler Lear (Lena) — Brantford, ON
Widlaski, Harry — Michigan–Hungary
Wiktorsky, Stanislaw — Michigan–Russia
Wilcocks, Henry — England
Wilkes, Charles — Moose Jaw, SK
Witiaz, Fonio — Michigan–Hungary
Wojtowicz, Mike — Michigan–Hungary
Wolcziuk, Jakym — Michigan–Russia
Woodard, Eliza Butcher — Toronto, ON
Woodard, May Florrie — Toronto, ON
Woodard, Mr. Walter — Toronto, ON
Woodwards, Sarah — England
Woodwards, Sarah White — England
Worobien (Worobiow), Maria — Missouri–Russia
Worobiow (Worobiow), Nicolai — Missouri–Russia
Worobien (Worobiow), Timofei — Missouri–Russia
Worrall, Herbert Horace — Prince Albert, SK
Zaleva, Marczin — Ontario–Hungary
Zolotorow, Wasili — Chicago, IL–Russia
Zrotam, Toader — Michigan–Hungary
Zsuffa, Stefan — Fernie, BC
Zuk, George — Michigan–Russia
Zuk, Josefa (6) — Michigan–Russia
Zuk, Kirilio — Michigan–Russia
Zuk, Maria — Michigan–Russia
Zuk, Wladislaw (child) — Michigan–Russia

APPENDIX 2
Crew List

Boldface indicates that the crew member was rescued. Out of the 423 crew members, 245 survived and 178 were lost.

Name	Position
Absolon, Victor	bedroom steward
Ainge, Edward	linen keeper
Anderson, James William	trimmer
Baker, Samuel Charles	bellboy
Baker, Thomas Henry	assistant stewart
Bailey, George	fireman
Bamford, Edward	marconi operator
Barber, John	fireman
Baxter, George R.	musician
Bell, Robert Williams	deck boy
Bent, James	seaman
Bishop, Thomas Henry	assistant cook
Boyd, Edward	fireman
Braine, Edward William	bedroom steward
Braithwaite, Isaac	baker
Bray, William Edward	kitchen porter
Brennan, Robert Henry	junior second engineer
Briard, Henry	engineer (*Empress of Asia*)*
Brown, John	assistant steward
Brown, Patrick	trimmer
Brown, William	seaman
Bruin, Thomas	seaman
Burns, Charles	assistant storekeeper
Burrows, Thomas	bedroom steward
Byrne, John Patrick	bedroom steward
Caley, Frederick John	junior 9th engineer
Campbell, John	fireman
Campbell, Michael	trimmer
Canepa, William Lazarus	assistant steward
Carroll, John	seaman
Chadwick, John Arthur	assistant steward
Challis, Montague	assistant steward
Chance, William George	staff steward
Cheetham, John McIntosh	assistant saloon steward
Childs, Harold Bertram Hope	musician
Clague, Robert Henry	assistant steward
Clandon, Henry	cook
Clare, William	assistant steward
Clarke, J.	seaman
Clarke, John Joseph	trimmer
Clarke, William	fireman
Cochrane, Andrew Leslie	engineer's boy
Cody, Michael	trimmer
Connor, James	donkeyman
Connor, John	greaser
Cooke, Thomas	assistant steward
Coombs, Charles William	2nd saloon pantryman
Cooper, Walter	assistant steward
Cope, Hector Allan	assistant steward
Cope, John	assistant pantryman
Copplin, George	assistant pantryman
Corfe, John Eustace	scullion
Corrigan, Thomas	seaman
Cottle, Samuel	trimmer
Cox, Samuel Alan	writer
Crabb, Joseph	assistant steward
Craik, Alexander Christopher	2nd steward
Crayton, Robert	seaman
Crellin, Robert William	assistant steward
Crowther, John George	leading fireman
Cunningham, James	cook
Cure, Albert Edwin	assistant steward
D'Arcy, Patrick	greaser
Davidson, George	storekeeper
Davies, John	trimmer
Davies, John	barman
Davies, John	fireman

* CPR crew from the *Empress of Asia* on the Pacific route, returning to Liverpool but not working on the *Empress*

Davies, Peter — fireman
Dawson, Alfred — butcher
Dawson, Edward — assistant steward
Deery, William John — trimmer
Dehnel, Charles Henry — interpreter
Delaney, Austin — assistant saloon steward
Dennehy, Edward — seaman
Dennis, Thomas — seaman
Derbyshire, Anthony Muir — bedroom steward
Dinwoodie, Agnes Ethel — stewardess
Disley, John — seaman
Dixon, Arthur Henry — assistant steward
Dixon, Harold — bedroom steward
Dolan, Paul — trimmer
Donaldson, John — trimmer
Donegan, James — assistant trimmer
Douglas, Thomas — baker
Downey, Thomas Shaun — seaman
Duckworth, William Barrett — electrician
Duffy, John — fireman
Dugan, Patrick — greaser
Duggan, John — assistant printer
Dumbell, Thomas Baker — assistant steward
Dunn, John — trimmer
Durkin, John — café steward
Eliott, Alfred Douglas — baker
Evans, Albert — seaman
Evans, John — seaman
Faulkner, Reginald — assistant pantryman
Fawcett, William Wright — seaman
Fayle (Taylor), Robert — assistant saloon steward
Fereday, Arthur William — assistant steward
Ferguson, Ronald — marconi operator
File, Osmond — ex-2nd officer
Fisher, Samuel Charles — bellboy
Fitchett, Edward — fireman
Fitzgerald, H. — seaman
Fitzpatrick, Alexander — assistant steward
Fitzpatrick, John — seaman
Flagel, J. — seaman
Flinn, George Fitzroy — assistant steward
Flood, Thomas — leading fireman
Foster, Ernest — trimmer
Fournier, Henri — fireman
Furness, John William — musician
Gaade, Augustus William — chief steward
Gale, Thomas John — assistant steward
Gallagher, William — deck boy
Galway, James Francis — quartermaster
Gardiner, William — scullion
Gavigan, Bernard — assistant steward
Gee, Percy — assistant saloon steward
Gerrard, Thomas Joseph — smoke room steward
Gibson, John Victor — assistant steward
Gill, Nathaniel — saloon pantryman
Gill, James Philip — bedroom steward
Gillespie, Robert Walls — senior 4th engineer
Glasberg, Rudolph — barber
Glover, Thomas Henry — cook
Grant, Edward — trimmer
Grant, James Frederick — ship's surgeon
Grant, John — electrician
Gratwick, Thomas William — seaman
Gray, Arthur — assistant saloon steward
Gray, Whit William — assistant steward
Green, Frederick George — assistant steward
Gregory, Frederick — assistant steward
Grieves, George — assistant steward
Gutcher, James Duncan — quartermaster
Hadfield, William James — assistant saloon steward
Haigh, Samuel Ernest — assistant steward
Hamilton, Frank William — ticket agent
Hamilton, James Alfred — bellboy
Hampton, William Joseph — junior 2nd engineer
Haran, Patrick — cook
Harford, N. — seaman
Harrison, Francis — grill cook
Harrison, Frank — bedroom steward
Harold, William — bedroom steward
Hayes, Edward — trimmer
Hayes, Ernest C. — 1st assistant purser
Hayes, Joseph Arthur — assistant steward
Healey, James — greaser
Hepburn, John David — fireman
Herbert, William — assistant steward
Highfield, William Duncan — printer
Hird, William — steward
Hobson, Sidney Francis — assistant steward
Holden, S. — greaser
Hollies, Harriet Ellen Coombs — stewardess
Holt, Robert Armor — bedroom steward
Hopwood, William — assistant steward
Houghton, James — trimmer
Hudson, John Henry Couch — seaman
Hudson, William Daniel — barman
Hughes, Hugh — bedroom steward
Hughes, William Henry — assistant steward
Hughes, William Lawrence — assistant steward
Hunt, Thomas William Dean — assistant steward
Hutchinson, George — fireman
Jackson, Charles E. — fireman

Name	Position
Jacob, Alfred Henry	assistant steward
Jaques, Henry	assistant steward
Jeffries, Joseph Frederick	seaman
Johnson, Harold	cook
Johnson, James	cook
Johnston, John Alexander	8th engineer
Jones, Clark	assistant steward
Jones, Daniel Henry	seaman
Jones, Edward John	1st officer
Jones, Ellen Eliza Birch	stewardess
Jones, Harold	bedroom steward
Jones, Henry	barber
Jones, Henry Andrew	saloon steward
Jones, Hugh	assistant steward
Jones, John Jameson	assistant steward
Jones, John Mackenzie	senior 2nd engineer
Jones, Miriam Roberts	matron
Jones, Owen	assistant steward
Jones, Percy Reginald	bellboy
Jump, John Thomas	trimmer
Jump, Joseph	fireman
Kane, Thomas	trimmer
Keegan, John	trimmer
Kendall, Henry George	ship's captain
Kirwin, James H.	trimmer
King, John	trimmer
Knight, Robert	butcher
Knill, Arthur	cook
Lally, James	fireman
Lang, Benjamin	seaman
Lappin, William Henry	cook
Lawrie, James	assistant steward
Learmonth, George Seaton	seaman
Leary, Charles	cook
Leders, Elizabeth Turnbull	stewardess
Lee, Sydney	cook
Lennon, George Henry	assistant steward
Leonard, Mark	seaman
Leonard, Thomas	seaman
Lewis, Charles	chief 3rd class steward
Lewis, Henry	assistant steward
Lewis, John	assistant cook
Liddell, Robert Roberts	junior 2nd engineer
Lightfoot, George	officers' steward
Lyons, William Henry	seaman
Macdonald, Lawrence Kay	assistant steward
Madden, Bertha Emma Brown	stewardess
Madden, Frank John	assistant steward
Maguire, James	trimmer
Maguire, John Thomas	seaman
Maguire, Joseph	fireman
Maguire, Patrick	greaser
Malone, Bernard	fireman
Malone, Peter James	fireman
Manderson, Walter George	assistant saloon steward
Mathews, John Edward	chef
Matthews, John	trimmer
McAdam, William	greaser
McAleavey, Michael	greaser
McAleavey, Patrick	scullion
McBride, William Frederick	trimmer
McCabe, James	fireman
McCabe, Richard	trimmer
McCabe, Thomas	trimmer
McCowan, James	fireman
McCoy, John William	seaman
McCoy, R.L.	assistant pantryman
McCready, Thomas	fireman
McDonald, Alexander Betteley	purser
McDonald, Charles Keven	junior 4th engineer
McDonald, Louis Adam	steward
McDonnell, Michael Joseph	butcher
McDougall, Duncan	seaman
McEnroe, Edward	trimmer
McEwan, James	junior 4th engineer
McEwan, John	seaman
McGuinness, John	trimmer
McGuinness, Michael	leading fireman
McGuiness, Richard	fireman
McGuinness, Thomas	leading fireman
McGrath, John	assistant steward
McMahon, Peter	fireman
McManus, John Henry	fireman
McOnie, George Randolph	junior 3rd engineer
McSherry, James	assistant steward
McWilliams, Robert	assistant saloon steward
Megson, John	greaser
Mellor, Herbert James	deck steward
Metcalfe, George Joshua	assistant saloon steward
Metcalfe, Thomas	assistant steward
Mitchell, James	trimmer
Mitchell, Robert	bedroom steward
Mohring, Guy	assistant pantryman
Moore, Charles Alwyn	3rd officer
Moran, James	seaman
Morgan, James	trimmer
Morl, William	boots
Morland, Harold Reginald	assistant steward
Mountain, Thomas	fireman
Muir, Charles William	assistant steward
Mulvaney, William	trimmer
Munroe, William Anderson	2nd class pantryman

Murden, Reuben Joseph — trimmer
Murphy, Jack — assistant steward
Murphy, John — quartermaster
Murphy, Peter — leading fireman
Murphy, Peter — trimmer
Murphy, William Bristow — trimmer
Murtagh, Matthew — bedroom steward
Murtagh, William Joseph — bellboy
Myers, Frank — assistant steward
Myers, John Jameson — assistant saloon steward
Neale, Henry — trimmer
Negus, Matilda Ibbotson — stewardess
Neilson, Cornelius — greaser
Nelson, George — assistant steward
Newham, Henry — assistant saloon steward
Norman, Frank S. — musician
Nugent, William James Christopher — bedroom steward
O'Connell, David — trimmer
O'Donnell, Daniel — greaser
O'Donovan, George Stephen — junior 3rd engineer
O'Neill, Nicholas — fireman
Orford, George Leonard — assistant steward
O'Sullivan, James — seaman
O'Toole, Patrick James — trimmer
Owen, Robert — pantryman
Owen, William Salisbury — assistant steward
Page, Clarrie May — stewardess
Parkinson, Charles Richard — assistant steward
Parkinson, Frederick George — assistant steward
Parry, D. — assistant steward
Passmore, Charles Joseph — bedroom steward
Paterson, John — butcher
Pearson, Sophia Jane Varley — stewardess
Pelton, Benjamin David — assistant steward
Pemberton, Albert — musician
Perry, Harold — assistant steward
Peterson, William Victor — carpenter
Phenna, Frederick Jones — assistant steward
Pierce, Augustus — cook
Pinner, Charles — assistant steward
Pitts, William Henry — assistant steward
Powell, Leonard Amos George — assistant boots
Preston, John Edwin — inspector
Price, John Henry — seaman
Price, Thomas — assistant saloon steward
Price, William — assistant pantryman
Pritchard, Ernest — assistant cook
Pritchard, John — assistant steward
Pritchard, Oliver — assistant steward
Prowse, James Bebbington — assistant steward
Quinn, John — trimmer
Quinn, William — trimmer
Radley, Alexander Christie — boatswain's mate
Rankin, Alexander Carmichael — second writer
Rankin, James — engineer (*Empress of Asia*)
Ratcliffe, Jack — assistant steward
Reardon, Daniel — greaser
Regan, Michael — fireman
Reich, Joseph Alexande — assistant steward
Reid, H. — fireman
Reid, James — trimmer
Reid, James — fireman
Rice, Edward — fireman
Richards, Sidney Edward — steward
Riddell, Alice — stewardess
Riley, John — seaman
Roberts, James — engineer's steward
Roberts, William — assistant steward
Robertson, John — 2nd class steward
Robinson, William — trimmer
Rockford, Michael — fireman
Rohr, Arnold — confectioner
Ross, William — greaser
Rowan, William Henry — assistant steward
Rowlands, Joseph Samuel — fireman
Rushton, Joseph Albert — assistant steward
Ryan, John — fireman
Ryan, Thomas — trimmer
Sampson, William — chief engineer
Saunders, Robert — master at arms
Scott, Walter — engineer (*Empress of Asia*)
Shannon, Edward — fireman
Shannon, Francis Joseph — assistant steward
Sharkey, Martin — cook
Sharples, William Henry — quartermaster
Shaw, Henry Edward — baker
Sheridan, Robert — greaser
Simms, John — seaman
Simon, Albert Henry — assistant cook
Singer, Joseph Edward — assistant steward
Skerritt, Leonard Paul — assistant steward
Smith, Alfred E. — 6th engineer
Smith, Albert E. — assistant steward
Smith, Albert E. — engineer (*Empress of Asia*)
Smith, Charles Hopley — assistant steward
Smith, Harry — assistant saloon steward
Smith, Henry K. — assistant steward
Smith, James — trimmer

Smith, Joseph — assistant steward
Smith, Thomas John — baker
Smith, Walter Beaumont — bedroom steward
Smythe, James — fireman
Snowdon, John Robert — assistant steward
Somers, Matthew — fireman
Spencer, Charles Herbert — bellboy
Sprague, Thomas William — boatswain
Starr, Edmund — greaser
Steede, Mansfield Richard — chief officer
Stephens, John — fireman
Stephens, John — greaser
Stratton, Lucilla Kennerley — stewardess
Summers, John — greaser
Swan, John H. — 10th engineer
Swinton, Alexander (John Black) — chief baker
Taylor, Walter — carpenter's mate
Terry, John — assistant steward
Thomas, William — assistant steward
Thompson, Gerrard James — plumber
Thomson, Archibald — assistant steward
Toole, John — fireman
Trainor, Nicholas — boots
Tumilty, Bernard James — fireman
Tunstall, Bertram — 4th officer
Tunstall, Harry — assistant steward
Turner, Joseph — assistant cook
Ventre, Joseph — cook
Vivian, Bertie Adams — assistant steward
Wakeford, Charles — assistant purser
Walden, David Heron — fireman
Walker, Thomas Lyle — bedroom steward
Welsh, Thomas — trimmer
White, Henry — trimmer
White, John Bell — 7th engineer
Whitty, James — fireman
Whitty, John — leading fireman
Wildman, James Alison — storekeeper
Williams, Arthur Clement — saloon steward
Williams, David — cook
Williams, Gwilym Caradoc — assistant steward
Williams, Joseph — assistant steward
Williams, Richard — bedroom steward
Williams, Roger — 2nd officer
Williams, Thomas — chief 2nd cabin steward
Williams, William — greaser
Williams, William — lamp trimmer
Williamson, Percy Robert — senior 5th engineer
Willis, George Oswald — smokeroom steward
Wilson, F. — assistant steward
Wilson, J. — trimmer
Wilson, John — trimmer
Worthington, P. — fireman
Wright, Alfred — assistant steward
Wynne, Thomas — scullion

ACKNOWLEDGMENTS

THANK YOU, HUGH VERRIER, because without you this book would not exist. Along the way, I connected with several experts on the *Empress of Ireland* who generously gave me their time. A huge thank you, David Saint-Pierre, for generously sharing your knowledge of the *Empress* and the Rimouski area, sharing photographs and sources, and being such a thoughtful early reader. Along the way I was welcomed into the *Empress* community and received help from Sébastien Hudon in Quebec, Kjetil Saugestad in Norway, Geoff Whitfield in Liverpool, and Greg Nesteroff in Nelson, BC.

Much gratitude to Guy D'Astous in Montreal for sharing so much of his impressive collection with me, and a thank you to Pierre Champagne, president of the Société d'Histoire du Bas-Canada.

I am extremely grateful to the archivists and librarians who helped me with various aspects of this book: Eyvind Bagle, Norwegian Maritime Museum; Kira Baker, City of Vancouver Archives; Annemarie Bourassa, Site Historique Maritime de la Pointe-au-Père; Peter Boyle, CPR Archives; Cameron Bridge, Nicola Valley Museum and Archives; Olivier Côté, Benoît Thériault, and Dominique Taylor, Canadian Museum of History; Charles Dagneau, Parks Canada; Gina Dewaele, Elgin County Archives; Allisa Dullemond, Peace River Museum and Archives; Lori Wenerstrom Grua, FamilySearch Library; Chantal Guérin, Exporail, the Canadian Railway Museum; Stuart Hill, British Columbia Provincial Archives; Brian Hubner and James Kominowski, University of Manitoba Archives and Special Collections; David Humphrey, Cranbrook History Centre; Kent Kikot, Archives of Ontario; Brynne Martin, Provincial Archives of Saskatchewan; Ron and Donna Millar, Salvation Army Archives; Eric

Mineault and Margaret Couper, Library and Archives Canada; Steven Schwinghamer, Canadian Museum of Immigration at Pier 2; Brett Swanson, City of Victoria Archives; Karen Wahlund, Stettler Town and Country Museum; Erwin Wodarczak, UBC Archives.

Help also came in different forms from Mike Babiski, Olivier Barthell, Christopher Best, Sharon Britz, Tom Carter, Jon Duthie, Heidi Hay, Stefan Kiener, Barry Leinbach, Geoff Langley, Mary McDermott, Shelagh Mahoney, Matt Mandziuk, Nigel Molaro, Jan Hauge Nilsen, Peggy Patmore, Andrey Pavlov, Denise Reynolds, Lauren Robilliard, Darlene Ruckle, Susan Safyan, Jonathan Scotland, Doug Secord, Mike Soegtrop, Terje Toftenes, Wesley Wakefield, and Jim Wolf. And thank you, Mike Dunn, for doing such a great job of organizing the travel and for doing all the driving on our three research trips back east.

My deep gratitude goes to the Canada Council for their funding through the Explore and Create Grant, which made much of the research, travel, and writing possible.

Much gratitude to the team at Arsenal Pulp Press—Brian Lam, Robert Ballantyne, designer Jazmin Welch, editor Catharine Chen, Cynara Geissler, JC Cham, Erin Chan—and ZG Stories for all your attention and for making the whole process so much fun.

ENDNOTES

1. Captain Kendall and the London Cellar Murder

1 "The Arrest of 'Dr.' Crippen," *London Daily Mail,* July 29, 1910.

2 Henry G. Kendall, *Adventures on the High Seas* (London: Hurst & Blackett Limited, 1939), 169.

3 Kendall, *Adventures on the High Seas*, 114.

4 Kendall, *Adventures on the High Seas*, 143.

5 Kendall, *Adventures on the High Seas*, 163.

6 Kendall, *Adventures on the High Seas*, 165.

7 "Arrest of 'Dr.' Crippen."

8 Kendall, *Adventures on the High Seas*, 168.

9 Henry Kendall, "Special Marconi Wireless Message to the Montreal Star," *Montreal Star*, July 29, 1910.

10 "Dramatic Arrest of Dr. Crippen and Miss Le Neve Aboard ss Montrose," *Montreal Star*, August 1, 1910.

11 Henry G. Kendall, August 14, 1963 letter, Canada and Bermuda Territory Salvation Army Archives, Toronto.

12 Kendall, *Adventures on the High Seas*, 188.

2. Travelling to Quebec

13 Wreck Commissioner's Inquiry, Seventh Day (testimony of Captain Walsh), Empress of Ireland Inquiry Project, accessed July 4, 2024, https://www.titanicinquiry.org/eoi/07walsh1.php; Testimony of Hugh Staunton, Wreck Commissioner's Inquiry, Fourth Day, June 19, 1914.

14 "Despatch Arrives Mailed at Rimouski. Message from Dead Captain Dodd Intended for Use in War Cry," *Toronto Star*, June 1, 1914.

15 George Attwell, "The Night the Empress of Ireland Foundered," *War Cry*, December 26, 1925.

16 "Despatch Arrives Mailed at Rimouski."

17 Hal Beckett, "Memories of the 'Empress,'" *War Cry*, May 28, 1955.

18 Attwell, "The Night the Empress of Ireland Foundered."

3. Departing Quebec City

19 Bert Greenaway, May 29, 1914 letter.

20 Attwell, "The Night the Empress of Ireland Foundered."

21 Frances Kelly, "Empress Shipwreck Still Haunts Survivor, *Toronto Star*, April 2, 1984.

22 Beckett, "Memories of the 'Empress.'"

23 "Mrs. Attwell's Story," *Toronto Daily Star*, June 8, 1914.

24 Florence Barbour, "The True Story of My Life," unpublished memoir, August 25, 1964, Canadian Museum of History, Gatineau.

25 Ken McIntyre, April 1958 letter, Canada and Bermuda Territory Salvation Army Archives, Toronto.

26 McIntyre, April 1958 letter.

4. The Storstad

27 Wreck Commissioner's Inquiry, Day 2 (testimony of Captain Thomas Andersen), Empress of Ireland Inquiry Project, accessed July 4, 2024, https://www.titanicinquiry.org/eoi/02anderson1.php and https://www.titanicinquiry.org/eoi/02anderson2.php.

28 Exhibit placard, Site Historique Maritime de la Pointe-au-Père, Rimouski.

29 Wreck Commissioner's Inquiry, First Day (testimony of Henry George Kendall), Empress of Ireland Inquiry Project, accessed July 4, 2024, https://www.titanicinquiry.org/eoi/01header1.php and https://www.titanicinquiry.org/eoi/01kendall2.php.

30 "Case of Importance to Underwriter's," *Birmingham Post*, June 26, 1916.

31 Wreck Commissioner's Inquiry, Day 2 (testimony of Captain Thomas Andersen).

32 "Captain Andersen's Wife Tells Her Version of Wreck on St. Lawrence," *Toronto Daily Star*, June 1, 1914.

5. The Collision

33 Wreck Commissioner's Inquiry, Eighth Day (testimony of Percy Hillhouse), Empress of Ireland Inquiry Project, accessed July 4, 2024, https://www.titanicinquiry.org/eoi/08hillhouse1.php and https://www.titanicinquiry.org/eoi/08hillhouse2.php and https://www.titanicinquiry.org/eoi/08hillhouse3.php.

34 Wreck Commissioner's Inquiry, Third Day (testimony of Ronald Ferguson), Empress of Ireland Inquiry Project, accessed July 4, 2024, https://www.titanicinquiry.org/eoi/03ferguson1.php.

35 "Vancouver Survivors Welcomed Home," *Vancouver World*, June 5, 1914.

36 "Vancouver Survivors Welcomed Home."

37 "The Ill-fated Empress of Ireland: Touching and Pathetic Stories," *Bristol and Exeter Journal and Western Advertiser*, July 1, 1914.

38 "Moose Jaw Man Tells of Terrible Experiences on Empress of Ireland," *Moose Jaw Weekly Times*, June 11, 1914.

39 "Stories of the Survivors Told at the Union Station," *Toronto Star*, June 1, 1914.

40 "Stories of the Survivors Told at the Union Station."

41 Bert Greenaway, May 29, 1914 letter.

42 Margaret Greenaway, letter, courtesy of Denise Reynolds.

43 Rufus Spooner, May 31, 1914 letter, Canada and Bermuda Territory Salvation Army Archives, Toronto.

44 Margaret Greenaway, letter.

45 Margaret Greenaway, letter.

46 Frank Morris, letter, Canada and Bermuda Territory Salvation Army Archives, Toronto.

47 McIntyre, April 1958 letter.

48 "Stories of the Survivors Told at the Union Station."

49 McIntyre, April 1958 letter.

50 "Put Lifebelt on Woman," *Chicago Examiner*, June 1, 1914.

51 McIntyre, April 1958 letter.

52 Kelly, "Empress Shipwreck Still Haunts Survivor."

53 Barbour, "True Story of My Life."

54 Barbour, "True Story of My Life."

55 John Langley, May 31, 1914 letter, private collection of Langley family.

56 Langley, May 31, 1914 letter.

57 J.W. Langley, "Merritt Man Relates His Amazing Experiences of Big Wreck, on Anniversary," *Merritt Herald*, May 26, 1933.

58 Langley, May 31, 1914 letter.

59 Langley, "Merritt Man Relates His Amazing Experiences."

60 "Gordon Davidson Dived Off the Keel of the Empress of Ireland and Swam About Naked Until Rescued," *St. Thomas Daily Times*, June 3, 1914.

61 "Gordon Davidson Dived Off the Keel."

62 Interview with Mary McDermott (Martin Gill's daughter) about his story, as told to her in 1964.

63 Interview with Mary McDermott.

64 Interview with Mary McDermott.

65 "Alberta Survivor of Empress Wreck Tells Story of Experiences," *Calgary Herald*, July 9, 1914.

66 "Passed by One Boat," *Western Morning News*, June 10, 1914.

6. Everyone for Themselves

67 "Irving and Wife Died in Each Other's Arms," *Detroit Free Press*, May 31, 1914.

68 Wreck Commissioner's Inquiry, Ninth Day (testimony of Miss Townshend), Empress of Ireland Inquiry Project, accessed July 4, 2024, https://www.titanicinquiry.org/eoi/09townsend1.php.

69 "These Cars Were Made in Canada," *Ottawa Citizen*, November 26, 1999.

70 Clayton Burt, letter to the editor, *Republican Northwestern*, June 8, 1914.

71 Burt, letter to the editor.

72 Wreck Commissioner's Inquiry, Ninth Day (testimony of Miss Townshend).

73 "The Daily Province's Page of Social and Personal News," *The Province*, July 9, 1914.

74 "Helen O'Hara Tells of Her Daddy's Death," *Toronto Daily Star*, June 2, 1914.

75 "Helen O'Hara Tells of Her Daddy's Death."

76 "Mrs. E. Paton's Escape," *Montreal Gazette*, May 30, 1914.

77 "Woman Driven from Lifeboat by Sailors," *Toronto Daily Star*, June 1, 1914.

78 "Stories Survivors Told at the Union Station Are Without Parallel," *Toronto Daily Star*, June 1, 1914.

79 "Dr. J.F. Grant's Story of Empress Disaster," *Daily Colonist*, June 28, 1914.

7. Heroes

80 Wreck Commissioner's Inquiry, Fifth Day (testimony of Aaron Syvertsen), Empress of Ireland Inquiry Project, accessed July 4, 2024, https://www.titanicinquiry.org/eoi/05syvetsen1.php.

81 "Captain Andersen's Wife Tells Her Version."

82 "Captain Andersen's Wife Tells Her Version."

83 "Dr. J.F. Grant's Story of Empress Disaster."

84 "Gordon Davidson Dived Off the Keel."

85 McIntyre, April 1958 letter.

86 Wreck Commissioner's Inquiry, Day 1 (testimony of Henry George Kendall).

87 "Dr. J.F. Grant's Story of Empress Disaster."

88 "Alberta Survivor of Empress Wreck."

89 "Death Ended Romance," *Montreal Gazette*, June 4, 1914.

90 "O'Hara's Gallant Death," *Hamilton Spectator*, May 30, 1914.

91 "Gordon Davidson Dived Off the Keel."

92 "Vancouver Survivors Welcomed Home."

93 "Major Morris Tells of Rough Treatment," *Toronto Daily Star*, June 3, 1914.

94 Margaret Greenaway, letter.

95 Margaret Greenaway, letter.

96 "Gordon Davidson Dived Off the Keel."

97 "Woman Driven from Lifeboat by Sailors."

98 "Captain Kendall Puts Blame Squarely on the Storstad," *Boston Globe*, May 31, 1914.

8. Identifying the Bodies

99 Beckett, "Memories of the 'Empress.'"

100 Beckett, "Memories of the 'Empress.'"

101 Wreck Commissioner's Inquiry, Sixth Day (testimony of Captain Pouliot), Empress of Ireland Inquiry Project, accessed July 4, 2024, https://www.titanicinquiry.org/eoi/06pouliot1.php.

102 "Identified 100 Bodies," *Boston Globe*, June 1, 1914.

103 "Identification of the Dead at Quebec Yesterday," *Montreal Star*, June 1, 1914.

104 "Loss of Father Lingers Decades After Disaster," *Toronto Star*, May 30, 2001.

105 "Wreck Survivor on Liner Makura," *Honolulu Advertiser*, July 16, 1914.

106 "Leonard Delmont Gave Up His Lifebelt to His Mother and Then Died," *Moose Jaw Weekly Times*, June 11, 1914.

107 Archie Brown, "Moose Jaw Man Tells of Terrible Experiences on Empress of Ireland," *Moose Jaw Weekly Times*, June 11, 1914.

108 Kelly, "Empress Shipwreck Still Haunts Survivor."

109 Langley, "Merritt Man Relates His Amazing Experiences."

9. Burying the Dead

110 Langley, May 31, 1914 letter.

111 Herbert P. Wood, *Till We Meet Again: The Sinking of the Empress of Ireland* (Toronto: Imaging Publishing Inc., 1982), 138.

112 "A Family of Nine. Awful Blow to Cambusnethan Home," *Daily Record*, June 2, 1914.

113 "Twenty Brantford People Were Aboard the Doomed Empress of Ireland," *Brantford Daily Expositor*, June 4, 1914.

114 "James F. Dandy Is Dead," *Free Press Prairie Farmer*, December 8, 1915.

115 Annie McKinnon, letter to the editor, *Broadview Express*, June 4, 1964.

116 Francis Rask, *The Story of Broadview and Area* (Broadview: Broadview Pioneer History Society, 1982), 399–401.

117 "Gordon Davidson Dived Off the Keel."

118 "The Empress Disaster, Survivors Welcomed," *Liverpool Daily Post and Mercury*, June 12, 1914.

10. Salvaging the Wreck

119 Wreck Commissioner's Inquiry, Eighth Day (testimony of Wilfred Whitehead) Empress of Ireland Inquiry Project, accessed July 4, 2024, https://www.titanicinquiry.org/eoi/08whitehead1.php.

120 Telegrams and letters from Charlie Young to Fred Cullen, Cullen-Shepherd Family Fonds, Canadian Museum of History, Gatineau.

121 Charlie Young, telegrams, Cullen-Shepherd Family Fonds, Canadian Museum of History, Gatineau.

122 Ian Kinder, *The 96th Voyage: The Truth About the Empress of Ireland Tragedy* (self-pub., 2017), 135.

123 "Funeral of Commissioner Rees," *War Cry*, July 25, 1914.

124 "Personal Stories," Empress of Ireland Commemorations, accessed July 4, 2024, http://www.empress2014.ca/seclangen/testimonies.html.

11. The Inquiry

125 "Storstad Is Seized by Montreal Officials," *Toronto Daily Star*, June 1, 1914.

126 "Big Liner Rammed and Sent to Bottom by Collier, Conflicting Reports as to Loss of Life," *Ottawa Citizen*, May 29, 1914; "Collier's Anchor Tore Through Liner's Steel Like Giant Can-Opener," *Winnipeg Tribune*, June 1, 1914.

127 Wreck Commissioner's Inquiry, Eleventh Day, Empress of Ireland Inquiry Project, accessed July 4, 2024, https://www.titanicinquiry.org/eoi/11header1.php.

128 Wreck Commissioner's Inquiry, Eleventh Day.

129 Wreck Commissioner's Inquiry, Eleventh Day.

130 Wreck Commissioner's Inquiry, Eleventh Day.

131 Wreck Commissioner's Inquiry, Eighth Day (testimony of Wilfred Whitehead).

132 Wreck Commissioner's Inquiry, Seventh Day (testimony of Captain Kendall), Empress of Ireland Inquiry Project, accessed July 4, 2024, https://www.titanicinquiry.org/eoi/07kendall1.php.

133 Langley, "Merritt Man Relates His Amazing Experiences."

134 "The Wreck and the Survivors," *Toronto Daily Star*, June 1, 1914.

12. Myth Busting

135 "How the Wreck Was Reported for the Star," *Toronto Daily Star*, June 5, 1914.

136 "Commissioner Rees' End," *Montreal Gazette*, May 30, 1914.

137 Morris, letter.

138 "Survivors Describe Terrible Scene as Vessel Was Sinking," *St. Louis Post-Dispatch*, May 30, 1914.

139 "Mr Lawler Had to Fight for Life of Young Son," *Brantford Daily Expositor*, June 2, 1914.

140 "Back from the Jaws of Death, Philip Lawler and His Son Reach Brantford," *Brantford Daily Expositor*, June 11, 1914.

141 "Preparing Evidence for Empress Inquest," *Vancouver Daily News Advertiser*, June 4, 1914.

142 "No Doubt Number Were Dead Before Entering Water. Undertaker Confirms Report that Many Bodies Bear Knife Wounds," *Saskatoon Daily Star*, June 2, 1914.

143 "Preparing Evidence for Empress Inquest."

144 "Back from the Jaws of Death."

145 "Big Black Shape Loomed Suddenly Out of Foggy Darkness," *Ottawa Citizen*, *Brantford Examiner*, and *Star Phoenix*, May 30, 1914.

146 "Vancouver Survivors Welcomed Home."

147 "Crippen's Curse. Murderer's Remark to Kendall Recalled by Disaster," *Windsor Star*, June 26, 1914.

148 Henry Kendall, August 14, 1963 letter, Canada and Bermuda Territory Salvation Army Archives, Toronto.

149 "He Swam Ashore as Empress Sank," *The Province*, June 1, 1914.

150 "Swims Four Miles to Shore," *Berkeley Daily Gazette*, June 2, 1914.

151 "Gordon Davidson Dived Off the Keel."

13. Survivors in World War I

152 Gordon Davidson, November 16, 1917 letter, private collection of Margaret Patmore.

153 *London Gazette*, 30507, February 4, 1918.

154 Gordon Davidson, December 31, 1917 letter, private collection of Margaret Patmore.

155 Douglas Archer, August 11, 1998 letter, Cullen-Shepherd Family Fonds, Canadian Museum of History, Gatineau.

156 Robert Cunningham, September 22, 1918 letter, *MANAGRA* (University of Manitoba Faculty of Agriculture), January 1919.

157 "Lieutenant Langley Home from France," unnamed newspaper, August 29, 1919, Merritt Archives.

158 "Lieutenant Langley Home from France."

159 "Canada at War," Canadian War Museum, accessed July 4, 2024, https://www.warmuseum.ca/firstworldwar/history/going-to-war/canada-enters-the-war/.

14. The Captains' War

160 Kendall, *Adventures on the High Seas*, 193.

161 "Jack Afloat: Interesting Letter from a Llanellyite," *Llanelli Star*, October 31, 1914.

162 Kendall, *Adventures on the High Seas*, 231.

163 Kendall, *Adventures on the High Seas*, 239.

164 Kendall, *Adventures on the High Seas*, 244.

165 Kendall, *Adventures on the High Seas*, 192.

166 "Empress Sank," *Star Weekly Toronto*, May 30, 1964.

167 "Belgian Relief Ship Sunk Without Warning. Crew Shelled in Boats," *Daily Telegraph*, March 12, 1917.

168 "Belgian Relief Ship Sunk Without Warning."

169 Ingrid Toftenes, postcards translated by Kjetil Saugestad, private collection of Jan Hauge Nilsen.

170 Obituary, *Norges Handels og Sjofartstid-ende*, May 1, 1918.

15. Shell Shock

171 Vancouver City Morgue, May 31, 1922 Inquisition, BC Archives, Victoria.

172 Vancouver City Morgue, May 31, 1922 Inquisition.

173 Vancouver City Morgue, May 31, 1922 Inquisition.

174 Vancouver City Morgue, May 31, 1922 Inquisition.

175 Vancouver City Morgue, May 31, 1922 Inquisition.

176 Vancouver City Morgue, May 31, 1922 Inquisition.

177 "Bullet Fired in Flanders," *The Province*, June 3, 1922.

16. Arthur Delamont's Musical Legacy

178 "Vancouver's Music Man Dies at 90," *Vancouver Sun*, September 13, 1982.

179 "New York Hears Vancouver Band," *Edmonton Journal*, July 22, 1939.

180 "Kitsilano Boys' Band Land Zig Zagged to Avoid U-Boats," *The Province*, September 11, 1939.

181 Denny Boyd, "Legendary Mr. D Excited with Fanfare," *Vancouver Sun*, September 13, 1982.

182 Christopher Best, "The Architect," Ambassadors of Empire Online, accessed July 26, 2024, https://kitsband.ca/the-architect/.

183 Christopher Best, *The Life and Times of the Legendary Mr. D* (Vancouver: Warfleet Press, 2014), 263.

184 Boyd, "Legendary Mr. D Excited with Fanfare."

17. Women and Children

185 Ninette Kelley and Michael Trebilcock, *The Making of the Mosaic: A History of Canadian Immigration Policy* (Toronto: University of Toronto Press, 2010), 115.

186 Mikael Elinder and Oscar Erixson, "Every Man for Himself! Gender, Norms and Survival in Maritime Disasters" (April 10, 2012), IFN Working Paper No. 913, 2012, http://dx.doi.org/10.2139/ssrn.2051006.

187 Paul Murray, "1,012 Drowned, but Grace Lived," *Toronto Star*, May 23, 1993.

188 Barbour, "True Story of My Life."

189 Barbour, "True Story of My Life."

190 Barbour, "True Story of My Life."

18. Homesteading and Immigration

191 "Stettler: a Tribute to Her Pioneers," *Stettler Independent*, May 10, 1962, Stettler Archives.

192 "Donor of Stettler Memorial Outlines Life," unnamed newspaper, n.d., Stettler Archives.

193 *Stettler Independent*, March 11, 1915.

194 Annie Elena (Rask) McKinnon, "The Rask Family History: The Early Days," unpublished manuscript, 1980, Rask family archives.

195 Francis Rask, *The Story of Broadview and Area*.

196 McKinnon, "The Rask Family History."

197 Kelley and Trebilcock, *The Making of the Mosaic*, 111–12.

19. Rediscovering the Empress

198 Auf der Maur, "Cousteau and Crew Tackle St. Lawrence," *Montreal Gazette*, August 25, 1980.

199 Monique Polack, "Forgotten Empress," *Montreal Gazette*, May 29, 2014.

BIBLIOGRAPHY

Books, Journals, and Articles

A Shipwreck's Centennial: The Family Stories. Rimouski: Site Historique Maritime de la Pointe-au-Père, 2014.

Ballard, Robert D., and Rick Archbold. *Ghost Liners: Exploring the World's Greatest Lost Ships*. Boston: Little, Brown and Company, 1998.

Bensley, Edward, H. "James Grant: Ship's Surgeon on the Ill-Fated Empress of Ireland." *Canadian Medical Association Journal* 126, no. 3 (1982): 318–19.

Best, Christopher. *The Life and Times of the Legendary Mr. D.* Vancouver: Warfleet Press, 2014.

Brylske, Alex. "A Brief History of Diving: Free Divers, Bells and Helmets." *Dive Training Magazine*. Accessed August 22, 2024. https://dtmag.com/thelibrary/a-brief-history-of-diving-free-divers-bells-and-helmets/.

Cleasby, Henry Standley. *The Nicola Valley in Review*. Published by the author, 1958.

Creighton, David. *Losing the Empress: A Personal Journey*. Toronto: Dundurn Press, 2000.

Darke, Eleanor. *Call Me True: A Biography of True Davidson*. Toronto: Dundurn Press, 1997.

Daschuk, James. *Clearing the Plains: Disease, Politics of Starvation, and the Loss of Indigenous Life*. Regina: University of Regina Press, 2014.

Elinder, Mikael, and Oscar Erixson. "Every Man for Himself! Gender, Norms and Survival in Maritime Disasters" (April 10, 2012). IFN Working Paper 913.

Ellsberg, Edward. *Men Under the Sea*. New York: Dodd, Mead & Co, 1939.

Grout, Derek. *RMS Empress of Ireland: Pride of the Canadian Pacific's Atlantic Fleet*. Toronto: Dundurn Press, 2014.

Kelley, Ninette, and Michael Trebilcock. *The Making of the Mosaic: A History of Canadian Immigration Policy*. Toronto: University of Toronto Press, 2010.

Kendall, Henry G. *Adventures on the High Seas*. London: Hurst & Blackett Limited, 1939.

Lazarus, Eve. *Blood, Sweat, and Fear: The Story of Inspector Vance, Vancouver's First Forensic Investigator*. Vancouver: Arsenal Pulp Press, 2017.

Jones, David Laurence. *Railway Nation: Tales of Canadian Pacific, the World's Greatest Travel System*. Vancouver: Heritage House, 2020.

McMurray, K.F. *Dark Descent: Diving and the Deadly Allure of the Empress of Ireland*. Toronto: McGraw-Hill, 2004.

Marshall, Logan. *The Tragic Story of the Empress of Ireland*. New York: Berkeley Publishing Group, 2014. Originally published in 1914.

Moyles, R.G. *The Blood and Fire in Canada: A History of the Salvation Army in the Dominion 1882–1976*. Toronto: Peter Martin & Associates, 1977.

Widds, Randy William. "Saskatchewan Bound: Migration to a New Canadian Frontier." *Great Plains Quarterly* 12, no. 4 (1992).

Willis, John. *Canada's Titanic: Empress of Ireland.* Gatineau: Canadian Museum of History, 2014.

Zeni, David. *Forgotten Empress: The Empress of Ireland Story.* Fredericton: Goose Lane Editions, 1998.

Websites

Canadian Museum of History: historymuseum.ca

Canadian Museum of Immigration at Pier 21: pier21.ca

Canadian War Museum: warmuseum.ca

Empress of Ireland Commemorations, "Personal Stories": empress2014.ca/seclangen/testimonies.html

Empress of Ireland Inquiry Project: titanicinquiry.org/eoi/01header1.php

Government of Canada, "Battle of Passchendaele": veterans.gc.ca/en/remembrance/wars-and-conflicts/first-world-war/battle-of-passchendaele

Library and Archives Canada, "Passenger Lists": bac-lac.gc.ca/eng/discover/immigration/immigration-records/passenger-lists/Pages/introduction.aspx

Library and Archives Canada, "Personnel Records of the First World War": library-archives.canada.ca/eng/collection/research-help/military-heritage/first-world-war/Pages/fww-personnel.aspx

Peter's Empress of Ireland Page: empressofireland.wordpress.com

Provincial Archives of Saskatchewan: saskarchives.com

INDEX

Illustrations and photographs indicated by page numbers in italics

T

U

V

W

Y

Z

Photo credit: Rebecca Blissett

EVE LAZARUS is a reporter, author, and the host and producer of the true crime podcast *Cold Case Canada*. Her bestselling books include *Cold Case* BC (2022), *Vancouver Exposed* (2020), and *Murder by Milkshake* (2018). Eve's books have garnered eight nominations, including an Arthur Ellis Award (Best Non-Fiction Crime Book), a City of Vancouver Book Award, and a BC Book Prize (Bill Duthie Booksellers' Choice Award). *Sensational Vancouver* (2014) was the recipient of a City of Vancouver Heritage Award. Eve blogs at *Every Place Has a Story*.

evelazarus.com

ALSO BY EVE LAZARUS

At Home with History: The Untold Secrets of Greater Vancouver's Heritage Homes (Anvil Press, 2007)

Blood, Sweat, and Fear: The Story of Inspector Vance, Vancouver's First Forensic Investigator (Arsenal Pulp Press, 2017)

Cold Case BC: The Stories behind the Province's Most Sensational Murder and Missing Person Cases (Arsenal Pulp Press, 2022)

Cold Case Vancouver: The City's Most Baffling Unsolved Murders (Arsenal Pulp Press, 2015)

Frommer's with Kids Vancouver (CDG Books Canada, 2000)

The Life and Art of Frank Molnar, Jack Hardman and LeRoy Jensen (Mother Tongue Publishing, 2009)

Murder by Milkshake: An Astonishing True Story of Adultery, Arsenic, and a Charismatic Killer (Arsenal Pulp Press, 2018)

Sensational Vancouver (Anvil Press, 2014)

Sensational Victoria: Bright Lights, Red Lights, Murders, Ghosts & Gardens (Anvil Press, 2012)

Vancouver Exposed: Searching for the City's Hidden History (Arsenal Pulp Press, 2020)